Finding Help When Your Child Is Struggling in School

Finding Help When Your Child Is Struggling in School

Lawrence J. Greene

Golden Books
New York

Golden Books®

888 Seventh Avenue
New York, NY 10106

Copyright © 1998 by Lawrence J. Greene
All rights reserved, including the right of reproduction
in whole or in part in any form.
Golden Books® and colophon
are trademarks of Golden Books Publishing Co., Inc.

Designed by Suzanne Noli

Manufactured in the United States of America

10 9 8 7 6 5 4 3 2 1

Library of Congress Cataloging-in-Publication Data

Greene, Lawrence J.
    Finding help when your child is struggling in school / Lawrence J.
Greene.
        p. cm.
    Includes index.
    ISBN 0-307-44075-3 (alk. paper)
    1. Home and school–United States.   2. Special education–Parent
participation–United States.   3. Learning disabled children–
Education–United States.   4. Underachievers–Education–United
States.   5. Problem children–Education–United States.   I. Title.
LC225.3.G74   1998
371.19′2–dc21   98-19128
                                                                              CIP

For my son, Joshua Ryan Greene. Your spirit and zest enthrall me. I shall always be thankful for the joy you have brought into my life.

Acknowledgments

I am indebted to the many experts who have provided me with invaluable information, guidance, and support. The list includes:

Kenneth Bloome, M.D., Ph.D., pediatrics and developmental pediatrics
Joan Cayton, M.A., educational therapy
Dana Dworsky, L.C.S.W., L.M.F.C.C., clinical social work and marriage, family, and child counseling
Leah Ellenberg, Ph.D., neuropsychology
William Garvey, Ph.D., clinical psychology
Audry Griesbauch, M.D., developmental pediatrics
Tony Hoffman, Ph.D., clinical psychology and developmental psychology
Pamela Jacobson, M.S., CCC, speech and language pathology
Judy Jesson, L.M.F.C.C., marriage, family, and child counseling
Walter Jesson, Ph.D., clinical psychology
Susan Knox, Ph.D., occupational therapy
Sherry Kolbe, Executive Director, National Association of Private Schools for Exceptional Children (NAPSEC)
Paul Kourkari, M.D., pediatric neurology
Beverly Metcalf, M.S., CET, educational therapy
Brad Murray, O.D., developmental optometry
Mark Steinberg, Ph.D., educational and clinical psychology

I am also thankful to the others who provided feedback, insight, and encouragement: Shimon Naftel, Shira Naftel, Alison Lucas, Dr. Gerald Walker Smith, Daniel Greene, Evelyn Greene, Evan Greene, and David Hungerford.

Contents

Introduction   1

Part I: Identifying the Problem

  1. Communicating with the Teacher and Getting
       Vital Information   9
  2. Focusing Your Observations and Impressions   27
  3. Communicating with Your Child and Getting
       Vital Information   37

Part II: Using the Resources at Your Child's School

  4. Getting Your Child Assessed   51
  5. Understanding Test Results   61
  6. Handling the Individual Educational Plan
       Conference   79
  7. Understanding the Law   95

**Part III: Finding the Right Person to Make
          an Evaluation**

  8. Diagnosticians: Pediatricians, Developmental
       Pediatricians, Pediatric Neurologists, Educational
       Psychologists, and Neuropsychologists   113

Part IV: Finding the Right Person to Treat the Emotional Fallout

9. Mental Health Professionals: Psychiatrists and Child Psychiatrists, Clinical Psychologists, Child Psychologists, Marriage and Family Counselors, and Clinical Social Workers   137

Part V: Finding the Right Person to Provide Specialized Services

10. Learning Assistance Providers: Tutors, Educational Therapists, Learning and Reading Centers, Privately Funded Specialized Private Schools, and Publicly Funded Nonpublic Schools   163
11. Specialized Clinicians: Speech and Language Pathologists, Occupational Therapists, and Developmental Optometrists   195

Part VI: Defining Your Role in the School Success Equation

12. Assessing the Effectiveness of the Intervention Program   221
13. Motivating Your Child to Set Academic Goals   229
14. Providing Support and Building Morale   247
15. Supervising Homework and Studying   261

Afterword   275

Appendix   279

Index   283

Finding Help When Your Child Is Struggling in School

Introduction

Your child is struggling in school, and your heart is breaking. Every parental instinct within you screams, "I want to help my child and protect him* from the pain he's experiencing! I want my child to like school, not hate it."

You see your child's frustration as he tries haltingly to decode the words and letters when he reads. You watch him struggle to write legibly. You feel his demoralization when he gets another bad grade on a spelling test even though you both spent hours drilling the assigned words. You see him wince when you become exasperated with him because he cannot concentrate and follow directions. You know his teacher is also frustrated with him, and you fear that the continual negative feedback is ravaging his self-concept. You see your child's pain, and you despair because you feel powerless to help. You feel guilty, and at the same time you feel angry. Your instincts tell you that the problems are solvable if you can only get your bearings and track down the right resources. You must do something!

The fundamental premise of this book is that you should trust your parental instincts. If you believe your child is hurting, you are undoubtedly right. If you observe your child becoming discouraged, your observations are undoubtedly accurate. If you feel compelled to provide help and protection, your reaction is undoubtedly appropriate.

Children are being damaged every day in school because of inadequate programs, incompetent teaching, classes that are too large, inflexible criteria for admission to special programs, and myopic, insensitive thinking on the part of school district personnel and government agencies that provide funding and oversight. No, it's not a conspiracy. It's basic

---

*Male and female pronouns will be used alternately to describe teachers and children.

economics. There isn't enough money to go around, and the spending priorities of schools shift depending on which interest group is the most vocal and has the most effective lobbyists and the greatest political leverage.

You don't have to be a passive bystander and watch your child being bruised and battered in school, and you don't have to accept that your child's level of educational achievement will be diminished because of insensitive or incompetent educational bureaucrats. You can learn how to identify your child's learning problems accurately and how to find skilled remedial help. You can acquire information that will allow you to fight the school bureaucracy and make certain that your child receives his fair share of the educational resources available in your school district. Although you may ultimately conclude that you need to go outside the public education system to find answers and get assistance, you'll know what to look for and how to assess the effectiveness of private remedial programs.

You must never forget that you are your child's most important ally and advocate. You have a legitimate right and, in fact, a solemn obligation to play a proactive role in helping him overcome the obstacles that stand in his way at school.

Is it unreasonable for you to believe that your child deserves to develop his academic skills and acquire self-confidence? Is it unreasonable for you to believe that your child deserves to actualize his full potential and develop his abilities? Is it unreasonable for you to believe that your child deserves to have positive associations with learning? Is it unreasonable for you to believe that your child deserves the opportunity to go to college and have a satisfying and rewarding career? The answers to these questions are the same: No! Any educator who says differently does not have your child's best interests at heart.

Like tens of thousands of other concerned parents, you may feel helpless as you watch your child's self-image being damaged as he falls further and further behind in school. He may not admit it openly, but you know he feels "dumb." You see the demoralization. You see that the daily battle in school is taking a devastating emotional toll. You see your child becoming resistant to doing his homework, turned off to learning, and school-phobic. You see the deterioration in his self-concept, and you see him becoming increasingly frustrated, demoralized, and angry.

Perhaps you've had the following experiences: You attempt to talk with your child about school and about his problems and feelings, and he either denies anything is wrong or tells you that he hates school because it's boring. He blames the teacher for being unfair and picking on him. He tells you that he doesn't want to do the work because it's stupid. Each evening you're forced to spend hours helping him do his assignments, and as you sit by his side, you realize that he's becoming more and more dependent on you. You also realize that he's becoming increasingly resentful of your help. Each morning you must coax him to get out of bed and get ready for school. You're caught in a bind. If you don't help him, he cannot do the work. He'll fall further behind and conclude that he's "stupid." If you do help, he'll become more helpless or more resistant.

Although learning, reading, and concentration problems are statistically more prevalent in boys, girls are not excluded from having academic deficits. Your daughter may not act out in the same way a boy might, but she may procrastinate, not complete her homework, or not hand in her assignments. She may struggle to read accurately or understand what she is reading. She may have difficulty following verbal or written directions. Her work may be chronically sloppy, incomplete, or filled with silly errors. She may have difficulty staying on task, and she may daydream or disturb other students. Perplexed by her marginal performance, the teacher may suggest that she's lazy or immature, and you may be tempted to agree. But intuitively you sense this explanation is too simplistic. Her difficulties reflect more than a lack of effort. You're certain she has the intelligence to do the assigned work, but you can plainly see that she's unable to do what's expected of her. You suspect that something isn't gelling properly inside her head. There must be an explanation as to why she's struggling, but no one has been able to tell you what's causing her problems and counterproductive behavior.

In frustration you throw your hands in the air. Countless questions course through your mind. Should you try to get her into a resource program at her school? Should you find her a tutor or seek the help of an educational therapist? Should you trust the educational assessment done by the school, or should you have her privately evaluated? Should you follow the school's recommendations, or should you get another opinion? How can you pinpoint the source of her problems? How can you intervene most effectively? Can you trust the school psychologist to identify her problem accurately and the school resource specialist to provide first-rate assistance? How do you evaluate the efficacy of the school remediation program, the tutor, the educational therapist, or the private reading or math center? How do you determine if she's making reasonable progress? How can you be sure she's getting all the help she needs?

The stress experienced by concerned and responsible parents who try to provide appropriate assistance for their child can be overwhelming. In the back of your mind is the most unsettling question: Am I doing the right thing? You realize that if you don't make the right moves now, your child's future may be adversely affected. Her natural talents may never be developed and her earning power may be drastically reduced. The likelihood of her finding a satisfying and rewarding career might be squelched, literally at the starting gate. By the time your child enters the fourth grade, she may be already "disqualified" from participating in the race, and she may never experience the thrill and satisfaction of having competed and won the coveted medal.

This book was written in response to the calls and letters I receive virtually every day from parents all over the United States. Concerned and, often, frantic parents who have read my previous books want me to advise them about how to provide help for their struggling child. They want me to make a quick diagnosis on the telephone, suggest an effective remediation strategy, and give them the name of someone in their community who can provide top-notch assistance. Unfortunately, I can rarely provide them with the specific recommendations they want. Making a meaningful "telephone diagnosis" is risky if you don't have all the information needed, and recommending someone in their local community who works effectively with children is implausible. I am not familiar with the resources available in Wheeling, West Virginia; Billings, Montana; or Biloxi, Mississippi. The net result is frustration—for me because I want to help and cannot, and for the parents because I am unable to provide the information and answers they want.

I believe this book represents the most effective way to handle the long-distance questions. It offers a systematic and strategic plan of action for understanding your child's underlying problems, for procuring help, and for assessing the efficacy of this assistance.

I cannot personally speak with you on the phone, but this book contains the advice I would give you if I met with you in my office. If you follow the blueprint laid out on the following pages, you *can* take an effective and proactive role in altering the course of your child's life, and you can significantly reduce the risk of your child's ending up at an academic dead end.

Now let's get down to finding out what to do to help your child succeed in school.

Part I
Identifying the Problem

Chapter 1
Communicating with the Teacher and Getting Vital Information

The classroom teacher is the captain of your child's ship each school day. She plots the course and navigates on both calm and turbulent seas. Because it's a small ship, she must also assume another key role. She is the lookout, the person standing at the helm who is responsible for activating the fog horn in inclement weather and for sounding the alarm, sending up flares, tossing over the life preserver, and lowering the lifeboat when a student tumbles over the side.

If it's your child who is teetering near the railing, you want to be certain the teacher is vigilant. Your child's academic survival and emotional well-being could be at stake. If the teacher is not observant or fails to alert you about problems, you won't have the information you need to make decisions about your child's education. This withholding of vital data can have serious consequences.

But the teacher is not the only source of information about your child's educational status. If your child has been struggling in school, he may already have been assessed by the school psychologist or the resource specialist (see chapter 4). You may also have had him privately evaluated (see chapter 9). And, of course, you've undoubtedly drawn conclusions from your own observations. You know if he's having problems with math or reading, and you know if his papers are sloppy and illegible. Your personal perceptions don't tell the full story, however. If the teacher fails to provide you with a precise description of his specific problems, you may not be able to discover what might be causing them. This lack of data could prevent you from developing effective remedies. Certainly, report cards provide information, but by the time you're "officially" made aware of the problem, it may be too late to control the damage.

Children who are academically deficient can pose a monumental challenge to the classroom teacher. Most teachers have twenty-five or more students in their classes who need their help and guidance. If your child is significantly below grade level and is resorting to counterproductive behavior to compensate for his deficits, he can easily test his teacher's skills and patience. Each student in a class of thirty should require approximately three percent of her time. If your child requires ten percent, there's clearly an imbalance. How can the teacher provide your child with the help and support he requires without cheating the other students? Despite the best of intentions, the teacher may feel frustrated and even resentful that your child is placing her in this bind.

The need to establish and maintain an effective, ongoing dialogue with the classroom teacher is all the more critical when your child has learning deficiencies. Without effective, focused communication and precise information, you could easily become overwhelmed by your child's problems. This could produce stress, frustration, confusion, demoralization, and resentment. In desperation, you may resort to counterproductive nagging, feeble threats, ineffective punishment, excessive involvement in monitoring homework, and unproductive tutoring. Or you may succumb to a sense of futility and simply hope that your child can somehow survive his ordeal.

To assure that your child gets back on target, you must assess his situation carefully and objectively, identify the factors responsible for his academic problems, evaluate the resources available at his school and in your local community, and intervene intelligently and proactively. In order to do this, you need specific information about your child's academic progress and needs.

The Issue of Teacher Competency

Let's begin by setting the record straight about good and not-so-good teachers. There are many teachers in American schools who work hard, teach with exceptional competence, and deserve to be acknowledged and acclaimed for their skills and dedication. Well-trained, insightful, and empathic, these gifted educators delight in teaching. Their joy and enthusiasm inspire students to learn and motivate them to develop their academic and intellectual capacity.

Good teachers realize the importance of positive learning experiences in building a child's academic self-confidence and expectations of success, and these teachers find countless creative ways to help students master the curriculum. Keenly aware of each youngster's strengths and weaknesses, they capitalize on abilities and shore up deficiencies. They capti-vate. They nurture. They coax. With consummate skill they nudge children out of their comfort zones, prod them to stretch academically and intellectually, and motivate them to develop their skills.

Whenever possible, first-rate teachers individualize their instructional methods and tailor their lesson plans and academic demands to the needs and skill level of their students. They are committed to developing the best in each child and do everything possible to help *all* their students achieve. They make the subject matter interesting and teach dynamically. They intentionally orchestrate successful learning experiences. They af-firm and praise. They make accommodations and astutely engineer how the material is presented and reinforced. Because they want their students to experience that special glow and sense of satisfaction derived from skill mastery and achievement, they do everything humanly possible to help struggling children succeed in their classrooms. These efforts do not go unnoticed or unappreciated. Their students intuitively perceive that these teachers are their allies and not their enemies. When asked years later about the people who had a positive impact on their lives, students who struggled in school almost invariably place an inspirational, demanding, and empathetic teacher high on the list.

Good teachers recognize when things are not going well. If a child isn't learning properly, they realize the importance of alerting the child's parents and involving all the key players in the process of identifying the learning problems, pinpointing the causal factors, and developing effec-tive solutions. They understand the risks of letting the situation get out of hand.

Talented teachers have clearly chosen their profession for more than its often meager monetary rewards. Their payoff is seeing their students become excited about learning and watching them puff up with pride when they succeed and achieve. They realize that children are genetically programmed to learn and the teacher's job is to nurture each child's in-nate instinct to assimilate information and acquire new skills. Watching these teachers interact with their students can be deceptive, because they make the job seem so simple and effortless. A meticulous analysis of the remarkable talents they use in the course of a typical school day would dispel any illusion about their job being simple.

If your child has the good fortune to have an exceptional teacher, you are also fortunate. This is especially true if your child is having problems in school. But let's not fool ourselves. There are also *unexceptional* teachers in our schools. They may do their job and follow their lesson plans, but they do little more than the minimum. Although they may not be incompetent or actually damage students, they certainly don't infuse children with the joy of learning.

When students are not motivated and struggle to master the fundamentals, the marginally competent teacher often blames the students. Blaming is certainly less threatening than looking objectively at her own teaching skills. The teacher who is insecure and defensive will frequently perceive concerned, inquisitive, involved parents as intrusive. The probing questions of an anxious parent can be unsettling to someone who doesn't have any answers.

Of even more concern are those teachers who are truly incompetent and who haven't a clue about how children learn or what might cause them not to learn. Some of these teachers are rigid and harsh. Some are actually cruel and denigrating. Others are passive and permissive. Some hate teaching, and others are burned out. Children with learning, attitude, or behavior problems who find themselves in the classroom with such teachers are in jeopardy. The requisites for resolving their problems—sensitivity, creativity, empathy, patience, and skillful instruction—are not present, and the struggling child is at risk for becoming increasingly discouraged and demoralized.

If you conclude that your child's attitude, behavior, or academic deficiencies are causing his teacher to become overwhelmed or resentful, you must be prepared to intervene. By helping the teacher better understand your child's situation and learning needs, and by diplomatically suggesting ways in which she might provide assistance or better manage his behavior, you can defuse a situation that could be damaging to your child. If you are skillful, you can achieve this objective without causing the teacher to become defensive or resentful.

If you conclude that the situation is unfixable, talk with the principal or, if necessary, the superintendent. Argue forcefully to have your child transferred to another class. You cannot afford to be complacent if the teacher is unable to meet your child's legitimate learning needs. You must take a proactive role in protecting your child from psychological damage and academic shutdown.

Inspired Teaching

During the course of his education, your child will experience teachers who range from excellent to marginal. If he's unlucky, he may suffer through a year with an incompetent teacher. But if he's fortunate, he may have the life-altering experience of being inspired by an extraordinary teacher.

Perhaps you've seen the movie *Mr. Holland's Opus*. If you haven't, you should do so. Mr. Holland epitomizes the very best in teaching, and his professional life testifies to his love and respect for children. The central metaphor rings true. The inspired teacher is indeed a conductor who stands each day on the podium, faces her orchestra, and tries to make beautiful music. She identifies the raw talents of her students and shows each one how to use the abilities God has provided. Perhaps she will occasionally stumble upon a genius, a potential Isaac Stern or Leonard Bernstein, but most of her students will have far less natural ability. It doesn't matter. She will coax and cajole until she gets the best out of each young musician. Her ultimate goal is to hand a baton to the student so that he can continue pushing, prodding, and inspiring *himself* to create his own beautiful music.

Yes, good teachers are underpaid and frequently underappreciated. Working conditions in many schools are abysmal. Classes are typically too large. The challenges are awesome, and the expectation that the teacher should be held responsible for shaping children's values, work ethic, and goals is illogical. This responsibility rightfully belongs to parents. Unfortunately, because of other obligations and priorities, far too many parents have either abdicated or severely limited their critical role in nurturing in their children a love of learning. These parents don't read with their children. They don't discuss and review what is being studied in school. They don't clearly communicate their guidelines and values. They don't establish expectations and actively encourage goal setting.

Many children today carry societal and family problems into the classroom, and these problems can undermine their ability to function efficiently. Unlike previous generations, too many parents are either not supportive of teachers or simply give lip service to being supportive. It should not surprise us when students mirror their parents' attitudes and become resistant to being educated and disrespectful of their teachers. Some even become downright dangerous, as attested to by the fact that fifty thousand teachers are actually physically assaulted each year!*

Good teachers deserve respect and active support. If your child's

---

*The National Educational Association estimates that every day 100,000 students bring weapons to school, 6,250 teachers are threatened, and 260 are assaulted. Source: Jon D. Hull, "The Knife in the Book Bag," *Time* (Feb. 8, 1993, p. 37).

teacher is talented, dedicated, and vigilant, be sure to let her know that you appreciate her and value her skills. You and your child are very fortunate.

Teacher Feedback

How does teacher competency and diligence affect your child? The impact is direct and profound. The more astute the teacher and the more insightful her observations, the more likely your child's difficulties and needs will be accurately identified and addressed.

It is the classroom teacher who should communicate her concerns if your child is not submitting his homework or is handing in sloppy, incomplete, illegible, or inaccurate work. It is the teacher who should alert you as soon as your child begins to struggle academically. It is the teacher who should call and indicate the specific deficiencies. It is the teacher who should send you a note advising you that your child is not paying attention in class, is struggling to read and comprehend, or is failing to develop effective language arts skills. This feedback should be provided before a full-blown crisis develops.

There are obviously a great many *shoulds* that unfortunately may never translate into action. One thing is certain: The teacher is a critical link in the communication chain.

If your child is floundering in school, you must develop an effective strategy for getting the information you need to understand his situation and make wise decisions about helping him resolve his problems. Certainly, the observations and impressions of a highly competent and insightful teacher are more valuable and reliable than those of a less-than-competent teacher. But even if your child's teacher is marginal or inadequate, you can still learn how to extract vital information, and you can learn how to assess objectively the value and validity of this information.

Your child's teacher may not be fully aware of her key role in the problem identification/resolution process. In fact, she may not even want this responsibility. Nevertheless, the obligation to sound the alarm is hers. And it's your job to remind her—diplomatically if possible, and more assertively if necessary—of her duty to keep you apprised as to how your child is doing and to advise you about problems before they become incapacitating. Even admitting that she doesn't understand why your child is struggling is preferable to not saying anything until it's too late.

The objective of the information-gathering process is to obtain substantive information about your child's educational status. You don't want platitudes or generalizations, such as "I think your son's immature" or "He doesn't seem ready to learn." You want precise observations, such as:

"He's reversing his letters."
"He's highly distracted."
"His spelling is inaccurate."
"His reading comprehension is poor."
"He has difficulty understanding verbal instructions."
"He has difficulty copying accurately from the chalkboard."
"He has trouble identifying important information when he studies."
"He has difficulty managing time and being organized."

You also want reasonable explanations, such as:

"I think he may be fooling around in class because he feels frustrated and can't do the required work."
"His handwriting is sloppy because he's holding his pencil too tightly and appears to have poor fine-motor control."
"His work is inaccurate because he has difficulty attending to visual details, and he doesn't take the time to check over his assignments."

Helpful Hints for Communicating with Your Child's Teacher

Express that you have concerns about your child's academic work. Tell her that you don't want him to fall behind and become discouraged and resistant to learning.

Communicate that you want to work together to solve your child's academic problems. If your expectations are positive and your communication style is not hostile or accusatory, you'll have a much better chance of winning the teacher's active support.

Show respect even if you have doubts about the teacher's competence. You want the teacher on your team. You don't want to make her your enemy. Express appreciation for her skills, contributions, and efforts, and let her know that you recognize the challenges she faces. Communicating respect can be extremely difficult, however, if you're convinced that the teacher is inadequate, unable to provide meaningful feedback, or damaging your child by being insensitive or unfair. You must do everything in your power to help her better understand the issues and become more insightful about your child's problems and more empathetic to his feelings.

Explain that you're prepared to do all you can at home to support her efforts. If additional assistance is required after school, you'll somehow manage to provide this assistance within the limits of your financial resources.

Make sure she knows that you are not going to take your child's side simply because he's your child. You want to get the problems resolved, not take sides. If your child is at fault, you're prepared to look at this objectively. If he's acting out or being irresponsible, you want to identify what's causing this behavior. If he's feeling inadequate, he may be unconsciously using the counterproductive behavior to deflect attention from his learning problems.

If you can't communicate effectively with the teacher, if you question her competence, judgment, or objectivity, or if you notice defensiveness or bias against you or your child, request that the principal, vice principal, school counselor, or school psychologist get involved. You want the school personnel to recognize your commitment to helping your child. You also want them to participate in finding solutions to your child's learning problems. If the teacher is damaging your child, you must intervene. Don't be afraid to make waves or be branded a neurotic, interfering parent. You are your child's most important advocate. If you can't enlist the help and support of the school administration, make an appointment to speak with the superintendent. Don't be intimidated. Your taxes pay this person's salary. Let the district know that you are a force to be reckoned with and that you will do whatever is necessary to ensure that your child gets a decent education and is not harmed by an incompetent or uncaring teacher. Try to work within the system, but be prepared to exercise your full range of options, including due process and hearings if necessary (see chapter 5).

Getting Critical Information

As the parent of a child who is struggling in school, you must see yourself as a detective. Like Sherlock Holmes, you must examine the available data, look for important clues that hide beneath the surface, and logically and objectively assess your child's situation.

The best detectives are tenacious and dedicated. They invariably develop an efficient and consistent method of investigation.

If you use the seven-step information-gathering/teacher communication system that follows, your efforts to help your child will be more focused and effective. You'll also be serving notice to the school personnel that you are committed to getting your child on track in school.

Seven Steps for Getting Vital Information from Your Child's Teacher

Step 1: Request brief and periodic updates from the classroom teacher if you or she observe that your child is struggling academically.

A. Tell the teacher that you're concerned about your child's poor academic performance and the negative impact this can have on his self-confidence.

B. Explain that you don't want to wait for the next report card to find out how your child is doing. And you certainly don't want to be told in April, after it's too late to do anything, that the teacher is recommending your child repeat the grade!

C. Explain that you believe parent/teacher communication is vital and that you're relying on her to inform you if your child falls behind, fails to master key skills, or is unable to do the assigned class work or homework.

D. Request brief updates every two or three weeks. Mini-conferences need not be person to person. A telephone call may be sufficient. Ask the teacher if she has any ideas about what's causing your child's difficulties, but don't be highly critical if she cannot identify the causal factors. Some teachers are better at this than others. They may have years of "front-line" classroom experience, good intuition, and/or formal or informal training in assessing academic problems. The classroom teacher is not a school psychologist or a learning disabilities specialist. Your expectations should be realistic.

Step 2: Ask the teacher to complete the Teacher Checklist on the following pages prior to your next parent–teacher conference.

A. This checklist is designed for children in grades 1–8 and should ideally be completed four to six weeks after the beginning of the new school year and again after six months to gauge academic progress or lack of progress. The checklist is designed to focus the teacher's observations, stimulate vigilance, and avoid generalities, such as "Tamara appears to be too social and doesn't seem to be very serious about her schoolwork." The more specific and precise the input, the more meaningful it is. If your child's academic problems primarily involve reading accuracy or letter reversals, this key information would indicate to a resource specialist or educational therapist what remediation approaches are appropriate. If your child is already well into the school year, ask the teacher to complete the checklist as soon as possible. If your child is in middle school, ask each of his teachers to complete the checklist. Please note that most teachers

Teacher Checklist for Elementary School Students
A Proprietary Diagnostic Inventory

Student's Name: _____ Date: _____ Teacher: _____

Please place the appropriate number after each item listed. If the student's behavior or performance falls between two numbers in the following code, use a dash. Example: 3–4.

Code: 0 = Never   1 = Rarely   2 = Sometimes   3 = Often   4 = Always

Motor Skills

Appears Clumsy _____ Poor Handwriting _____
Poor Gross-Motor Coordination _____ Poor Balance _____
Awkward _____ Right/Left Confusion _____
Poor Eye-Hand Coordination _____ Avoids Sports _____

Behavior

Overactive _____ Slow in Completing Work _____
Unpredictable _____ Impatient _____
Sensitive _____ Unpopular with Other Children _____
Daydreams _____ Excitable _____
Easily Distracted _____ Easily Frustrated _____
Appears Immature _____ Disturbing to Others _____
Resistant to Help _____ Impulsive _____
Forgetful _____ Poor Self-image _____
Difficulty Working Independently _____ Difficulty Concentrating _____
Short Attention Span _____ Hard to Discipline _____
Projects Not Completed _____ Accident Prone _____
Negative Attitude Toward School _____ Unhappy _____
Difficulty Accepting Guidelines _____ Defiant _____
Reckless _____ Temper Tantrums _____
Hostile _____ Moody _____
Resistant to Help _____ Lies _____
Procrastinates _____ Disorganized _____
Teases _____ Irresponsible _____
Blames Others _____ Manipulative _____
Poor Self-control _____ Gives Up Easily _____

Apathy About School Performance ___	Makes Up Excuses ___
Acts Out in Class ___	Chronically Confused ___

Academics

Difficulty Keeping Up with Class ___	Inaccurate Assignments ___
Slow in Completing Work ___	Sloppy Work Habits ___
Difficulty Spelling ___	Letter or Number Reversals ___
Inaccurate Reading ___	Poor Phonics ___
Difficulty with Written Directions ___	Poor Reading Comprehension ___
Difficulty with Verbal Directions ___	Difficulty Blending Sounds ___
Difficulty Identifying Sight Words ___	Difficulty with Word Attack ___
Difficulty with Language Arts ___	Difficulty with Math Concepts ___
Difficulty with Math Computations ___	Incomplete Assignments ___
Inaccurate Copying at Desk ___	Sloppy Work ___
Inaccurate Copying at Chalkboard ___	Poor Grades ___

Study Skills (Not Relevant in Grades K–3)

Poor Time Management ___	Difficulty Planning Projects ___
Doesn't Identify Key Information ___	Poor Test Preparation ___
Irresponsible About Deadlines ___	Difficulty Memorizing ___
Difficulty Taking Notes in Class ___	Difficulty Establishing Goals ___
Doesn't Establish Short-term Goals ___	Frequent Study Interruptions ___
Doesn't Establish Long-term Goals ___	Rushes Through Assignments ___
Difficulty Recording Assignments ___	Difficulty Reviewing for Tests ___
Difficulty Using a Study Schedule ___	Difficulty Setting Priorities ___
Overwhelmed by School Demands ___	Takes Little Pride in Work ___
Difficulty Taking Textbook Notes ___	Doesn't Learn from Mistakes ___

How would you evaluate my child in the following areas?

Self-esteem: 1 2 3 4 5 6 7 8 9 10
               (low)   (high)

Responsibility: 1 2 3 4 5 6 7 8 9 10
               (low)   (high)

Happiness: 1 2 3 4 5 6 7 8 9 10
               (low)   (high)

Ability: 1 2 3 4 5 6 7 8 9 10
               (low)   (high)

Performance: 1   2   3   4   5   6   7   8   9   10
                            (low)   (high)

Effort/Motivation: 1   2   3   4   5   6   7   8   9   10
                            (low)   (high)

What are your primary concerns about my child?

What specific changes would you like to see?

What are my child's strengths?

What should I be doing to help my child?

What additional services can the school provide?

want a release form signed by parents before they will fill out any form that provides information about a student. Even though the child's parent may request the checklist for her own use, the information could end up in someone else's possession. By requiring a release, the teacher is protecting herself. The release would consist of a simple statement in writing: "I authorize to complete the attached checklist that provides information about my child." You would then sign and date the release.

B. Complete the checklist yourself. It will help focus your observations and allow you to compare your impressions with those of the teacher. You may perceive the same strengths and weaknesses, or you may disagree on key points. The checklist will provide a context for comparison, discussion, and brainstorming.

Step 3: As you interpret the teacher's evaluation, look for specific deficits areas (3s and 4s on the checklist) that need to be corrected and for a pattern of deficits that suggests an underlying learning disability.

A. Don't be alarmed if your child has a few deficits (that is, a 3 in "Easily Frustrated" and a 3 in "Inaccurate Copying"). Isolated deficits can generally be remediated easily. Your child might simply need extra help from the teacher in writing more legibly, or you might hire a tutor for a few sessions of handwriting instruction. The frustration issue might be resolved by alerting your child to the behavior and brainstorming ideas and options for dealing more successfully with setbacks, errors, and disappointments. If, however, you observe a pattern of chronic academic or behavioral deficits as indicated by many 3s and 4s, this clearly suggests that your child is at risk. Chronic explosions of anger are atypical and suggest the need for a professional assessment and possible counseling (see chapter 9).

B. Deficits flagged with 3s and 4s on the Checklist should be discussed with the teacher, especially if she has flagged more than one or two problem areas. You want to know, for example, what the teacher proposes to do about a 4 in "Difficulty Keeping Up with Class" and a 4 in "Letter or Number Reversals."

C. A pervasive pattern of 3s and 4s is a red flag, and you need to take action. The starting point in the process is the teacher. You must ask him or her three critical questions:

What can you do to help correct my child's problem?
Will this help be enough?
Who else needs to be brought into the equation? Do we need to involve the school psychologist, a tutor, a private educational therapist, the pediatrician, or some other expert?

Step 4: Once the teacher identifies specific academic, attitudinal, or behavioral deficit areas, ask for suggestions about how to correct the deficiencies.

A. The teacher may have supplemental materials that could be used at home to correct specific deficits identified on the checklist (for example, finding common denominators, working more legibly, or recording assignments).

B. Ask if the teacher would be willing to spend some extra time helping your child before or after school.

C. If there is a pattern of deficits on the inventory that suggests a learning disability (or learning difference), request an assessment by the Child Study Team, the school psychologist, and/or the resource specialist (see chapters 5, 6, and 7).

• School districts are required by law to provide learning assistance for learning disabled students. Request a parents' rights manual (all districts are required to have one) that spells out the criteria and procedures for testing.

• Communicate clearly that you place great value on education and that you're committed to making certain your child acquires a good education and masters the skills he needs to support himself and, if he desires, go on to college. Express that you're committed to helping remove any academic or emotional roadblocks that might stand in his way.

• Communicate diplomatically that the school is responsible for helping identify your child's learning problems before they become debilitating, and explain that you're not willing to let the situation deteriorate. Inform the teacher that it's your responsibility to be your child's advocate and that it's the school's responsibility to provide an adequate education. (Ideally, this education will be more than simply adequate.)

• If your child has skills deficits or an attitude problem, state that you believe it's reasonable to expect the school to help you identify the causative factors and to work with you in resolving the problem.

Step 5: If you and the teacher agree that your child cannot keep up with the class because of specific learning deficits targeted on the checklist, inquire if the workload and difficulty level of in-class and homework assignments are too demanding. Request that the work be modified (see chapter 7 for accommodations required by federal law) so that your child doesn't become discouraged and demoralized.

A. Explain that this adjustment is only a temporary fix until headway can be made in remediating the deficits.

B. Ask the teacher how much time she realistically expects students to spend doing their homework. If your child is doing less than expected and the quality of his work is poor or marginal or he's not completing his assignments, you'll need to discuss this issue with him and require that he allocate more time. If, on the other hand, he appears to be working hard, you will need to determine if he's wasting time or cannot do what is expected of him within a reasonable time frame. No fourth grader should spend four hours each evening doing homework. If he is, something is amiss, and the situation needs to be examined carefully.

C. Ask the teacher not to make your child feel guilty for his learning problems and to make every effort not to embarrass him in class. If he's struggling to read aloud and is very self-conscious, ask that she tell him in advance what section he'll be reading so that he can prepare with your help or the help of his resource specialist (see chapter 4), tutor (see chapter 10), or educational therapist (see chapter 10). If your child's skills are very poor, he should not be asked to read aloud at all, since this might make him feel ridiculed. These emotionally wrenching negative associations can last a lifetime and should be avoided at all cost.

D. If your child has been identified as having a learning disability, ask the teacher if she is communicating regularly with the resource specialist. If appropriate, explore ways in which this communication might be enhanced. It would be beneficial if the resource specialist participated in this discussion.

E. If your child has a significant learning disability and is in a special day class, ask his teacher if the specific deficits highlighted on the checklist are being addressed.

F. If you and the teacher conclude that extra help from a private educational therapist or tutor is advisable (and financially feasible), ask if she can make a referral to someone with a good reputation (see chapter 10). Some school districts discourage or even forbid teachers to make referrals to private practitioners or private agencies for fear that it might be construed that the district is admitting it cannot provide for the student's educational needs and therefore should pay for private services.

Step 6: Ask to review your child's scores on standardized tests that have been given, such as the Stanford Achievement Test, the California Tests of Basic Skills, or the California Achievement Test.

A. Ask the teacher to explain your child's test results in terms you can understand. If you're not sure what the 37th percentile or the 4th stanine means, ask for clarification. If your child's grade expectancy is 4.7 (fourth grade, seventh month) and he is in the third month of fifth grade, ask how to interpret the information and ask for specific suggestions to help your child get up to grade level (see chapter 6).

B. If your child is more than one year below grade level, ask if he would qualify for the resource program (remedial assistance during the school day), the Title 1 Program (special tutorial help for children in "disadvantaged" schools), or a special after-school tutorial program (see chapters 4 and 5).

C. If you're dissatisfied with the teacher's explanation and interpretation of your child's standardized test scores, request that the school psychologist or resource specialist explain and interpret the scores.

Step 7: Periodically ask for updates about your child's progress.

A. A telephone call to the teacher can provide key information about the efficacy of the remediation strategy. If everything is going according to plan, you'll feel relieved. If there are glitches, you and the teacher can discuss adjustments and alternatives.

B. An in-class visit can provide invaluable information, and most teachers will have no objection to such a visit. (If your child's teacher does object, tell her such an observation will help you better understand your child's academic problems and needs.) The visit will offer you an opportunity to observe your child as he does his class work. You'll be able to see firsthand whether he's distractible or has difficulty following directions. You'll also see if he can do the work expected of him. Initially, your child may be self-conscious having you observe, but he should quickly become less aware of you. The observations should last at least an hour. At home you might discuss what you observed. Do so nonjudgmentally. You might say, "It looked as if those math problems were easy for you. Was the reading more difficult? Could you use some extra help with your reading?"

C. Send notes to communicate with the teacher. You might write, "Kelly had difficulty with the two-place division problems. Any suggestions? Do you recommend additional worksheets that might explain and reinforce the concepts and procedures? Do you want me to correct the problems or try to explain the material to her?"

D. Periodic, informal conferences can provide an update and a follow-up on suggestions and strategies for working with your child in school and at home. You could apprise the teacher about progress with the tutor or educational therapist. If your child is taking medication for attention deficit disorder, you could compare notes about improvement in concentration, follow-through, and academic performance. These conferences need not last more than ten or fifteen minutes.

Considering Your Options

If you have gone through the seven steps described above, you undoubtedly have a better sense of your child's situation in school and the challenges he faces. Each of the steps will be examined in later chapters.

You have many legally guaranteed options as you advocate for your child's educational rights. Let's take a brief look now at some of the possibilities. By the time you finish this book, you will know how to exercise each of these options skillfully.

Options for Parents

1. Request an assessment by the Child Study Team, the school psychologist, or the resource specialist (see chapters 4–7).
2. If your child doesn't qualify for testing in school or has been ex-

cluded from the resource program, consider having him privately evaluated (see chapters 8–10).

3. Discuss your concerns about your child's academic deficits with your child's pediatrician or family physician. This is especially important if your child has chronic concentration difficulties (possible attention deficit disorder or attention deficit hyperactivity disorder). If appropriate, request a referral to a specialist (see chapters 8–12).

4. Consider discussing your concerns with a private educational consultant, educational psychologist, or educational therapist who may provide important insights about your child's problems and suggest remediation strategies (see chapters 8 and 10).

5. Consider hiring a qualified private tutor or educational therapist. Request a referral from the teacher, resource specialist, or school psychologist. School personnel may be reluctant to make referrals if there is the possibility that the district will have to pay for these services (see chapter 10).

6. Consider enrolling your child at a learning center (see chapter 10).

7. Discuss the issues with your child in language he can understand and involve him in the process of resolving the problems (see chapters 3, 13, 14, and 15).

8. Seek counseling if a pattern of counterproductive attitudes and behaviors are compounding your child's learning problems (see chapter 9).

9. Continue to monitor the situation in school and meet regularly with the classroom teacher (see chapter 2).

10. If your child is receiving special help in school, request periodic meetings with the specialist providing this help so that you can gauge progress and pinpoint areas needing improvement. Explain that you want to be alerted if your child experiences unanticipated difficulties and that you also want to be informed if your child has made a breakthrough (see chapters 7 and 12).

Chapter 2
Focusing Your Observations and Impressions

Imagine that you're having car problems and that you can't rely on your old Nissan to start in the morning. The car has begun to stall in traffic at the most inopportune times. You can no longer deny that the valves and the transmission are making strange noises. You're faced with a difficult decision: invest in fixing the car or sell it and buy a new one.

To determine how bad the situation is, you take the car to your trusted mechanic. Your worst fears are confirmed. He hands you a long list of needed repairs and an estimate of how much they will cost. Just to be safe, you decide to have another mechanic check out the car. While wrestling with what to do, you decide to visit some auto dealerships and get prices on a new car. As you stare in disbelief at the stickers on the back windows, you shudder involuntarily. The cars cost as much as your parents paid for their house!

In an effort to do a thorough job of investigating your options, you pore over consumer reports about performance, safety, and reliability, and you test-drive several different makes and models. You make comparisons and begin the unpleasant job of negotiating prices with salespeople. You also query friends who own the models you're considering. You talk to several banks to find the best financing package. And, of course, you spend many hours thinking about the pros and cons of each car and the pluses and minuses of repair versus replacement. You must make a decision. You have a final discussion with your spouse, reexamine your choices, and agree on what to do.

It's interesting that many parents fail to go through a similar systematic process when they conclude that their child is not working properly in school. Parents don't have the option of selling the old model, but they do have other options. They can:

- choose to disregard the problem;
- deny the problem exists;
- live with the situation and hope the problem goes away;
- commit themselves to making the necessary "repairs."

Just as your malfunctioning car will ultimately break down unless you attend to the repairs, so, too, will your malfunctioning child. The longer you wait before fixing the problem, the more expensive it will be. This assumes, of course, that the problem is still fixable. Serious, perhaps irreparable damage may already have occurred.

Key Questions

Before you can come to grips with your child's learning problems and resolve the difficulties, you must ask and answer three key questions:

1. What is the problem that is causing my child to struggle?
2. What do we need to do to fix the problem?
3. Who is the best "academic mechanic" in town?

These questions are challenging because the most difficult problems to define are those in which you are emotionally enmeshed. There is a tendency to focus on the symptoms ("She's highly resistant when I try to help her") and not the underlying causes ("Her dyslexia and attention deficit disorder make it difficult for her to do the assigned work. She resists because she's trying to avoid having to deal with the problem. To ask her to work in her deficit areas causes her to feel inadequate and defensive. She'll do anything she can to escape the pain").

Even if you succeed in defining your child's problem, you face another challenge: figuring out what needs to be done to fix it. You may conclude that you lack the knowledge to evaluate the advice and recommendations given by friends and professionals. One expert may tell you, "Your daughter seems immature. I think we should retain her in third grade and give her time to grow up and become serious about her schoolwork." Another expert may tell you, "Your daughter has significant auditory and visual processing deficits, and requires intensive educational therapy." Whom do you believe? What do you do?

Finding the best person to provide help can pose another dilemma. Should you rely exclusively on the school resource program? Should you seek a private tutor or an educational therapist? Should you enroll your child in a private school or a private learning center? Should you consider counseling or medication for attention deficit disorder? Sorting out your options, evaluating the skills of the professionals, and finding an intervention/remediation program that meets your child's needs can sorely test your emotional, reasoning, financial, and problem-solving resources. The most effective strategy is to begin with what is most concrete: the specific information you acquired about your child's academic strengths and weaknesses.

Crunching the Data

If you've followed the information-gathering strategy described in chapter 1, you should have some data about your child's academic strengths and weaknesses. The completed Teacher Checklist and your discussions with the teacher will have pinpointed your child's specific academic, behavior, and attitude deficits, and the severity of those deficits. You have probably deduced whether you need to be somewhat, moderately, or urgently concerned.

Possessing data is one thing; interpreting it accurately and using it effectively is another. The situation is once again similar to the malfunctioning car. If the mechanic says you need a valve job, a transmission overhaul, a new timing belt, and a complete brake job, you must assess the information and recommendation to decide whether you trust the mechanic's skills. If you conclude that the repairs are needed and appropriate, the price is right, and the mechanic is honest and skilled, you authorize the job.

Why wouldn't this same decision-making procedure be applicable in assessing a school problem and deciding on a plan of action? You evaluate the data analytically and objectively (a left brain function) and intuitively and subjectively (a right brain function). You then determine the degree of urgency. You have two basic choices: monitor your child closely, keep on top of the situation, and be ready to intervene aggressively if the situation doesn't improve or begins to deteriorate *or* pull out all the stops because your child is in crisis and at serious academic and emotional risk.

Reacting to the Signals

Recognizing the danger flags is the first step in solving a problem. Figuring out a systematic strategy for addressing the underlying causative issues is the next step.

Let's assume you've determined the urgency in your child's school situation. You're now faced with three additional challenges:

1. to make certain your child's academic deficiencies are effectively remediated
2. to respond appropriately to the psychological fallout: procrastination, laziness, late assignments, irresponsibility, sloppy work
3. to build your child's self-confidence.

If you conclude that your child's learning problems are being adequately addressed with school and/or outside-of-school assistance, you can relax somewhat. Because your child appears to be responding positively to the assistance program, your primary role is now to provide emotional support and encouragement, and make certain the progress continues. You'll need to monitor the situation carefully and communicate regularly with the teacher until your child is definitely out of the woods. If, on the other hand, you conclude that your child's learning deficits are *not* being adequately addressed and that your child is falling further and further behind, you may need to become more aggressive and perhaps intrusive.

Parental Intuition

Human intuition is one of the top rungs on the ladder of human intelligence, and yet this remarkable capacity to size up situations and respond effectively is often dismissed as nothing special. You might be thinking, "Intuition is no big deal. Everyone has it. So does my dog." Well, your dog certainly has instincts, but this is not the equivalent of human intuition. Your dog cannot integrate insights, emotions, analytical thinking, logic, critical thinking, and strategic thinking. And your dog can't use these capabilities to assess situations and predict future consequences. You have these remarkable abilities, however, and they will serve you well in your search for answers to your child's learning problems.

Intuition results from the sum of your life experiences—both the positive and negative. Having learned from the good choices and the flawed ones, your intuition in tandem with your wisdom, analytical thinking, and judgment is the beacon that helps you make choices, respond to challenges, and solve problems. This beacon should be your guide as you devise a strategy for helping your struggling child.

Your intuition will tell you when your child is hurting, despite her unconscious attempts to hide her feelings from you. It will tell you if the advice offered by experts should be heeded and if your child's difficulties have been accurately diagnosed and are being properly treated. Your intuition will also tell you if the remediation program is working.

Listen to your inner voice and trust it as you labor to make the right decisions about your child's education. Don't allow anyone to persuade you that this voice is unreliable when you intuitively conclude that what you're being told simply doesn't add up.

Cause and Effect

Let's examine a hypothetical scenario. You ask your child's teacher to complete the Teacher Checklist in chapter 1, and he indicates that your child *always* has poor reading comprehension and *often* has poor handwriting. Realizing that the poor reading comprehension is an academic deficit, you assume that the problem can be corrected with a good remediation program. You note that the handwriting problem is listed under the motor skills category on the checklist. Although you may not fully understand why handwriting is considered a motor skill, you reason that it has something to do with the muscles in the hand that control the way a pencil or pen is used. You're not certain about how to correct the problem, but you presume it's correctable with instruction from someone who has had the proper training.

Let's say that the teacher has also indicated on the checklist that your child is *always* impulsive, *often* has difficulty accepting guidelines, *always* leaves projects incomplete, is *always* irresponsible, *always* disturbs others, and is *often* resistant to help. This feedback suggests that your child has acquired a pattern of counterproductive attitudes and behaviors. Although you have no idea why she's manifesting these behaviors and attitudes, you conclude that they are related to her academic deficiencies.

Differentiating academic problems from behavior and attitude problems can be difficult, even for professional educators and school psychologists. Deficiencies in one area tend to overlap with those in another. Trying to sort out and classify the deficits and establish a pattern of cause and effect can be a complex process because the symptoms of a problem may be mistaken for the causes of the problem. For example, a child with reading comprehension deficits may be struggling because she never acquired a good foundation in phonics or because she's dyslexic, chronically distractible, cannot recall visual information, or is unable to form mental images of what she's reading. It's also possible that she might have difficulty comprehending because she's preoccupied with family problems (an impending divorce or separation), social problems (difficulty making friends), or emotional problems (insecurity and internal conflict). She may write illegibly because she has fine-motor problems and a poor sense of spatial relationships, or because she's chronically impulsive and distractible and lacks the requisite self-discipline to make certain her letters are well formed. The child may also have acquired the habit of doing shoddy work because she lacks self-esteem and may actually feel undeserving of turning out work that produces pride and a sense of accomplishment.

Because the factors causing your child's problems in school are often complex or difficult to identify, you must acquire as much data as possible about her specific deficits. You'll want input from her teacher and, if your child has been assessed, from the school psychologist, the resource specialist, and any other professionals who are providing assistance.

Differential Diagnosis

When children are struggling academically, there are frequently multiple overlapping symptoms and several possible explanations for the difficulties. The red flags signaling problems in scholastic performance, attitude, and/or behavior can be difficult to differentiate, so you must be prepared to do some sleuthing. An *attitude* problem ("School is dumb!") can negatively affect a child's school performance and behavior. A *performance* problem ("When I take a test, I can't remember what I studied!") can negatively affect a child's attitude and behavior.

One of the greatest challenges you face is determining what the red flags mean. The most effective way to define your child's problem accurately and identify the causes is to eliminate systematically what the problem *isn't* through a process called *differential diagnosis*. This procedure is also used in medicine. When a patient goes to the doctor complaining of excruciating pain and restricted motion in her shoulder, she is describing the presenting symptoms. The doctor realizes that the problem might be caused by tendinitis, bursitis, arthritis, or a host of other factors. By means of a careful examination and appropriate blood, X-ray, and MRI tests, the physician uses differential diagnosis to rule out what is *not* causing the problem. Through this process of elimination, the doctor determines the source of the pain and then prescribes the most effective treatment.

You can use this same method to get a handle on the factors that are causing your child's learning problem. Because your child's school difficulties may be multifaceted, you'll probably need help in differentiating the symptoms of the problem (such as chronic spelling errors) from the source of the problem (such as visual memory and auditory discrimination deficits). Providing this help is the function of the school psychologist, resource specialist, and the Individual Educational Plan (IEP) team (the school personnel who meet with you to discuss your child's diagnostic test results and recommend a remediation plan—see chapter 6).

If the staff at your child's school is not helpful or if your intuition tells you the staff is not competent, you may need to seek differential diagnosis and treatment elsewhere (see chapters 4–8 and 10).

Deciding If Your Perceptions Are Accurate

If you feel unsure of the accuracy of your observations, impressions, and conclusions, there are two steps you can take to confirm your perceptions:

1. Complete the Teacher Checklist yourself and compare your assessment with that of the teacher.
2. Complete the following Parent Perceptions Inventory.

After you complete the Teacher Checklist, it may be apparent that your assessment of your child's skills, strengths, and weaknesses is not the same as her teacher's. This should be discussed. You might say: "I've observed that my child has difficulty following directions at home. You've indicated on the Teacher Checklist that this is rarely a problem in the classroom. I'm curious about our different perceptions, and I'm trying to understand why my child appears to have problems in this area at home but not in school. Do you have any ideas about this discrepancy? If you're doing something that's effective in helping him understand directions in class, I would like to borrow the technique and use it at home."

If your perceptions are consistent with those of the teacher, you now have concurring input from two sources that indicates your child's current level of performance in specific areas. You, the teacher, and the resource specialist can use the checklist to establish realistic performance goals and gauge improvement. If your child is working with a tutor or educational therapist, the feedback on the checklist can also serve as a baseline in the remediation process. It can be used to highlight deficits and gauge your child's progress in overcoming them.

The following inventory is designed to help you assess your child's attitudes, behavior, emotional state, and academic situation. Your responses to the statements will either substantiate or allay your concerns about your child. A pattern of "true" responses are cause for concern, and you can refer to the specific deficits you've identified on the inventory to support a request that your child be diagnostically evaluated and, if appropriate, provided with remedial assistance in school.

This inventory can help you clarify key issues that may be preventing your child from working to her full potential. Even one or two *true* responses should be interpreted as a warning signal.

Identifying your child's specific academic, attitude, and behavior deficits and pinpointing your concerns about her school situation represent only the first leg of the journey. You must continue your search for effective assistance and ultimate resolution of the learning difficulties. The next critical step is learning how to communicate more effectively with your child about her problems, feelings, and perceptions.

Parent Perceptions Inventory

	True	False
My child's academic skills are below grade level.	_____	_____
My child dislikes school.	_____	_____
My child is losing enthusiasm for learning.	_____	_____
My child is not working up to full potential.	_____	_____
My child is not working diligently in school.	_____	_____
My child does not submit completed, legible assignments.	_____	_____
My child does not submit assignments on time.	_____	_____
My child's self-concept is being damaged by repeated negative experiences in school.	_____	_____
My child has developed a pattern of self-sabotaging coping mechanisms, attitudes, and behaviors.	_____	_____
My child's problems have not been adequately diagnosed.	_____	_____
My child's attitudes and behaviors appear to be linked to underlying, unresolved learning deficits.	_____	_____
My child feels inadequate.	_____	_____
My child is defensive.	_____	_____
My child has a poor understanding of cause and effect and makes chronically flawed choices.	_____	_____
My child has become very dependent on me to help with homework and studying.	_____	_____
My child appears to be crying out for help but is intent on denying that he/she has a problem.	_____	_____

	True	False
My child resists my efforts to help.	___	___
My child blames others rather than takes responsibility for actions.	___	___
My child has poor organization and time management skills.	___	___
My child does not know how to study efficiently and effectively.	___	___
My child is not receiving enough help to overcome his/her academic problems.	___	___
My child is not responding positively to the help being provided in school.	___	___
My child is not responding positively to the help being provided privately after school.	___	___

Chapter 3
Communicating with Your Child and Getting Vital Information

*"How'd it go today in school?" you ask your ten-year-old at the dinner table.
"Good," your son replies nonchalantly. He looks away, and every parental
instinct screams that he's not telling the truth.*

Perhaps this vignette doesn't describe how your child responds
when you ask him about what's happening in school. Perhaps he
openly replies to your inquiries and willingly shares his frustra-
tions, fears, and doubts. He may tell you that he was embarrassed when
his teacher asked him to go to the chalkboard and solve a math problem
that he couldn't do. He may recount how self-conscious he felt when the
kids began to laugh as he stood in front of the class trying to remember
how to add mixed fractions. He may reveal how dumb he feels because
he can't keep up or a classmate teases him about being stupid.

Having a child who discusses his problems, shares his perceptions, and
expresses his feelings is a blessing. This feedback can play a key role in
helping you identify the issues that are causing the academic difficulties
and emotional upsets.

Unfortunately, many struggling children are unwilling to express their
feelings and perceptions openly. It's far more common for a demoralized
child to be uncommunicative and guarded. As you confront this evasive-
ness, you may find yourself becoming frustrated, angry, and sad. You
want to provide support and play an active role in helping your child
resolve his school-related problems. No parent likes being kept at arm's
length when his or her child is hurting.

Your child's unwillingness to communicate can be very disconcerting,
but you must keep his reaction in perspective. The behavior is not a con-

scious rejection of you as a parent. The defensiveness is instinctual. Your child is unconsciously driven to protect himself from feeling inferior. By refusing to discuss his upsets in school, he's trying to cope as best he can with his demoralization and sense of failure. He's shutting you out because he feels guilt and shame, and because he doesn't want to expose his inadequacies to the most important person in his life.

The Pain Factor

Your child spends more than one thousand hours each year in the classroom, and it's understandable that chronic academic problems will cause him to feel frustration, embarrassment, and distress. The classroom is the arena where he is expected to perform and where he receives continual feedback about his abilities. If he can't function effectively in this venue, he'll inevitably conclude that he's in some way flawed and incompetent. To protect his fragile self-image, he'll probably devise a range of coping behaviors. He may resort to rationalizing ("School is boring"), minimizing the implications ("Who cares about getting good grades?"), denying ("Stop bugging me. I'm doing fine"), deflecting ("Why do you always complain about me and never about Kelly?"), blaming ("The teacher never told us to study that"), running away ("Who cares about doing well in math? I want to be a professional skateboarder"), hiding ("My stomach hurts. I want to stay in bed"), evading ("I don't think I have science homework"), and even lying ("I didn't sign your name to the report card!"). Because he is immersed in the compelling need to protect himself, he may not realize that his problems are still visible. Unfortunately, you and his teacher may become so preoccupied with reacting to his self-sabotaging behaviors that you may lose sight of the fact that the behavior is actually a *sign of despair*.

Most children cry when they're upset. Some bounce back quickly from their upsets. These youngsters typically have healthy self-esteem. Those who are more emotionally fragile tend to internalize a bruising setback or demoralizing defeat and often resist showing their pain. They may repress their feelings by retreating into their room or escaping into a fantasy world of video games, TV cartoons, toy action figures, or dolls. Other distressed children externalize their frustration by raging against the perceived injustice: "When the dumb teacher came back into the classroom, he blamed *me* because the kids were talking and fooling around. It's not fair! Everyone was fooling around. I hate the teacher!" Frustrated youngsters may vent their anger by hitting a younger sibling, slamming doors, throwing tantrums, hurling a toy across the room, or kicking the dog. They may also express their anger with passive resistance or passive aggression. They might hide something that belongs to a sibling, sabotage a family project by not cooperating, or cause stress by never being ready to leave on time.

Children who are convinced they're incompetent are especially vulnerable to real or imagined criticism. They may misconstrue their parents' noncritical statements and observations as being judgmental. Their tenuous self-confidence and self-esteem often cause them to associate any negative feedback from their teachers ("I'd like you to recopy this paper and make it neater") and any efforts by their parents to help ("Do you want me to help you figure out how to do these two-place division problems?") as further confirmation of their inadequacies. They may respond by becoming resistant, resentful, discouraged, manipulative, or oppositional.

A child's defensive behavior is quite logical. He doesn't want to talk about a bad grade, a punishment for misbehavior, or a teacher's remark that hurt his feelings, because the discussion would be too agonizing. He's unwilling to tell you that he was mortified when he was asked to read aloud and couldn't read the assigned paragraph without making mistakes. For fear of disappointing you, he doesn't want to reveal how ashamed he felt when he received a bad grade on a spelling test after having studied with you for two hours. Nor does he want to tell you how humiliated he felt when someone called him retarded as he left the classroom to see the resource specialist. Rather than express these feelings, he locks them inside and tries to pretend they don't exist.

For a child who wants to block out the miserable experiences of the day, it's far less threatening simply to respond "Good" when asked "How'd it go today?" than to dredge up bad feelings. Pretending problems don't exist can be a coping mechanism for an emotionally bruised child. If your child automatically responds "Good" when asked how his day went and resists your attempts to communicate, you must find the keys that can open the closed door, even slightly.

The next challenge is to help your child acquire analytical thinking tools that will allow him to participate actively in the process of identifying and resolving his problems. To provide the most meaningful assistance, you'll need more than test scores and completed evaluation forms from his teacher and resource specialist. You want to know: how your child perceives his school situation and how he feels about himself and his abilities; if he is convinced that he's dumb; if he considers his situation hopeless; if his teacher is embarrassing him in class; if he's being teased by other children because of his reading problems or because he has to leave class to go to the resource specialist; if he is jealous of his younger sibling who can read better than he can.

There is another compelling reason for learning how to communicate more effectively with your child: You want to teach your child that he can't run away from problems. Children who fail to learn this may spend their lives fleeing from their difficulties and may never come to grips with the doubts, fears, and insecurities that are causing their unhappiness.

Knocking on the Door

The likelihood of your child's overcoming his learning problems improves significantly if you can help him become an active, voluntary participant in the process of identifying and resolving the issues impeding his academic progress. Figuring out how to convince him that it's safe to let down his guard can be a severe test of your parental mettle.

In your effort to obtain information, you must avoid a trap that ensnares many concerned parents. You don't want to assume the role of a detective interviewing a suspect. Interrogation is not communication! Be forewarned that if your child believes you're "grilling" him, he'll turn off and shut down.

The antidote to a communication impasse is to create a safe, nonthreatening, nonjudgmental context that is conducive to discussing problems and upsets. Initially your child may not appreciate your efforts and may resist you actively or passively. Don't be deterred. You must help him realize that you're committed to being his ally and that your curiosity about school is not meddling but, rather, a desire to provide him with the resources he needs to succeed in school. You're saying: "Your impressions and feelings count. I value your feedback and insights. They're vital to getting a handle on the problem. I'm not here to judge or criticize you." By patiently helping him realize that you're on his team, you can earn his trust. This should make him more receptive to your efforts to provide help.

Opening the Door

The following communication and problem-solving strategy is designed to help you create a context that will help your child feel secure and safe discussing his emotions and perceptions. Each child is different, and you'll need to tailor your communication strategy to your child. If the method doesn't work, don't give up immediately. Make adjustments and fine-tune the system so that it can work. If you are unsuccessful in getting your child to communicate, consider consulting a professional counselor.

School-Related Issues: A Parent-Child Communication Strategy

1. Ask your child to complete the following self-evaluation. It is designed for children ages six to twelve. Do not comment about your child's responses at this point; you don't want to make him self-conscious about his answers and inhibit him. This includes nonverbal reactions such as a frown, a raised eyebrow, or a smile. If the temptation to react is too great, do something else while your child completes the evaluation.

2. Ask your child to list his best subject and his worst subject in school. Explain that you're interested in academic subjects such as mathematics and reading, not P.E. If your child has difficulty selecting his best subject, substitute "favorite subject" and "least favorite subject."

3. Explain what a "one to ten scale" is. This explanation is especially important if you have a younger child. For example, you might say that if "ten" is the most intelligent child in your class, "one" is the least intelligent child in your class, and "five" is in the middle, what number describes how smart you are—a nine or a five or a seven . . . ? Don't dispute his self-assessment, even if he considers himself unintelligent. For now, you might simply say, "Hm, that's interesting." Later you'll use his assessment as a springboard for discussion.

4. Remind yourself that your goal is to draw out your child and stimulate a discussion about impressions and reactions. You might say to your child, "These are interesting responses. Let's take a look at two of them now. We can discuss the others later." Keep the interactive sessions short—five minutes at most—especially with children in grades 1 to 4. "You say that math is your best subject. What things in math are fun and easy for you? How does it make you feel when you get a problem right or a good grade on a math test? Is it the same feeling you have when you get a hit in baseball? What's different and what's similar? How does it make you feel if you miss a problem you know how to do? Is it the same as striking out or making a fielding error?" If your child says simply "Good" or "Bad," you might respond, "In what way does it make you feel good? Do you feel proud [or ashamed] if you do poorly on something? Are there any types of math problems that are difficult for you? For example,

How I See Things

My best subject in school: _____

My worst subject in school: _____

Quality of My Work in My Best Subject

1	2	3	4	5	6	7	8	9	10
Poor				Fair					Excellent

Quality of My Work in My Worst Subject

1	2	3	4	5	6	7	8	9	10
Poor				Fair					Excellent

How Intelligent I Think I Am

1	2	3	4	5	6	7	8	9	10
Low				Average					Superior

How Much Effort I Put In

1	2	3	4	5	6	7	8	9	10
Poor				Fair					Excellent

How Happy I Am in School

1	2	3	4	5	6	7	8	9	10
Poor				Fair					Excellent

How Happy I Am at Home

1	2	3	4	5	6	7	8	9	10
Poor				Fair					Excellent

do you think you make silly errors or copy numbers from the chalkboard incorrectly? Any ideas about how to fix this problem? Do you think you do well in math because you're smart?

5. If your child seems fatigued or saturated, you may want to discontinue the discussion and pick it up later. During this subsequent discussion, you might say, "Yesterday you said reading is your worst subject. What things in reading are difficult for you? If you have a difficult time,

how does that make you feel inside?" After your child responds, you might say, "Yeah, I think I'd feel the same way. When you struggle in reading, does that make you feel dumb? Does it make you feel frustrated?" Your child's comments may lead you to say, "Hm. Any idea about how we might put our heads together and fix the problem? For example, do you think a tutor might help? Let's think about it a bit, and talk about it more tomorrow."

6. Don't try to make everything okay. It's certainly painful for parents to see that their child is discouraged, but uncovering the pain and examining it is the first step in finding solutions. Children who are rescued and who do not become actively involved in the remediation process generally make slower progress and often become increasingly dependent and helpless. And you should not rattle off questions like a machine gun. Listen carefully to what your child says about his thoughts and feelings, and resist responding with a mini-lecture or a sermon.

7. The next day you might continue your discussion about the issues left unresolved from the previous day, or you might examine another of your child's evaluations on the scales. You may be able to discuss only one scale at each session. There's no rush. If the conversation is flowing, go with the flow. But remember to keep the discussions short unless you're sure that you're both enjoying it. Resist any temptation to be judgmental. It's acceptable for your child to give himself a three in his worst subject. It's also acceptable if his perceptions about the situation seem off base. And it's acceptable for him to experience some distress without your attempting to rescue him. Your child may give himself a ten in his best subject when you believe a five is more accurate. Remember, your goal is to encourage your child to open up and communicate his thoughts and feelings, and not to challenge his perceptions. Certainly, you want him ultimately to be realistic about his situation, but he may not be emotionally ready to be realistic now. If your child is in denial, he is resorting to a psychological defense mechanism. By getting him to talk about the problems and by developing strategies with him for correcting these problems, you're providing your child with the opportunity to replace his negative associations and expectations with more positive ones.

8. During a subsequent session, you might say to your child, "You indicated on a scale that the quality of your work in reading was a three. Let's make up a list of things that might be done to improve the situation. We're just going to brainstorm—put our heads together and try to come up with as many ideas as we can to solve a problem. I have one: We

might ask the teacher to tell you in advance what section you'll be asked to read aloud in class, and we could practice it together. Another idea is to get you a tutor. Now you think of an idea."

The preceding communication strategy is designed to help you get your child beyond the automatic knee-jerk response "Good" when you ask, "How did your day go?" The suggestions for enhancing communication are intended only as a model. If your child is exceedingly resistant or profoundly blocked emotionally, the strategy may not work, and you will need to seek a competent therapist to help him sort out his feelings and perceptions.

As a general rule, children are more willing to share their feelings when they're convinced their parents are listening to what they're saying and are not continually judging them. They're also more willing to communicate when they're convinced their parents will not try to *dictate* how to solve their problems.

In this respect, children's reactions parallel our own. We share our feelings with special friends who are empathetic, sensitive, and nonjudgmental. We trust these people because they listen attentively to what we say and don't attempt to impose their own perspectives and agendas on us. We are predisposed to accept their insights and advice because they have repeatedly demonstrated their loyalty, they aren't heavy-handed, and they understand and appreciate us for who we are. We trust them because we know they care about us.

Your child probably cannot articulate his feelings about trust, respect, appreciation, loyalty, and empathy, but he has the same intimacy requirements that you do. He will share his feelings when he's convinced you will accept him flaws and all, when he's convinced you are fair, and when he believes you are his ally.

Identifying Psychological Overlay

The counterproductive behavior and attitudes that are directly attributable to a child's struggle in school are called psychological overlay. The more serious and incapacitating the learning problems, the greater the risk of psychological overlay. And the longer the psychological overlay persists, the greater the risk of self-concept damage. The child who has difficulty reading accurately, recalling what he reads, or remembering what he's told is experiencing difficulty on the neurological level of perception. If the child's neurological inefficiency and learning problems cause him to become angry and demoralized, he is manifesting psychological overlay. As his frustration increases and his self-confidence deteriorates, the overlay usually becomes more extensive and more pronounced. He may compensate for his feelings of incompetence and hopelessness by acting out, giving up, or retreating into a defensive shell. He may also compensate by becoming irresponsible, unmotivated, resistant to help, helpless, manipulative, or hostile. He may conclude that school is useless, his teacher is the enemy, and you are in cahoots with her to make his life miserable. This emotional spillover can undermine your child's self-concept, your equanimity, and your entire family's happiness.

It's important to distinguish between psychological overlay and a psychological problem. The latter is typically caused by emotional trauma, such as physical abuse, molestation, feelings of abandonment, a profoundly terrifying experience, or chronic and emotionally debilitating family problems. The challenge of differentiating psychological overlay from a psychological problem is complicated by the fact that the symptoms are frequently similar, even though the actual origins of the symptoms are dissimilar. The child who is profoundly sad because of a trauma and preoccupied with surviving emotionally (a psychological problem) may shut down in school and become resistant and irresponsible. This child's learning difficulties and nonadaptive behavior are directly linked to the emotional trauma and the psychological problem triggered by this trauma.

A dyslexic child may also be experiencing emotional upset. He may be so frustrated and discouraged that he, too, may shut down academically and become resistant and irresponsible. In this instance, the child's counterproductive attitudes and behaviors are psychological overlay directly linked to learning problems. Because of the overlap of symptoms associated with psychological problems and psychological overlay, the actual source of a child's emotional distress must be accurately diagnosed before the underlying problem can be properly treated.

It's also possible for a child to be struggling with both a psychological problem and psychological overlay at the same time. Such a child will require educational therapy to resolve his learning deficits and psychotherapy to treat his emotional problem.

If you're uncertain about what might be causing your child's emotional distress, you should consult a professional who can evaluate your child and recommend the appropriate intervention (see chapters 8 and 9). The following chart summarizes the distinction between psychological problem and psychological overlay and may help you understand this distinction.

Learning disabled children who suffer psychological overlay may become accustomed and hardened to reprimands, poor grades, and punishment. Once these youngsters give up and accept failure as their lot in life, tragedy often ensues. They may actually become intent on proving to the world that they are incompetent so that nothing is expected from them by their parents and teachers. Such children sabotage themselves at every turn. Their defense mechanisms—denial, procrastination, laziness, blaming, acting out, resistance, passivity, and daydreaming—offer no real protection but only guarantee continued marginal performance. Children resorting to these behaviors are so enmeshed in their own drama that they do not see that their behavior and attitudes are only intensifying and prolonging the agony.

Handling Psychological Overlay

Psychological overlay rarely disappears on its own. Before most struggling children are willing to relinquish their self-protecting behavior, they must become convinced that they no longer need these behaviors to protect themselves from feeling incompetent and vulnerable. If your child is manifesting symptoms of psychological overlay attributable to school problems, he requires learning assistance from a resource specialist, edu-

Differentiating Psychological Problems from Psychological Overlay

Psychological Problem →	Overlapping Symptoms ←	Psychological Overlay
Possible Causes:	*Possible Symptoms:*	*Possible Causes:*
Molestation	Fears and insecurities	Learning disability
Physical or emotional abuse	Counterproductive behavior	ADD/ADHD
Traumatic experience	Negative attitude	Memory deficts
Serious family dysfunction	Poor self-esteem	Poor study skills
Feelings of abandonment	Social problems	Language disorder
Family dysfunction	Demoralization	Poor coordination
	Depression	
	Defensiveness	
	Denial	
	Shame	

cational therapist, or tutor. If the intervention is timely and effective, the overlay should diminish as your child's learning difficulties are corrected.

When a child has a protracted history of academic problems and has not received or responded to help, eliminating the psychological overlay can be challenging. Behaviors such as laziness, procrastination, and irresponsibility may become so embedded in a child's personality that he may be unwilling to relinquish them. If this is the case, professional counseling will be an essential element in the intervention strategy.

The symptoms of psychological overlay may assume different forms as children mature. An irresponsible fourth grader could become rebellious in ninth grade and a delinquent in tenth grade. Without intervention, the underlying issues will persist and continue to distort the child's emotions and conduct. Not seeking professional help could have catastrophic consequences for the child and the entire family.

If you observe symptoms that suggest psychological overlay or a possible psychological problem, the first step is to ask the teacher if she believes your child's unhappiness and/or self-defeating behavior and attitudes are being caused by school issues or by other factors. The teacher may have an opinion or may say she cannot answer the question. This in no way suggests she lacks competence. A teacher is not, after all, a trained psychologist, nor is she an educational diagnostician or therapist.

If your child is already receiving help in school, ask the resource specialist the same question you asked his classroom teacher. Inquire if the school psychologist can do some specialized testing that might pinpoint the source of your child's counterproductive behaviors and attitudes.

If you cannot draw a conclusion from the feedback provided by the school personnel, you may need to rely on your own impressions. If your intuition tells you there's a problem, seek a professional opinion from a private therapist or diagnostician.

Part II
Using the Resources at Your Child's School

Chapter 4
Getting Your Child Assessed

Your son's teacher informs you that your child has difficulty keeping up with his class. She requests that he be considered for an evaluation by the school psychologist. After reviewing his test scores and observing your child in class, the Child Study Team recommends that he be assessed to identify the specific causes of his academic difficulties and to determine if he qualifies for the resource program. You agree that he should be tested and give your authorization. The evaluation is scheduled in two weeks.

I t would be ideal if the system always worked this way. A vigilant teacher alerts you and the Child Study Team that there is an academic problem. The school authorities react quickly and say, "Let's find out what's going on." The evaluation procedure is set in motion. The Child Study Team reviews the data, does an in-class observation, makes an initial assessment, and refers your child for formal diagnostic testing by the resource specialist and the school psychologist. With your approval, they administer a comprehensive battery of tests to determine if your child has a learning disability and qualifies for remedial help. The tests pinpoint the specific deficit areas, and an effective and focused remediation plan is promptly designed and implemented.

In tens of thousands of cases each year throughout the United States, the assessment procedure does work as described above. Typically, the process of identifying, evaluating, and placing children in special education programs is as follows:

- A concerned teacher and/or parent sounds the alarm.
- The student is referred for initial assessment by the Child Study Team.
- The Child Study Team evaluates standardized test scores and classroom performance and determines suitability for further testing.

- The student is referred for a comprehensive diagnostic assessment.
- The school psychologist administers a battery of tests.
- The resource specialist and, if appropriate, speech and language pathologist administer additional tests.
- An Individual Educational Plan (IEP) conference is scheduled.
- The qualified child is placed in the appropriate special education program.

Once the classroom teacher refers a child to the Child Study Team, which may consist of a school psychologist, resource specialist, a school administrator, and perhaps a representative of the district office and/or a master teacher, the team uses district-prescribed procedures and assessment criteria to determine if formal testing is appropriate. The initial evaluation process typically involves making an in-class observation, consulting with the child's teacher, and reviewing samples of the child's work and standardized test scores. If there are sufficient indicators of a possible learning disability, the team refers the student to the resource specialist and the school psychologist for comprehensive testing. (Some of these diagnostic tests are administered by the resource specialist. Other tests, such as the Wechsler Intelligence Scale for Children–WISC III, and the Bender Gestalt, are administered exclusively by the school psychologist. See the test descriptions in chapter 5.)

Parental approval is required before diagnostic testing can proceed. In most states there is a prescribed time frame for completing the evaluation, although districts may disregard their own timetable when their school psychologists are overloaded with children to test.

The diagnostic assessment may span several days depending on how many tests are being administered and the amount of time allotted for each testing session. To avoid fatigue and to increase the likelihood of testing accuracy, most schools break up the assessment into several segments.

When the diagnostic testing is completed, the IEP (see chapter 7) conference takes place. During this meeting, the child's deficits are identified and examined. A remediation strategy is then designed, and specific educational goals are defined. The child's parents are encouraged to participate actively in the development of the strategy and the definition of the educational objectives. Once the plan and the goals are approved, the child is then assigned either to a special day class (for children with more serious learning problems) or to a resource program that typically involves having the child work with a specialist one or more hours each day. The school is also required by federal law to make reasonable and appropriate modifications in the regular curriculum and instructional methods to accommodate the child's specific learning problems and special educational needs. These adjustments must be implemented whether or not the child qualifies for a special education program.

When the special education program works as intended, the teacher and the resource specialist coordinate their efforts in helping the learning disabled student overcome his deficits and catch up with his class. Ideally, the assistance program would not only help the child with his current schoolwork but would also address and help alleviate the underlying sensory processing deficiencies causing the student's academic problems. The long-term objective is to integrate the child fully into the mainstream.

This ideal learning assistance scenario is not always implemented in the real world despite the provisions of federal law that require children with learning handicaps be tested and placed in remediation programs. One explanation for why some struggling children are not being identified, tested, and treated can be traced to classroom teachers who fail to identify students who are candidates for assessment. Because these teachers may not have been adequately trained to recognize such learning problems as dyslexia, auditory discrimination deficits, visual memory deficits, and visual tracking problems, they may erroneously attribute the child's learning difficulties to immaturity, misbehavior, or lack of motivation. In other cases, children are not being targeted quickly because of school district administrative procedures. Child Study Teams may be so beleaguered with referrals that they are unable to observe and screen a student for months or, in nightmare scenarios, even years.

Other factors can also contribute to the backlog. In many districts school psychologists are assigned so many students that it may take months to test them. In fact, some struggling children may never be formally evaluated or may be evaluated only after emotional and educational damage has occurred. By then, their learning problem can no longer be overlooked. There are also children who are evaluated, but who do not meet the criteria for placement in a resource program or a special day class. These children, who are often labeled underachievers, are relegated to the no-man's-land of special education. Little or nothing is done to help them, and the consequences are often tragic. Children's lives can literally be destroyed when the system doesn't work the way it's supposed to work.

Parents have procedural and legal recourses when their school district is not in compliance with the law. Unfortunately, many parents who find themselves in conflict with their local school district are uninformed about these procedural and legal options (see chapter 7).

There are four additional reasons why children may not be tested quickly and provided with help immediately:

1. Limited financial resources: Restricted resources to fund special education programs may cause children to be placed on long waiting lists. (A school district would never officially admit this, however, given the strict federal mandates for providing assistance for disabled children.)

2. Staffing limitations: Qualified personnel may not be available to teach special education programs, thus limiting the number of children who can be served.

3. Defensiveness about inadequate programs: School districts may have distorted priorities and may minimize the importance of providing first-rate special education resources for struggling students.

4. Restrictive bureaucratic procedures: School district policies and guidelines may impede the efficient testing and placement of children in special education programs.

In some school districts, all of these conditions exist. This unwholesome situation can cause concerned parents to despair. Those who must deal with a myopic, incompetent, or bureaucratically entrenched school district have their work cut out for them. To protect their child's legitimate interests and to make certain he is provided with appropriate federally mandated educational services, these parents will need to fight the system and become proactive, assertive, aggressive, and even confrontational.

Confronting the Bureaucracy

Bureaucracy can be more than a simple annoyance; it can be infuriating, obstructive, and insidious. All these adjectives apply when you're forced to do battle with a highly codified, inflexible educational system and insensitive administrators who care more about conforming to their procedural policies and protecting themselves from federal scrutiny and charges of noncompliance than about providing for children's educational and emotional needs.

Bureaucratic edicts serve a pragmatic function: They are designed to create order and provide guidelines for handling recurring issues. As anyone who has had to deal with an entrenched bureaucracy can attest, edicts and procedures can assume a life of their own. When the rules become rigid, they can undermine the very programs they are designed to support. Unfortunately, the spoken and unspoken procedures can prevent deserving children from getting the help they need.

It can be argued that without systematic procedures, school districts and special education programs would be in chaos. Maintaining objectivity about the advantages of these procedures is not realistic, however, when you've concluded that your child is being deprived of a decent education because of them. Aggrieved parents can easily panic when they realize the clock is ticking and their child is falling further and further behind every day in school. Rather than address the child's learning problems, the system may rationalize its failings with convenient platitudes and recommend flawed, simplistic solutions such as:

"Your child is immature and needs to repeat second grade."

"He'll outgrow his reading problem."

"Lots of second graders reverse their letters and numbers."

"He's not two years below grade level, and he doesn't qualify for the resource program."

"Your child is lazy and unmotivated."

"We have children with far more serious problems and we have to save the places in the resource program for them."

"He needs to take more responsibility for doing the assigned work. Let him sink or swim on his own."

"You may need to accept the possibility that she will never be a good student."

School policies for evaluating students vary. Although in theory these policies must conform to federal laws, state mandates, and local school district policies, in reality the procedures are often bent so that the school can cope with the volume of children requiring special services. The net effect is that some schools are in blatant noncompliance with the guidelines. Informed parents are the first line of defense against this intolerable situation. If no one legally challenges a school that does not comply, the situation can persist for years, and successive generations of students may be irreparably harmed.

If you know or suspect that your child is struggling in school because of learning problems, you want him evaluated. You want his problems accurately identified, and you want him placed in an effective remedial program. You don't want to be told that he doesn't qualify because he fails to meet one or more specific criteria. Nor do you want to be told that there are only a limited number of spaces available in the school resource program or special day class, and that these spaces are reserved for students with more serious and chronic problems.

If the school authorities decide that your child's learning problems are not serious enough to warrant testing, you must determine your next step. Do you accept this decision, or do you vigorously refute it? If you conclude that your child is struggling academically despite the decision that his deficits do not meet the testing eligibility criteria, you should be prepared to do battle. Even if you don't feel like fighting, you must do so anyway! You owe it your child to find out what is causing his learning difficulties. If you begin to vacillate, remind yourself that your taxes support public education and that you have every right to insist that your child's learning problems be taken seriously. That these problems do not appear to be severe should be a blessing, not a curse. Logic suggests that with effective remediation, your child's deficiencies could be quickly resolved. Yes, learning dysfunctions involving nonspecific or intermittent deficits can be difficult to diagnose, but to exclude children who manifest atypical or hard-to-define problems from testing and special education programs is unfair. You should not acquiesce to this discrimination.

Below you will find a facsimile of the eligibility guidelines used in a California school district for placement in special education. The specific guidelines used in your local district may differ somewhat.

Facsimile of Typical Eligibility Guidelines for Special Education

Criteria:

A pupil shall qualify as an individual with exceptional needs (specific learning disabled) if the results of the assessments demonstrate *all* of the following:

1. The pupil has a disorder in one or more of the basic psychological processes that include:
   - Attention
   - Visual processing
   - Sensory motor skill
   - Cognitive abilities including *association, conceptualization,* and *expression*

2. The pupil has a severe discrepancy (at or greater than 1.5 standard deviations*) between intellectual ability and achievement in one of the following academic areas:
   - Basic reading
   - Reading comprehension
   - Mathematics reasoning
   - Written comprehension
   - Listening comprehension
   - Oral expression

3. At least two individually administered, nationally normed examinations shall be used.

4. The academic delay cannot be due to any of the following:
   - Limited school experience
   - Poor school attendance
   - Environmental, cultural, or economic disadvantages or differences
   - Nonattendance (truancy)
   - Noncompliant behavior (such as refusal to do classwork or homework)
   - History of inappropriate instruction or frequent moves so that continuity is disrupted
   - Social maladjustment
   - Behavior disorder

5. The specific learning disability is affecting the pupil's educational performance (such as receiving D's or failing grades)

6. The degree of the pupil's specific learning disability requires special education and related services which cannot be provided with modification of the regular school program or through categorical instructional programs.

Getting Down to Business

In good schools, struggling learners are often identified by the classroom teacher in kindergarten, or first or second grade. In some cases, however, alert parents are the first to recognize that a child may have a learning

---

*There must be at least a 22-point difference between IQ score and, say, achievement in math. If the student's IQ is 100 and his math standard score is 78, the 22-point difference equals one-and-one-half standard deviations. One standard deviation equals 15 points, and one half of a standard deviation equals 7 points. Added together they equal 22 points.

problem. Parents may observe chronic distractibility, difficulty following directions, memory deficits, letter reversals, reading problems, spelling difficulties, or handwriting deficits. These parents may not fully understand the issues and implications, but they intuitively realize something is wrong and request an evaluation.

School districts have a range of standardized tests that are used to diagnose learning disabilities. Many districts use a similar standard "testing package." (See chapter 5 for a description of the more widely used diagnostic and achievement tests administered by school psychologists and resource specialists.) Because there may be several well-respected tests designed to detect the same learning deficits, states and local school districts often stipulate the specific components of the diagnostic assessment. Some districts require that these tests be used in all schools, while others allow school psychologists and resource specialists a degree of latitude in determining certain components of the battery.

Some school districts do an extensive multidiscipline assessment; it may include an evaluation by the resource specialist, speech pathologist, school psychologist, occupational therapist, and school social worker. Other districts do less comprehensive assessments. The testing procedure may also have two tiers. If the initial battery of tests indicates a learning problem, a more extensive assessment is then given to identify specific perceptual processing deficits and determine eligibility for special education resources.

Although there are general federal guidelines for determining the eligibility criteria for special education programs, these guidelines can be creatively applied by individual states, counties, and school districts. Disparities reflect local school district policies, priorities, and economics. In the final analysis, standards for placement in a special education program are not as uniform as many people might believe. The disparities parallel the lack of national uniformity in the American educational system. States have the final say in determining their educational standards, teaching procedures, grading criteria, and requirements for awarding high school diplomas. Although states must comply with federal mandates regarding disabilities and discrimination, in reality there is a great deal of subjectivity in interpreting these mandates.

If you are thwarted in your dealings with your local school district and believe your child is being unfairly denied legitimate educational services, you have legal options under federal law. These rights and remedies are described in detail in chapter 7.

Steps to Getting Your Child Tested

• Talk to your child's teacher. Explain your position clearly and present your reasons for requesting an evaluation. If you encounter resistance, ratchet up your assertiveness.

• Discuss your concerns with the principal and request *in writing* an initial evaluation by the Child Study Team (Education Code: E.C. 56321).

• If you are dissatisfied with the principal's response to your request for an evaluation, request a conference with administrators at the district office.

• If you are still blocked, request an appointment with the superintendent.

• Consider enlisting a qualified professional advocate to present your position (see chapter 6).

• Contact the school board and be willing to raise your concerns about the bureaucratic impasse during a board meeting that is open to parents. Be a squeaky wheel.

• If necessary, inform the district that you will be contacting an attorney, and be prepared to do so if there is no other alternative.

Alternatives to Dealing with the System

Some parents who find themselves in conflict with their school district may elect not to do battle. They may conclude that the payoff—enrollment in a resource program or special day class—does not justify the wear and tear on them and their child. Rather than exhaust their resources fighting for something in which they have little faith, these parents may decide to seek out-of-school help. If they lack confidence in the school's testing procedures or in the way the school interprets test results, they may want to have their child privately assessed (see chapter 8). They may conclude that the most effective way to help their child is to hire a tutor or educational therapist or to enroll their child in a local or nationally franchised learning center (see chapter 10). Some parents may elect to withdraw their child from the public school system entirely and enroll him in a private school that specializes in providing services for children with learning problems. Others may opt for home schooling.

Parents who lack the financial resources for private assistance have no other option but to fight for the publicly funded services their child requires. The angry parents of a child who is being institutionally damaged by a callous and/or myopic educational system can be a formidable enemy. Anyone who has seen footage of a mother bear protecting her cubs from real or perceived danger has witnessed the fury of the parental instinct to shield and safeguard the young. Perhaps we need to tap into this parental instinct without feeling social inhibition. Perhaps if more parents protected their children with the same intensity in society's supposedly civilized forest, our culture would be in less of a mess and our children would have fewer problems.

Chapter 5
Understanding Test Results

As you can see on this test summary, your son scored on the Woodcock Johnson at the 28th percentile in passage comprehension. His scaled score on this subtest was ninety-one, and his age equivalent was seven years and two months. To be at grade level his reading skills should be at an age equivalent of seven years and nine months, and he should be testing at approximately the 50th percentile. His broad reading score indicates that he's reading at the 19th percentile. He's testing nine months below his chronological age and more than one year below grade level. On the WISC III, there's a twenty-two-point discrepancy between his verbal and performance scores. He did extremely well on certain subtests, namely Information, Similarities, Vocabulary, Comprehension, Coding, Picture Arrangement, and Object Assembly. His full-scale IQ is 123. This discrepancy of twenty-two points is considered an indication of a possible learning disability.

As the school psychologist drones on, your mind begins to wander despite your efforts to concentrate on what she's saying. You know the information is important, but it's as if she's speaking a foreign language.

It's easy to feel overwhelmed and intimidated when you're presented with a mass of seemingly incomprehensible test data. Unless you're a professional in the field of education or psychology, you may conclude you can't possibly decipher and assimilate the information bombarding you. What does it all mean? She's talking about percentiles, stanines, standard deviations, scaled scores, grade expectancies, and age equivalents. She's using technical jargon that sounds as if it is coming straight out of a course on statistics.

Then there are the tests themselves: The Bender Gestalt, the WISC-III, the LAC, the WRAT, the PIAT, the Wepman, the Detroit, the ITPA, TAPS, the Slingerland, the GORT-3, the SORT-R, the Woodcock, and the others with acronyms and proper names you've never heard before. All you know is that these tests with their strange names have been used by the school psychologist and the resource specialist to diagnose your child's learning problems and determine her eligibility for assistance in school. When your child's test scores are discussed, everyone at the IEP seems to expect you to understand what it all means. Don't they realize that they're using language you've never heard before? Don't they realize that you're confused? Should you tell them? If you do tell them that you don't understand what they're saying, will they think less of you? Will they patronize you? If only they would talk in plain, comprehensible English!

Jargon and "Edu-babble"

Professional jargon serves a purpose. It allows those in a particular field to communicate with one another efficiently. A psychiatrist might say to another psychiatrist, "I'm treating her bipolar disorder with an antidepressant." The second psychiatrist will know exactly what she means.

A school psychologist might say to the resource specialist, "This child has a profound auditory discrimination problem. She scored considerably below grade level on the LAC. I think we should use the ADD program with her." The translation of this statement is: The Lindamood Auditory Conceptualization Test (LAC) indicates that this child is having a problem distinguishing the different sounds that letters and blends (a combination of letters) produce when verbalized. The recommended intervention is a systematic training program called Auditory Discrimination in Depth, or ADD (not to be confused with attention deficit disorder, which has the same acronym).

In referring to another child, the resource specialist might say, "He has serious kinetic tracking deficits and is manifesting indications of dyslexia on the Slingerland. Orton-Gillingham or Slingerland techniques would be the most effective remediation strategy." Translation: He reads inaccurately and flips letters (*b* becomes *d*), omits syllables, transposes words (*saw* becomes *was*), and loses his place. On the Slingerland test he reversed *b, d, g,* and *q* as well as *6* and *9*. The recommended intervention is a systematic Orton-Gillingham or Slingerland program designed for children who have dyslexia.

Certainly, jargon can expedite communication, but it can also be used intentionally or unintentionally by professionals to exclude nonprofessionals from participating in a meaningful discussion of the issues. As the parent of a child who is struggling in school, you must know all you can about your child's problem. You need to familiarize yourself with the jargon or insist that the jargon be explained to you. And if you don't understand the clarification the first time around, you must insist that the jargon be explained again. Admitting that you don't understand a technical term is not an admission of inadequacy. And you are not being unreasonable or difficult when you insist that the names and descriptions of tests, acronyms, and statistically based scores be translated into language you can comprehend.

Examining the Testing Battery

The components of a diagnostic test battery may vary somewhat from school district to school district. Federal law requires that it must include individualized testing (as opposed to group) of intellectual ability and academic achievement. The school psychologist and resource specialist may have some latitude in selecting testing instruments that are geared to the child's presenting academic deficits. The extensiveness of the testing may also be keyed to the resources of the district. Those with a smaller budget and fewer psychologists may do a more abbreviated assessment.

The tests available to psychologists are extensive and can pinpoint specific deficits with a high degree of accuracy. Unfortunately, the procedures for remediating these deficits are not as reliable. The explanation for this disparity can usually be attributed to three factors:

1. Too many children assigned to the resource program, too few resource specialists, and too little time allocated for students to work with the resource specialist.

2. Special education personnel who have not been trained in the most effective remediation methodologies

3. Conflicting priorities: Should the resource specialist focus on remediating the underlying perceptual processing deficits responsible for the student's learning problems, or should she devote the remedial time to helping the student complete assignments for his regular class?

Let's assume that a diagnostic assessment indicates a student is reading two years below grade level, is tracking words inefficiently (has poor ocular-motor pursuit, characterized by omissions, transpositions, and inaccurate reading), has auditory discrimination deficits (has difficulty hearing the difference between the sound that letters make), and has visual discrimination deficits (reverses letters such as *b* and *d* and *p* and *q* when reading or writing). Having this information about the child's perceptual processing deficiencies is of vital importance, because the data indicate what specific areas need to be addressed in the remediation program and what intervention methods should be used. The critical issue is whether the resource specialist has sufficient training and can spend enough time with the student to address and adequately remediate the deficits. Although there may be highly effective procedures for helping the child overcome the problems, the resource specialist may not be trained in these methods (see chapters 10–12).

The tests described below are commonly used to assess learning problems. Some of the tests overlap and assess the same skills; other tests are highly specialized and may not be used as a regular component of the school diagnostic testing battery. A description of these tests has been included, because they may be administered by private educational psychologists or educational therapists. It is also possible that some tests used in your school district are not described below. Don't hesitate to ask the school personnel for an explanation of these tests.

In most school districts, certain tests are administered by the school psychologist and others by the resource specialist. Many diagnostic tests can be given by either one, and the actual division of responsibilities will reflect district policy and pragmatic scheduling realities. IQ tests such as the WISC-III (see below) require specialized training and are administered by school psychologists (or by private educational or clinical psychologists). In fact, in many instances test publishers require examiners to have specific credentials before making certain tests available for purchase.

In most school districts a low score on an achievement test is not sufficient to assure eligibility for a resource program. Although some form of assistance may be provided, most schools require that a learning disability be confirmed by several diagnostic testing instruments.

Common Diagnostic Tests Used in American Schools

Typically Administered by the Resource Specialist

Woodcock Johnson Psycho-Educational Battery (Revised) of Academic Achievement. Four tests:*

1. The Reading Assessment (called *Broad Reading*)
   Two subtests:
   Letter/Word Identification: The child is asked to name letters, sight (nonphonetic) words, words containing short vowels, and words containing consonant and vowel combinations.

---

*There is also a cognitive (aptitude) section of this test that is not generally administered by public schools. When the test is used, the school psychologist usually administers this section. Private educational therapists are more likely to use this cognitive test.

Passage Comprehension: The child reads a passage and supplies a missing word in each passage.

2. The Mathematics Assessment (called *Broad Math*)
Two subtests:

Calculation: The child does problems involving addition and subtraction. Older students do problems requiring more advanced math skills.

Applied Problems: The child does problems involving counting, identifying shapes, addition, subtraction, and telling time. Older students do more difficult problems that correspond to their grade level in school.

3. The Written Language Assessment (called *Broad Written Language*)
Two subtests:

Dictation: The child punctuates and writes words containing short vowels, vowel combinations, and consonant combinations. Included are some phonetic irregularities, irregular plurals, and contractions.

Writing Sample: The child's use of complete sentences, subjects and predicates, capitals and periods, and descriptive detail is evaluated.

4. General Knowledge Assessment (called *Broad Knowledge*)
Three subtests:

Science: The child responds to a picture or verbal cue and accurately identifies scientific concepts.

Social Studies: The child responds to a picture or verbal cue and accurately identifies a concept that reflects the way society functions.

Humanities: The child responds to a picture or verbal cue and answers questions about music, history, or art.

Example of a score:

	Age*	SS**	PR***
Letter/Word Identification	6-11	84	14 low average

*This student's score statistically corresponds to the score a child of 6 years and 11 months would receive on the test.

**Scaled and standard scores are statistical rankings of a student's number of correct answers relative to other children of the same age and grade level. To generate the statistical norms, the test must be administered to a large number of students. The data collecting and number crunching process is called standardization or norming. The procedure allows a statistically derived score to be assigned to the child's test performance.

***Percentile: This is another statistical derivation of norming. It indicates that out of every 100 children taking the test, this student scored 14th from the bottom. The score indicates that the child is significantly below grade level.

Sample interpretation of this subject:

This child, whose chronological age is six years and eleven months, correctly named letters, some sight words, some words containing short vowels, vowel combinations, and consonant combinations. He correctly sounded out the first part of most words attempted and correctly sounded out the ending of some of these words. On most words, however, he sounded out the beginning but guessed at the endings. Of thirty items attempted, he read twenty items correctly.

The child's score on each subsection of the test would be analyzed and interpreted in a similar fashion. A score would also be generated that indicates the child's overall level of functioning or the major areas: Broad Reading, Broad Math, Broad Written Language, and Broad Knowledge. For example, the child's Broad Reading scores might be:

Age	SS	PR
6-11	87	19 low average

Whereas the subsection scores indicate a child's specific skill levels relative to other children in his grade and of his age, the broad score indicates the child's relative functional level in the content area as a whole. The above hypothetical child who receives a percentile score of 19 is testing in reading at least two years below grade level. This important data, in conjunction with corroborative data from other achievement and diagnostic tests, might lead to a diagnosis of a specific learning disability.

If your child had the above scores, you would be justified in requesting learning assistance. The school district might contend, however, that your child doesn't qualify for the resource program if other diagnostic tests fail to identify specific underlying perceptual processing deficits. Whether or not your child qualifies for the resource program, he would nonetheless qualify for accommodations under Section 504 of the Rehabilitation Act if he is two years below grade level (see chapter 7). You might also want to consider private tutoring, educational therapy, or enrollment in a learning center (see chapter 10).

Peabody Individual Achievement Test—Revised (PIAT-R)

This is another test of achievement in basic academic areas. Listed below are the subtests and sample scores:

Subtests	G.E.*	SS	PR
General Information	2.4	99	48
Reading Recognition	1.7	86	18
Reading Comprehension	1.7	86	17

Total Reading	1.6	85	15
Mathematics	2.0	91	27
Spelling	1.6	81	11
Total Test	1.9	89	21

*Grade Expectancy—the number of correct answers in the general information section correlates statistically with the performance of a child in the fourth month of second grade.

Sample interpretation of the scores

The PIAT-R shows that this child, who is currently in the seventh month of second grade, is functioning approximately one year below grade level in reading recognition, comprehension, spelling, and written expression. She is seven months below grade level in mathematics and three months below grade level in general information. Although her scores are below grade level, they would probably not qualify her for a resource program in many school districts. If the child's scores go down and there is other evidence of a learning disability, she might then qualify for assistance.

California Achievement Test (CAT)

This group test also measures academic achievement and basic skills. Although the test may be used to screen children for skills deficits, it is not used for determining eligibility for special education, as it does not meet the federally mandated criterion of "an individualized test." The Woodcock-Johnson does meet this criterion as is generally used for determining eligibility. The sample profile below indicates significant deficits in every area.

Subtests	PR
Reading:	
Vocabulary	11
Comprehension	1
Language:	
Mechanics	14
Expression	5
Math:	
Computation	18
Concepts and Application	10
Other Content Areas:	
Word Analysis	20
Spelling	12

Total Reading:	2
Total Language:	8
Total Math:	10
Total Battery:	5

Wide-Range Achievement Test (WRAT-3)

This test measures achievement in reading (word recognition only), spelling, and math. The child is asked to read words aloud, write down dictated spelling words, and write down the answers to printed math problems. This test generates the following: grade levels, standard scores, stanines (another statistical representation scaled from one to ten, with ten the highest score), and percentiles. For example, a child might test at the 1.9 grade level in spelling (first grade, ninth month). The age range is five to adult.

Peabody Picture Vocabulary Test (PPVT-R)

This test measures understanding of word meanings. The examiner says a word, and the child selects a picture that matches the word. The test generates the following scores: mental age (for example, a child who has a chronological age of six years and seven months but who tests at the mental age of eight years and six months is clearly above average in intelligence), a percentile, and an IQ equivalent. The age range is two to eighteen years.

Detroit Test of Learning Aptitude (DTLA-3)

This test measures general mental abilities. It generates a mental age and IQ score. The subtests measure reasoning, comprehension, practical judgment, verbal ability, time and space relationships, numerical ability, auditory attentive ability, visual attentive ability, and motor ability. The age range is three to nineteen years.

Lindamood Auditory Conceptualization Test (LAC)

This test assesses a child's ability to distinguish the sounds that letters produce when isolated and when used in words. This ability is vital to being able to read and spell accurately. The test would indicate how many correct answers (points) a child receives out of a possible 100. For example, a second grade child's score might be 35/100. This score indicates significant auditory discrimination deficits and strongly suggests that auditory discrimination training is advisable.

Wepman Auditory Discrimination Test

This test measures auditory discrimination skills. It has a rating scale that ranges from "very good development" to "below the level of threshold of adequacy." The examiner says two words (such as bid, bit), and the child is asked if they sound the same or different. The age range is five to eight years.

Brigance Diagnostic Inventory of Basic Skills

The inventory measures readiness, reading, language arts, and math skills, and can pinpoint a child's specific areas of strength and weakness. The tests generate a grade level (i.e., math skills: 3.4, or third grade, fourth month.) The elementary inventory is designed for children in grades kindergarten through sixth. A separate inventory is used to assess older children.

Illinois Test of Psycholinguistic Abilities (ITPA)

This test measures visual-motor and auditory vocal skills (listening and responding by speaking). The test generates age-level scores and a scaled score. The scale ranges from zero to sixty-eight, and a score below twenty-six is considered a potential danger signal of a learning disability. The age range for the test is two to ten years.

Subtests

Auditory Reception	Measures how well the student understands verbal questions. Example: "Do spiders fly?"
Visual Reception	Measures how well the student understands visual pictures. Example: "Find the pictures that are similar."
Auditory Association	Measures how well the student understands orally presented ideas: Example: "A butterfly has wings. A cat has _____."
Visual Association	Measures how well the student links visually presented ideas. Example: "Find the picture [a sock] that goes with this picture [a shoe]."
Verbal Expression	Measures how well a student describes familiar objects. Example: "A needle is round and thin, has a hole at the top . . ."
Manual Expression	Measures how well a student understands how objects are used. Example: "Look at this picture [a hammer] and show how it is used [a hitting motion]."

Subtests

Grammatical Closure	Measures how well a student uses correct grammar. Example: "Here is a peanut. Here are two _____."
Visual Closure	Measures how well a student identifies pictured objects when parts are missing: "Find all the butterflies in this picture." (Some butterflies are partially obscured.)
Auditory Sequential Memory	Measures how well a student remembers what he has heard. Example: "Repeat this number: 94376."
Visual Sequential Memory	Measures how well a student remembers (in order) what she has seen. Example: "Look at these shapes and draw them from memory when I cover them up."
Auditory Closure	Measures how well a student can identify a word when a part of it is not said. Example: ____aseball.
Sound Blending	Measures how well a student can blend individual sounds into a word. Example: *h, a, t* into "hat."

Slingerland Test for Identifying Specific Language Disabilities

This test, which provides guidelines for prescriptive teaching, does not generate a statistically based score. The test measures visual, auditory, and kinesthetic skills related to reading and spelling, and is used for diagnosing dyslexia. Subtests include copying, visual memory, visual discrimination, auditory memory, initial and final sounds, auditory discrimination, following directions, word finding, and storytelling. The age range of the test is six to twelve years.

Slosson Oral Reading Test (SORT-R)

This untimed test, which has no basal (minimum low) or ceiling (maximum high) score, generates an oral reading level. For example, the test might indicate that a child's oral reading level is 1.5 (first grade, fifth month).

Gray Oral Reading Test (GORT-3)

This test generates statistical data about a child's level of functioning in the following areas: rate, accuracy, and passage comprehension. It also generates an oral reading quotient. For example, a child in the seventh month of second grade may score as follows:

G.E.: 1.9
PR: 16th

This child is testing eight months below grade level on this subtest and is scoring sixteenth from the bottom for every one hundred children of his age who took the test.

Other achievement tests used to assess students' basic skills are the Iowa Test, the Stanford Achievement Test, the California Tests of Basic Skills (CTBS), and the Gates-MacGinitie Achievement Test. These group tests are comparable to the California Achievement Test and the Peabody Individual Achievement Test and may be used to *screen* children for possible learning disabilities.

Tests Administered by the School Psychologist

Wechsler Intelligence Score for Children III (WISC III)

The following is an example for a second grade child.

Areas Tested

Verbal		SS	Range
Information	Long-term memory or general factual information (What day comes after Thursday?)	9	Average
Similarities	Verbal abstract reasoning; knowledge of categories; concept formation (How are a coat and a sweater alike?)	10	Average
Arithmetic	Mental numerical reasoning; attention and concentration	9	Average
Vocabulary	Word knowledge and verbal fluency (What is a runway?)	9	Average
Comprehension	Social judgment; practical knowledge and reasoning (What should you do when you cut yourself?)	9	Average
Digit Span	Short-term auditory memory; attention and concentration (Repeat this number: 7324.)	10	Average

Performance

Picture Completion	Awareness of essential visual details (What's missing from this picture?)	7	Low Average

Verbal		SS	Range
Coding	Visual motor dexterity and writing speed, visual memory, attention, and concentration	7	Low Average
Picture Arrangement	Visual sequencing, logical thinking, and ordering	8	Low Average
Block Design	Spatial awareness, nonverbal abstract reasoning, and problem solving (Copy this design . . .)	8	Low Average
Object Assembly	Visual analysis and construction of objects (Can you put the pieces together?)	8	Average
Symbol Search	Visual-motor processing speed; visual discrimination	7	Low Average
Scores Derived:	Verbal IQ: 107 Performance IQ: 91 Full-Scale IQ: 101		

This test indicates a child's level of cognitive function. The verbal scale measures language expression, comprehension, listening skills, and the ability to use these skills to solve problems. The performance scale assesses nonverbal problem-solving, perceptual organization, speed, and visual-motor proficiency. A significant discrepancy between the Verbal and Performance scores (more than 17 points) and/or the Full-Scale IQ and academic achievement (such as a high IQ and low academic test scores on a standardized achievement test and/or poor achievement in class) is considered symptomatic of a learning problem.

Bender Gestalt Test for Young Children

This test measures visual-motor integration skills (how well the student can integrate something she sees), perceptual maturity, and fine-motor coordination. The student is asked to copy nine geometric and abstract designs. The test determines how well the student can link visual perception (what is seen) and fine-motor representational skills (what the hand is able to reproduce). Since there is a significant correlation between visual-motor integration deficits and learning disabilities, a score of two years or more below age expectancy is considered a red flag.

Beery Developmental Test of Visual-Motor Integration

This test also assesses a student's ability to match motor movements with perception and correlates with the Bender Gestalt Test. The student is asked to copy geometric forms that range from straight lines to complex and abstract designs. Administering both the Bender and the Beery might be considered redundant unless the second test is used to confirm the results of the first.

Motor-Free Visual Perception Test

This test measures visual processing skills. Specific skills that are assessed include visual matching, visual discrimination, visual closure, and visual memory without requiring a motor response or manipulation of stimuli. The test yields the Perceptual Age and Perceptual Quotient scores.

Test of Auditory Perceptual Skills (TAPS)

This test measures a student's functional level in specific areas of auditory perception and auditory processing skills, including auditory rote memory, concentration, discrimination, and interpretation of directions. The following is an example:

Subtests	Language Age	SS	PR
Auditory Number Forward	6–5	9	37
Auditory Sentence Memory	4–7	7	16
Auditory Word Memory	4–8	7	16
Auditory Interpretation of Directions	4–10	8	25
Auditory Discrimination	8–10	10	49
Auditory Processing	7–7	9	37

Goodenough-Harris Drawing Test

This test measures intellectual and emotional maturity. The student is asked to draw a complete picture of a man, a woman, and himself/herself. The test generates a standard score, a percentile score, and a quality scale. In some instances the child is asked to draw only one picture–a picture of a person. The age range is three to fifteen years.

Anecdotal Parent and Teacher Diagnostic Input

Parent- and teacher-supplied observations can be a very important component of the diagnostic process. Although anecdotal information is more subjective than the data generated by standardized and normed tests, the observations can provide invaluable information that should be factored into the diagnostic and prescriptive formula.

The observation by the classroom teacher that a student is having difficulty with phonics and with spelling will probably be confirmed by the Lindemood Auditory Conceptualization Test (LAC) or the Wepman Auditory Discrimination Test. The observation by a parent that a child is reversing *b* and *d* and *q* and *g* will probably be confirmed by the Slingerland Test.

Other deficits observed by parents and teachers would not necessarily be picked up on a standardized diagnostic test. For example, if a teacher reports that a child is chronically distractible and appears to have difficulty with far-point copying (copying accurately from the chalkboard), the possibility of attention deficit disorder and a vision efficiency problem becomes an important consideration. The child certainly should be assessed by an optometrist or ophthalmologist, and an ADD profile such as the Conner's Rating Scale should be completed. An assessment for ADD by a pediatrician, pediatric neurologist, child psychiatrist, child psychologist, or developmental pediatrician would provide information that should be factored into the educational diagnostic evaluation. If the child does have a visual impairment, corrective lenses would be necessary for the child to make academic progress. If the child has ADD, medication may be appropriate. (Please note: The diagnostic criteria for the term attention deficit hyperactivity disorder (ADHD) have recently been made more specific. There are now three categories: ADHD inattentive-type, ADHD hyperactive-impulsive-type, and ADHD combined type.

If a parent indicates that her child has food allergies or has a tendency to twitch or jerk his arms or head, these issues affect school performance and perceptual efficiency. Input from a physician who is treating the child for either condition is critical, and appropriate medical or pharmacological interventions would be a component in the intervention formula.

The following questionnaires are designed to elicit important information about a child's behavior and performance. The anecdotal data derived from the questionnaires can be used to assess learning efficiency and to indicate concentration deficits.

Child Behavior Checklist (CBCL)

Devised by Thomas Achenbach, these comprehensive questionnaires for parents, teachers, and adolescents contain over one hundred questions each. An analysis of responses can indicate conditions such as anxiety, depression, and hyperactivity.

The Anser System (Aggregate Neurobehavioral Student Health and Educational Review)

This information-gathering system is designed to help parents and teachers recall pertinent data and organize their observations. It consists of two in-depth questionnaires:

1. *The Parent Questionnaire for Developmental, Behavioral, and Health Assessment of the Elementary School Child*

This comprehensive questionnaire was created by developmental pediatrician Melvin Levine. By organizing medical and school history and previous interventions, the questionnaire helps parents gain an overview of the issues that may be causing their child to experience difficulty in school, focus their concerns, and develop a plan for providing medical and educational support.

2. *The Teacher Questionnaire for Developmental, Behavioral, and Health Assessment of the Elementary School Child*

Also developed by Dr. Levine, this comprehensive questionnaire helps teachers focus their observations and insights about students who are struggling. It pinpoints deficits in such areas as academic skills, motor output, language, visual-perceptual function, memory, and organization. The questionnaire also elicits behavioral observations about concentration and asks for a summary of academic strategies and interventions that have been used to address the student's learning problems.

Conner's Rating Scale

This questionnaire elicits comprehensive behavioral observations from parents and teachers, and is widely used by pediatricians, psychiatrists, school psychologists, clinical psychologists, and educational psychologists to diagnose ADD and ADHD.

Informed Choices

The wide range of testing protocols that have been developed to assess children's academic skills and learning efficiency are highly accurate instruments. If your child is having difficulty in school, these tests can usually identify the specific deficits causing the learning problems. Once the deficits have been identified, the next hurdle is to find remedies.

Qualifying for placement in the resource program is no guarantee of successful remediation. Key issues remain to be answered. Is the resource program going to be a "let's do the classroom handouts together, and I'll help you complete them" situation? Or is meaningful, focused intervention going to occur—remediation that targets your child's diagnosed perceptual processing deficits? Is the resource specialist going to use specialized methods to resolve your child's auditory discrimination deficits, auditory sequencing, and visual memory deficits? Or is he going to use the time to go over material that was taught in your child's mainstream class? The answers to these questions can determine whether or not your child overcomes his learning problems. If you are to be constructively involved in the process, you must understand the intervention strategy. Only then can you assess your options and make informed judgments about what is in your child's best interests.

In many cases, a resource specialist is faced with a dilemma. If your child is struggling to keep up with his mainstream classes and cannot do the regular work, the resource specialist may be forced into a crisis intervention mode. Realizing that if he focused exclusively on resolving the underlying deficits, it could take months (or, in extreme cases, years) before your child begins to show substantive improvement in the classroom, the resource specialist may decide that it would be most expedient to help your child with his classwork. He may rationalize this strategy by arguing that without crisis intervention, your child may become overwhelmed and demoralized by the material his classroom teacher expects him to complete each day, and would fall further and further behind. Your child might then be at risk for shutting down in school. Under the circumstances, the resource specialist may conclude that he has no alternative but to deal with the current crisis.

Let's examine this dilemma in concrete terms. Let's say that your child is in the sixth grade, and his math skills are at the third grade level. To require him to do sixth grade problems is clearly unreasonable. In an ideal situation, the resource specialist would have the time to go back to where your child first became "stuck" (the beginning of third grade math) and do an extensive and systematic review of the basics: addition, subtraction, multiplication, and division. Unfortunately, this may not be practical. If your child's classmates are working on multiplying and dividing fractions, the resource specialist may feel obliged to help your child with more advanced math so that he can do his assigned work. This stopgap strategy is, however, short-sighted. The far better solution is to remediate your child's underlying math deficits using alternative teaching methods, to modify the difficulty level of the work required in your child's mainstream math class until he masters the fundamentals, and to assign less advanced worksheets and fewer problems until his skills improve.

For those school districts that view the resource program as a means for rehashing what hasn't been learned in the regular classroom, a "go back to where the child is stuck" strategy represents a major shift in their remediation philosophy. To utilize the resource program exclusively for crisis intervention tutoring is not only myopic, it's also educationally unsound. The approach guarantees that the struggling child's foundation will remain weak. For meaningful remediation to occur and for your child to overcome his learning problems and improve his academic self-confidence, the foundation must be strengthened before any attempt is made to make repairs on the superstructure.

Chapter 6
Handling the Individual Educational Plan Conference

"You have a very nice child."

"Thank you. She is a very nice child, but she's suffering in school, and she's becoming discouraged. If her learning problems are not quickly resolved, I fear she may not remain nice for much longer. I want to make certain that everything possible is being done to help her."

Your child has just been evaluated by the school psychologist and resource specialist to determine her eligibility for the resource program. Or perhaps she's already in a resource program, and she's just been reevaluated to assess her progress. As prescribed by federal law, you've been asked to participate in a formal meeting to discuss the test scores and examine the school's proposed strategy for addressing her learning deficits and improving her performance. This meeting is held in order to develop an Individual Educational Plan, or IEP.

As you sit at the table waiting for someone to begin the meeting, you feel self-conscious and nervous. You sense that some of the teachers and administrators also feel uncomfortable, despite their having participated in numerous IEP meetings in the past. The amenities and small talk finally run their course, and you feel a sense of relief when the vice principal opens the meeting. He speaks in a modulated, professional voice, and his words seem carefully rehearsed: "As you know, we're here today to discuss your child and to discuss a program that will address her educational needs." The vice principal introduces everyone in attendance: the school psychologist, the resource specialist, your child's classroom teacher, the speech pathologist, and the school counselor. The meeting begins.

Perhaps this is your first IEP conference. Perhaps it's your fifth. The procedure is quite predictable, varying little from state to state and from school district to school district. The school personnel will look for positive things to say about your child. The school psychologist will discuss the results of the diagnostic evaluation. The teacher and resource specialist will examine your child's current academic strengths and weaknesses. If this is a reevaluation, you'll be apprised of your child's progress and the specific educational objectives that have been attained. The resource specialist will outline new goals for the current year and discuss methods to be used to help your child achieve these goals. The teacher will share her perspective about your child's performance, deficits, and improvement.

The tone of the discussion will be upbeat. You'll ask a few tentative questions, which will be answered using educational jargon that may or may not be explained. Everyone is cordial and helpful. If your child is making progress, the meeting will be reassuring and probably allay any concerns you have. You'll leave the meeting feeling that your child is on track and in good hands and will prevail over her learning difficulties.

If you're satisfied with the professional competence of the school personnel participating in the IEP conference, and you concur with the remediation plan they're proposing, consider yourself fortunate. The evaluation and intervention systems are functioning effectively, and your child's needs are being met.

Some parents, however, are very dissatisfied with the IEP conference. However well orchestrated the meeting may be, these parents continue to have grave concerns about their child's educational future and serious misgivings about the intervention strategy.

If you are one of these dissatisfied parents, you may question your child's progress, despite her having ostensibly attained the objectives outlined in previous IEPs. You may doubt the assurances you're given and mistrust the overall efficacy of the learning assistance program. In spite of your misgivings, you may be reluctant to appear negative or unappreciative. To avoid controversy, you may suppress your concerns and resist making any statements that might appear challenging or provocative. Fearing that you might alienate the school staff and your child might suffer the consequences, you bite your tongue. You smile at the appropriate moments and agree with the reassurances.

Finally, you're asked to sign the IEP document. You realize that by doing so, you're formally concurring with the recommendations, agreeing to the defined educational goals, and authorizing the implementation of the proposed plan. Quickly reading over the official paperwork you've been handed, you sign the document. Questions nevertheless run through your mind: Is my child getting what she needs? Is the program really working? Will my child truly overcome her learning problems? Will she graduate from high school with good skills? Will she ever be able to keep up with the regular curriculum? Is her self-concept being permanently damaged by her learning difficulties? Am I being neurotic by having these concerns? Do I have the right to express my apprehensions? Should I be more patient and trusting? These people are the professionals. How can I presume to challenge someone who knows far more than I do about dealing with learning problems?

Yet, you may intuitively sense that your child is not doing as well as everyone is implying. You can see that she's still struggling and that she's becoming increasingly demoralized, and you feel uncertain and apprehensive. You pray that the document you've just signed can attain the defined goals and that this will translate into decent academic skills and self-confidence. You also pray that the people providing help really know what they're doing.

The Function of the IEP Conference

The concept of the IEP is sound and pragmatic. Professionals assess a struggling child's academic strengths and weaknesses, pinpoint underlying causal factors, develop a systematic plan for resolving the underlying learning problems, and establish realistic educational goals.

The IEP meeting is one of the most critically important conferences you will ever attend. If your child's learning deficits are not accurately identified and if the proposed remediation program does not adequately address her learning deficits, your child will be at serious educational, emotional, and vocational risk.

Two of the primary functions of the IEP are to apprise you of your child's test results and to describe how the learning assistance program can address her educational needs. As the meeting progresses, one of the attending school personnel will record the specific recommendations and educational goals for the year in the school district's formal IEP document. A formal summary of the diagnostic tests administered by the school psychologist and resource specialist will either be given to you at the conference or mailed to you within a reasonable period of time (usually two weeks). This report will also contain the results of any assessments done by the school district speech and language pathologist, occupational therapist, and/or social worker.

You want the IEP conference to provide you with substantive information about your child and an effective strategy for resolving her learning problems. You can't allow the meeting to become a mind-dulling pro forma exercise. You can't waste time on platitudes, and your child can't waste time on ill-conceived programs.

The IEP conference is a problem-solving forum. It allows you to participate directly in a methodical examination of your child's current educational status and needs. You are there as your child's representative and advocate. Your role is to make certain that the proposed remediation plan does what it's designed to do: resolve the learning problems.

To maximize the benefits of the IEP conference, you want to be certain that critically important issues are discussed to your satisfaction. The following checklist is designed to ensure that the IEP covers these key issues. You might want to bring the checklist to the meeting.

IEP Procedural Checklist

	Yes	No
The results of all diagnostic and academic tests given by the school psychologist, resource specialist, and other professionals have been discussed and explained.	_____	_____
My child's specific learning deficits and distinctive educational needs have been determined.	_____	_____
The remediation program being proposed adequately addresses my child's deficits and needs.	_____	_____
My child's eligibility for specialized interventions such as Slingerland, Lindamood, speech therapy, occupational therapy, and counseling has been explored.	_____	_____
Realistic, challenging improvement goals for the school year have been defined.	_____	_____
Guidelines for providing homework assistance and supervision at home have been discussed.	_____	_____
Guidelines for responding to counterproductive behavior in class and at home have been developed.	_____	_____
Objective criteria for evaluating progress in the special education program have been created.	_____	_____

Procedures for maintaining effective ongoing
communication have been developed.   _____ _____
The benefits and drawbacks of supplemental out-of-
school services have been examined.   _____ _____

Examining Diagnostic Tests Results

As you discuss the results of your child's diagnostic evaluation at the IEP,
you will undoubtedly want clarification about certain scores and the educational implications of these scores. The questions below are models.
You can use them as a guideline for formulating your own questions about
any testing issues that have not been explained to your satisfaction. If you
are intimidated by the technical educational jargon used in these questions and feel uncomfortable delving into the test scores, you may simply
state, "I'm not clear about what my child's result on this test means in
practical terms, and I don't fully understand how the proposed remediation plan will address the issues. Could you clarify this for me?" (Refer to
chapter 5 for descriptions of diagnostic and achievement tests.)

Questions About Your Child's Diagnostic Assessment

• You've indicated that my child showed auditory discrimination deficits on the Wepman. How do you intend to correct these deficits?

• Subtests on the ITPA (Illinois Test of Psycholinguistic Abilities) indicate that my child is having problems with auditory sequential memory,
visual sequential memory, and sound blending. The IEP objectives focus
on the reading and the sound blending, but I see no mention of what can
be done in the resource program to address my child's auditory and visual sequential memory deficits. Will these be corrected with the current
strategy?

• The Slingerland test indicates that my child makes letter reversals
and transpositions. It is my understanding that these are symptoms of
dyslexia. Are you saying that my child is dyslexic? Will the resource program remediate this problem? And if so, what program will you be using?

• On the Broad Written Language Assessment of the Woodcock Johnson, my child performed considerably below grade level on the dictation
and writing sample subtests. How are these deficits going to be addressed
in the resource program?

• On the PIAT (Peabody Individual Achievement Test), my child had
difficulty in the areas of general information and reading recognition. Can

you explain what these categories mean and what can be done to resolve these deficiencies?

• What could explain the discrepancy between my child's verbal and performance scores on the WISC III? You've indicated that the discrepancy is indicative of a learning disability. If my child is retested after completing the resource program, should I expect less of a discrepancy? Also, if my child's lower performance score is bringing down his full-scale IQ, may I assume that if the resource program improves my child's performance, my child's full-scale IQ will be higher than currently indicated? Do you readminister the WISC III after completion of the resource program to get a more current measurement of his ability and potential?

• The Bender Gestalt indicates visual-motor integration deficits. What does this mean, and how are these deficits addressed in the resource program?

• The TAPS (Test of Auditory Perceptual Skills) indicates that my child has difficulty interpreting auditory directions and is testing at the 6th percentile. She also has difficulty with auditory word memory. What can be done to correct these problems in the special day class program you've recommended? Is there anything I can do to help her at home?

If the questions you ask do not produce acceptable answers, you may conclude that your child's deficits are not going to be adequately addressed in the resource program. For example, the school personnel may state that the Slingerland test indicates your child has dyslexia. If they aren't prepared to use specialized teaching methods to address the problem, you have justification for concern. Simply reading with your child and correcting her mistakes is not going to resolve her dyslexia. Such a strategy is at best a stopgap measure.

If you believe that the IEP is not producing workable solutions to your child's problems or that your child had not made significant progress since her last IEP, you have several options for getting the remediation program on track:

• Consult a private educational therapist, developmental pediatrician, educational psychologist, or neuropsychologist. You may want to have this person independently evaluate your child, review the IEP, and make remediation recommendations.

• Suggest that highly specialized remediation techniques be used such as the Lindamood ADD program (a method for training children with auditory discrimination and reading problems), the Visualizing Verbalizing Program (a method for improving comprehension and recall), or the Slingerland method (a technique for teaching dyslexic children).

- If appropriate, suggest that your child be assigned to a different resource specialist on an experimental basis.
- Hire a specialist to work privately with your child.

Giving Your Approval

At the end of the IEP meeting you'll be asked to sign the IEP document that defines specific academic and remediation goals. By signing the document you're indicating that you concur with the recommendations that have been made. You should not agree to sign this document unless you do concur and fully understand the issues. If you wish, you can ask for more time to study the proposals more carefully at home. If, however, you do concur with the remediation program and sign the document, the IEP would then be immediately implemented, and your child would be provided with the agreed-upon assistance in either a special day class or in the resource room for the stipulated amount of time each day.

You want to leave the IEP conference convinced that all the issues have been carefully examined and that a plan will be set in motion that can reduce—and ideally eliminate—your child's academic deficiencies. You want concrete objectives, a well-conceived intervention strategy, effective remediation methods, and accountability. The more stringent the oversight, the greater the probability that your child's learning problems will be resolved.

By having highly focused goals for the IEP conference, you can significantly enhance the likelihood that the meeting will be productive and the learning assistance program effective. Although each struggling child has a distinctive mix of learning problems and underlying issues, there are common denominators that need to be addressed in every successful remediation strategy.

Basic IEP Objectives

- To provide first-rate remedial assistance and emotional support that will allow your child to acquire academic skills at or above grade level or at a level commensurate with her intelligence.
- To improve your child's academic self-confidence.
- To make certain your child applies the skills being taught in the resource program to her mainstream classes.

• To encourage your child to function with increasing independence and self-reliance.

• To resolve your child's underlying learning deficits so that she can successfully handle mainstream curriculum without requiring ongoing learning assistance.

The rate at which your child achieves these objectives will depend on the severity of her learning problems, the quality of the resource program, the effectiveness of your support at home, and the nature of your child's coping mechanisms (see psychological overlay, chapter 3). Some children make quick and dramatic progress, and others require more extensive and extended learning assistance (see learning curves, chapter 12).

If your child is already in a special program and your observations of her progress indicate that the educational plan is effectively addressing her learning deficits, you can be less anxious about the IEP conference. Because the program is on target and doing what it's intended to do, your child is likely to emerge from the resource program or special day class with adequate skills.

But if you conclude after a reasonable period of time that your child's program is not meeting its stated objectives, you should be prepared to take a more assertive role at subsequent IEP meetings. You have every right to ask penetrating questions and insist on incisive responses. Don't worry about upsetting people or about challenging statements or explanations that don't make sense. Don't worry about requesting clarification if you don't fully understand the issues or the rationale for the proposals being made. Don't worry about asking for explanations about why agreed-upon goals haven't been attained. This is your meeting, and this is your child's future you're discussing.

In most states an informal IEP review is scheduled annually, and a comprehensive reassessment of the child's progress is scheduled every three years. You don't need to wait for the next regularly planned review, however, to express your concerns. You have the right to request one at any time.

A note of caution is in order. Although you are justified in expecting improvement, you must also be realistic and reasonable. Some learning problems can be quite resistant to immediate cures, and you should guard against imposing arbitrary and unrealistic timetables. Your improvement expectations should be geared to the severity of your child's problems. You must also factor your child's age into the remediation equation. The longer your child has been struggling, the further behind he is likely to be. Older children also tend to be more resistant to assistance and quick academic fixes because of their more elaborate emotional defense mechanisms.

Making the IEP Conference Work

The composition of the IEP conference may vary somewhat from district to district and from state to state. The principal, resource specialist, classroom teacher, and school psychologist will, of course, be there. In some cases, the school nurse may also participate. If your child is in an occupational therapy program at school, the OT would also attend. The school social worker may also participate in the conference. You have the option of inviting your child's tutor, educational therapist, and/or counselor. You may also invite an advocate to represent you.

Your role during an IEP conference is to serve as your child's representative and make certain she receives the best assistance available. Your role is not to rubber-stamp whatever recommendations are made by the professionals in attendance. Even though a team of specialists is overseeing your child's program, you cannot assume that everything is under control and that the outcome will be positive. To do so is to place too much trust in a remediation system that in many cases has a spotty track record. Far too many children derive little or no meaningful benefits from in-school learning assistance, and they emerge from the resource program with inadequate skills and damaged self-confidence. Undoubtedly there are parents reading these words who can attest from personal experience that supposedly competent, well-intentioned professionals can make serious mistakes in diagnosing and treating children's learning problems and that these mistakes can have disastrous educational consequences.

Your objectives are to become informed about the educational deficits impeding your child's academic progress, to explore options for resolving these deficits, and to provide support and oversight. You must serve notice at the IEP conference that you're committed to helping your child and determined that she ultimately prevail over her learning difficulties. By so doing you're notifying the school personnel that you want your child's remediation program to be productive.

IEP conferences are generally not hostile, confrontative, or adversarial, and it's very unfortunate if they become so. The professionals are there to explain the test results, define the professional jargon, clarify the issues, and suggest a focused, reasonable, and realistic remediation plan.

Ideally, there will be a dynamic sharing of ideas and insights and everyone will agree to work together to achieve a mutually shared goal. In this scenario there is certainly no reason to be challenging, assertive, or insistent. You and the school personnel have established a good working relationship. You concur about what needs to be done, and you support and respect each other's efforts and commitment.

Sometimes, however, the IEP conference can be less than satisfying, and you may begin to think, "I've been down this road already, and nothing is happening. My child is still struggling and doesn't appear to be making much progress despite the assurances they're giving me." When your instincts tell you that your child's learning problems are not being adequately addressed, trust them. If the remediation program is not working, you may need to abandon the current plan and formulate an entirely new one. Your child may require a different type of assistance or may need to work with another resource specialist. He may also need private supplemental learning assistance after school from a skilled educational therapist or tutor (see chapter 10).

Although you may sense or know intuitively that something is wrong with the remediation plan, you may not be able to identify the weak links or determine what steps need to be taken to get the program on track. If this is the case and you have hard-to-define concerns about the intervention strategy, you may want to consider the following.

Questions to Pose at the IEP Conference When the Remediation Program Appears to Be Stalled

How would you rate the severity of my child's learning difficulties on a scale from one to ten, with one being subtle and ten being very severe?

Do you believe the proposed program will provide all the instructional resources my child requires to overcome her learning difficulties?

Are the resource specialist and classroom teacher working together to help my child resolve her learning deficits?

What is the realistic prognosis for my child? Do you believe she can overcome her learning deficits, or is the goal to help her learn how to compensate for them?

Is the proposed instructional plan designed primarily to help her with her current class work, or is it oriented toward resolving her underlying perceptual processing problems?

If the resource specialist is addressing the underlying learning deficits, how should the day-to-day challenges my child is experiencing in her regular classes be handled? Should the teacher reduce the difficulty level of the work she's expected to do in class until her skills improve? Should the quantity of assigned work be reduced?

If the resource specialist is working primarily on helping her do in-class and homework assignments, what is being done about correcting her underlying learning deficits? Does she need to return to where she became stuck in reading, math, and language arts?

Can my child graduate from a special day class and be successfully integrated into mainstream classes? If so, when can this happen?

Will my child continue to require learning assistance in one form or another throughout her education?

Are you observing behavior and attitude problems and lowered self-confidence? If so, do you have any suggestions about how we can work together to help her handle the fallout from her learning problems and improve her self-image?

Does my child require psychological counseling?

Would additional outside-of-school assistance from a tutor or educational therapist speed up the remediation process? If so, can you recommend someone?

What assistance should I provide at home? Should I help her with her homework? If she makes mistakes, should I correct them? Should I review skills that are being taught in the resource program? Should I study with her and help her review for tests?

How much homework should I expect her to do each evening? What should I do if she cannot complete her assignments in the allotted time? How do I prevent her from becoming overly dependent if I provide help?

How can I best support your efforts to help my child?

Do you see any ways to make the learning assistance program more effective?

IEP Reviews

When you attend your next regularly scheduled IEP review, the resource specialist will indicate the specific educational goals that have been attained. As you examine these accomplishments, it may be appropriate to ask certain key questions:

Have the checked-off skills been completely mastered?
What are the criteria for determining mastery?

Do the resource specialist and the classroom teacher share the same standards?

Could my child regress or forget what she has learned?

Is my child transferring the skills she has mastered in the resource program to her mainstream classes?

Are the defined goals sufficiently challenging to assure substantive academic gains?

Will my child's current skills allow her to keep up with her mainstream classes?

No one is suggesting that the school personnel would intentionally mislead you about your child's progress, but the standards for determining competence can be subjective. Skills that may appear to have been mastered may still be tentative. You want your child's progress to be solid and her skills to be consistent. If additional practice and reinforcement are needed to make this a reality, you want to be informed. You certainly don't want to discover later that learning deficits that were supposedly resolved are still problematic.

Periodic retesting is, of course, is the most objective means for determining your child's progress. If retesting has not been done prior to the IEP review, you have every right to request it. The scores can be mailed to you, and if you have questions, you can contact the resource specialist informally or schedule another meeting.

Advocates

If you find yourself in dispute with your child's school about placement in a special education program or about the efficacy of the program, you may conclude that it would be beneficial to have an experienced professional represent you and your child at the IEP conference. Such professionals, called advocates, specialize in clarifying issues, presenting your position, and resolving conflicts. They are knowledgeable about learning disabilities, school district policies, state guidelines, and educational codes. If the disagreements cannot be resolved at the IEP conference, the advocate would represent you in continuing discussions with school district personnel. If a compromise or negotiated settlement can be reached, the advocate would participate in the process of hammering out an acceptable agreement. The advocate would also represent your child if as part of due process you request an impartial hearing.

Should litigation become necessary, the advocate would coordinate his or her services with those of an attorney. The advocate should also be able to help you find a lawyer who is knowledgeable about federally mandated educational codes and who has represented other families in litigation with school districts.

There are generally two categories of advocates. The first is comprised of such professionals as educational therapists and psychologists who understand the educational issues associated with learning disabilities. These professionals are well informed about federal and state laws that pertain to children's rights, and they are willing to challenge a school district's inflexible policies or restrictive eligibility criteria for providing special education resources.

The second category is comprised of well-versed parents who have themselves done battle with a school district about their own child's rights. These individuals know the pertinent laws and are passionate about fighting for fair treatment of the learning disabled.

There are pluses and minuses to hiring an advocate. A strong and highly knowledgeable advocate can provide invaluable emotional and legal support when you find yourself in a seemingly unsolvable conflict with the school administration. This person can often make the difference between your child's getting or not getting the educational services she needs. At the same time, hiring an advocate to represent your child at an IEP conference can put the school district personnel on the defensive. If the advocate is abrasive or strident, he or she can cause the district to

---

Reasons for Hiring an Advocate

- You are in dispute with the school district about your child's eligibility for a resource program or special day class.
- You are in disagreement with the school district about whether or not your child is making adequate progress.
- You are dissatisfied with the services being offered by your child's school.
- You believe your child's classroom teacher is unwilling to make reasonable, federally mandated accommodations for your child's learning problems. (You should first discuss your concerns and complaints with the school district's Section 504 grievance officer. See chapter 7.)

Profile of the Ideal Advocate

- Able to interpret test results and evaluate the effectiveness of in-school remediation programs
- Enlightened about causes and academic and psychological implications of learning problems
- Able to negotiate effectively
- Articulate and diplomatic
- Forceful when appropriate
- Not easily intimidated
---

become even more intransigent. For this reason you must choose wisely when selecting someone to represent you and your child. Because the stakes are great, you want the very best person available.

Most advocates charge for their services, so you should discuss the issue of fees. It would also be advisable to request references and to discuss the advocacy procedure with parents who have gone through the process.

Pitfalls in Special Placement

Many parents are understandably relieved when their child qualifies for a special education program. However, there can also be problems with these programs.

Some struggling children are very self-conscious and sensitive about their learning difficulties, and they may feel humiliated when they have to leave the classroom to see the resource specialist. From the perspective of a child who is overly sensitive, leaving the classroom for special help is tantamount to wearing a big sign on her back that says DEFECTIVE.

Children with more severe learning problems who are placed in special day classes may also feel embarrassed and self-conscious. They may be convinced that other children in school consider them retarded. Their embarrassment is magnified when children are permitted to tease or denigrate students in special programs.*

---
*The most appalling behavior I encountered occurred at a middle school in an very affluent community where I practiced. Students would hide the cane of a blind eighth grader and laugh at her as she attempted to find it. They would also trip her. This child went on to graduate as valedictorian of her class. That this outrageous behavior was tolerated by teachers and administrators is incomprehensible. The situation represents a failure by the school to reinforce the fundamental values of a civilized society.

Many children are not resistant to being pulled out of class. Nevertheless, it would certainly be appropriate for the classroom teacher to explain to the entire class why some students may need extra help. Class discussions and activities might be used to make students more aware of the types of difficulties certain children face when they attempt to do schoolwork. For example, the teacher could have students try on a pair of someone else's prescription glasses and then ask them to read a passage in a textbook.

The purpose of the experiment is to demonstrate what it feels like to struggle to do something that others can do with little difficulty. To help students understand the effects of a learning problem and become more sensitive to those who have such a problem, the teacher might also draw an analogy about trying to watch television or work on a computer when static is causing the information on the screen to jiggle.

It is both sad and ironic that many children who participate in resource programs are penalized for receiving remedial help. The most common form of penalty is for the classroom teacher to hold these students accountable for all work missed when they are out of class. An even more insidious form of intolerance occurs when a teacher resents children being pulled out of class and communicates this resentment to students who are participating in the resource program. Although it seems inconceivable that any educator would be this narrow-minded, there are some teachers who cannot grasp the value of providing intensive help for struggling students.

Children with learning problems are already insecure and, in many cases, resistant to help. For a teacher to make them feel even more self-conscious only compounds the problem. These teachers need to be reminded that students are being pulled out of class because they're having difficulty mastering academic skills and require special help. To insist that all missed work be made up can be unfair and demoralizing to these children.

Teachers who express openly or through innuendo their disapproval of students participating in the resource program need to be enlightened by the school administration. Parents should not tolerate this misguided behavior. If the teacher refuses to cooperate, parents should not hesitate to contact the principal or superintendent. Teachers must also make reasonable accommodations in the assigned classwork and homework until the struggling child can catch up with her class (see chapter 5). The teacher who fails to do so defeats the purpose of the resource program and can damage the child who is trying to overcome her learning deficits. The teacher's failure to accommodate is also illegal.

Fortunately, most teachers are supportive of the resource program. They realize that learning assistance will not only help the poorly performing student but will also make their own lives easier.

Some districts actually send resource specialists into the regular classroom to help students with their assignments on site. This procedure is intended to reduce the student's self-consciousness about being pulled out of class and to allow the resource specialist to work with real-world problems that the student is facing. The rationale for this practice, however, is debatable. It's difficult to believe that the student would actually feel less self-conscious having the resource specialist in the classroom with her. And focusing exclusively on completing in-class assignments takes time away from addressing the underlying perceptual processing deficits that are responsible for the child's learning problems.

There may be no ideal solution to the challenge of providing learning assistance for struggling students without creating potential embarrassment for those who are self-conscious and lacking in academic self-confidence. Whatever the downside of providing help, the advantages clearly outweigh the disadvantages. The child who prevails over her learning problems may one day look back on her embarrassment and still feel the sting, but ideally she'll realize that this was the price she had to pay to acquire skills she needed to be successful in school and in life.

Chapter 7
Understanding the Law

Injustice: violation of the right or rights of another; iniquity or unfairness.

P erhaps you're satisfied with the support services your child is receiving in school. You've concluded that his resource specialist is dedicated, talented, creative, and dynamic. You're delighted that your son likes her, is making steady progress, and is proud of his accomplishments. Each month you see improvement in your child's skills, self-concept, and desire to learn. You're confident that the school psychologist and the IEP team have accurately identified the underlying academic and perceptual deficits and have put in place a well-conceived remediation plan. You're also pleased that the professionals are working together. Your child's motor coordination problems are being addressed by the school occupational therapist, and his articulation problems are being treated by the speech pathologist. The school social worker meets with your child periodically to discuss such issues as frustration and occasional misbehavior in class.

Your child's classroom teacher has made several effective accommodations. She has placed your child's seat closer to her desk, and she allows him extra time to take tests. She doesn't ask him to read aloud in class unless he's had an opportunity to prepare the material in advance. To reduce his frustration, she has modified his homework and in-class assignments so that he can complete them within a reasonable amount of time. Each day she initials his assignment sheet to make sure he knows what homework needs to be done.

If this scenario describes your child's situation in school, you should breathe a sign of relief. He is in good hands, and the system is working superbly. Because your child is receiving comprehensive assistance, his educational prognosis has been enhanced, and the risk of self-concept damage has been reduced.

Although the preceding description of special education resources may seem idealized, many school districts do a first-rate job of addressing the needs of their learning disabled students. These districts are in full compliance with the letter and the spirit of the federal laws that protect the rights of the learning disabled.

Unfortunately, some parents have a different impression of how the special education system works. These parents have been thwarted by their local school district when they requested help, and they're justifiably angry and frustrated. If you identify with these dissatisfied parents, you may have laughed cynically as you read the preceding description of an ideal educational support program. You may have thought, "If my child received only twenty-five percent of the services you described, I'd be ecstatic. My daughter is essentially being left to fend for herself."

For decades the special education guidelines in many school districts have limited participation in remedial programs to between three and four percent of the student population. This limitation was imposed despite the face that as many as thirty percent of the children in American schools are working below their full intellectual and academic potential. Even today many marginally performing students with hard-to-define academic deficits are not being provided with meaningful help. These students are labeled immature, irresponsible, lazy, unmotivated, oppositional, disadvantaged, or having an attitude, and their legitimate learning needs are conveniently swept under the carpet.

Becoming a Gladiator

The laws enacted by the federal government are designed to protect the rights of children with learning disabilities. These laws require school districts to provide assistance for students with documented learning disabilities and to make in-class accommodations that will prevent these children from being discriminated against because of their learning problems.

As parents who have butted heads with the inflexible and myopic school personnel can attest, federal law does not always translate into tangible, substantive help for the children whom the laws are designed to protect. Some school districts meticulously comply with the law, and others make only a halfhearted attempt to comply. And certain districts are in blatant noncompliance with federal mandates.

The legal position typically argued by lawyers representing school districts in litigation is that schools are only required to provide an adequate education and adequate services. They are not obligated to provide a superior education or superior services. At issue is what constitutes "adequate." Your definition of adequate may be very different from that of your local school district.

Despite the rationalizations offered by many school districts for inferior or marginal learning assistance programs, federal law guarantees that learning disabled children cannot be discriminated against and that their legitimate educational needs be met. Unfortunately, parents cannot rely exclusively on the law. To protect their child's interests, they must demand compliance with the law. The incidence of educational injustice drops significantly when parents are informed, prepared to fight the system, and willing to assert their child's legitimate rights.

Common Assumptions About the Obligations of the Educational System

• My child has the right to receive a decent education. *This right is guaranteed by federal law.*

• My child deserves to acquire positive associations with learning. *This is one of the guiding principles of all effective educational systems.*

• My child deserves to graduate high school with academic and thinking skills that will allow her to find employment or pursue a higher education. *This is a fundamental objective of all functional educational programs.*

• My child should be provided with reasonable learning assistance and accommodations. *These rights are guaranteed by federal law.*

If the preceding list accurately expresses your assumptions, be assured that your position is legitimate and justifiable.

The Provisions of Federal Law

In 1975, Congress enacted a law that prescribes specific procedures for providing assistance to children with learning disabilities and other handicaps and dysfunctions. This law, the Education for All Handicapped Children Act (PL 94-142), was subsequently renamed the Individuals with Disabilities Education Act (IDEA-PL 105-17). It requires that schools:

• provide a free and appropriate public education to all handicapped children, which includes special education and related services to meet their unique educational needs;

- provide handicapped children with an education in the least restrictive environment on the basis of individual needs;
- guarantee to each handicapped child an unbiased, valid assessment in a mode of communication normally used by the child;
- provide parents the opportunity to be involved in educational decisions concerning their child.

Another federal law protects children who are struggling in school. This law, Section 504 of the Rehabilitation Act of 1973, has proven to be a very useful resource for parents trying to procure help for children with mild to moderate learning disabilities who might not qualify for special education services. A key provision in Section 504 distinguishes it from IDEA: the law provides protection to people with disabilities *throughout their lifetime.*

Section 504 states: A not otherwise qualified individual with disabilities in the United States . . . shall not, solely by reason of his/her disability, be excluded from the participation in, be denied the benefits of, or be subjected to discrimination under any program or activity receiving federal financial assistance.

The preceding paragraph played a key role in shaping the regulations subsequently enacted in the Americans with Disabilities Act of 1990 (ADA, as distinguished from IDEA). A person with a disability is defined as someone who has a physical or mental impairment that substantially limits one or more major life activities; has a record of such impairment; or is regarded as having such an impairment.

Learning disabilities, attention deficit disorder (ADD), and attention deficit hyperactivity disorder (ADHD) are included as dysfunctions covered in both Section 504 and in the Americans with Disabilities Act. These inclusions have critically important legal significance.

The Intent of the Law

Section 504 and ADA are both, in essence, civil rights laws intended to end discrimination against people with disabilities in all programs and activities receiving federal financial assistance. The objective of the Individuals with Disabilities Education Act (IDEA) is to provide federal financial assistance to state and local school systems so that they can properly educate children with disabilities.

Whereas children under IDEA must meet certain diagnostic criteria (thirteen categories of disability are specified), under Section 504 this restrictive stipulation is not imposed. Section 504 applies whenever a functional impairment can be identified that "substantially limits a major life activity." A learning dysfunction qualifies as an impairment. Although both laws require that a *free and appropriate education* be provided by the Fair and Appropriate Education Act (FAPE), IDEA limits protection to those requiring and qualifying for special educational services. It also provides funding for support services and independent evaluations.

Section 504 offers broader protections than IDEA and includes students who do not qualify for special education but who may require in-class accommodations to meet their distinctive learning needs. Unlike IDEA, it does not require school districts to pay for independent evaluations, but it does require that school districts at the minimum *consider* reimbursement for such evaluations when appropriate.

Under the provisions of Section 504, school districts are mandated to provide a grievance procedure. Schools are also required to have a Section 504 official to assure compliance with the regulations and are prevented from passing on any associated costs to the student's family.

School districts cannot claim that they are unable to provide accommodations because of fiscal limitations, but they can attempt to prove that the adjustments would cause undue hardship for the district. This argument rarely succeeds, because most reasonable accommodations are relatively inexpensive.

There is another key difference between IDEA and Section 504. IDEA requires a formal written IEP that conforms to standard content and formatting criteria. Section 504 does not have this stipulation, but it does require that an accommodation plan be created and implemented. This plan must address the struggling child's specific learning needs and must be formatted so that it is clear and understandable. Another key feature of Section 504 is that no administrative hearing is necessary prior to seeking recourse from the Office of Civil Rights or from the courts. Individuals who believe their child has been damaged by discrimination can seek monetary compensation.

Please note: If your child does not qualify for a special education program, there may be another resource available to supplement the provisions in Section 504. Called Title 1, this federally funded program provides small-group reading and math assistance for children who are testing below grade level. The program is offered in schools where there is a significant proportion of children from financially disadvantaged homes. Parents should check with the principal to determine if this program is available at their child's school.

Making Reasonable Accommodations Under Section 504

Because Section 504 is essentially a civil rights law, its intent is to remove physical, organizational, and instructional/curriculum barriers that might prevent students with disabilities from fully participating in educational activities and opportunities. The act stipulates that reasonable accommodations be made in instruction and testing so that discrimination against students with disabilities is eliminated. Inflexible procedures that prevent students from demonstrating their abilities must be modified. Other accommodations might include permitting extra time for tests, providing a separate room for testing, and allowing children to take oral tests. The 504 plan might also incorporate books on tape, small group teaching, instructions that are delivered orally and/or in writing, modified seating placement, permission to use a computer in class, and adjustments in assignments, pacing, class environment, and presentation of subject matter. Reasonable efforts must be made not to embarrass handicapped students by asking them to spell or read aloud in class if their skills prevent them from doing so.*

Reasonable Accommodations for Struggling Learners

Classroom Instruction
- Using different sensory modalities when teaching (auditory, visual, tactile, kinesthetic)
- Using specialized, less difficult curriculum
- Taping lectures for students with auditory processing deficits
- Using manipulatives (hands-on materials) to reinforce learning
- Providing study guides
- Providing a written model for how assignments are to be completed
- Backing up oral directions with written directions
- Backing up written directions with oral directions
- Breaking instructions into smaller units
- Modifying reading level of in-class and homework assignments
- Using creative, less traditional techniques to help the student master course content, acquire skills, and maintain focus

---

*I am indebted to the *Learning Disabilities Association Newsbrief* (July/August 1995) for descriptions of the federal laws that protect the rights of learning disabled children.

- Identifying and capitalizing on the student's preferred learning style
- Utilizing visual aids to explain content of lectures and textbooks
- Reading directions to the student that appear on worksheets and in textbooks
- Reducing the emphasis on spelling accuracy
- Using taped textbooks
- Checking for understanding of newly introduced material
- Periodically reviewing material already covered
- Blocking off, masking, or highlighting assignments to facilitate focus and mastery
- Handing out printed homework assignments for the week
- Diversifying activities during each lesson
- Sending home simple daily and/or weekly progress reports
- Verifying that instructions and directions are understood
- Providing a written outline of textbook or lecture content
- Reducing pencil and paper tasks
- Asking the student to repeat instructions
- Having the student summarize information orally
- Providing tutoring before and after school
- Reducing the length of instructional segments
- Using computers to assist in learning, reinforcement, and mastery
- Allowing extra time to complete tasks
- Reducing the number of worksheets handed out at one time

Classroom Management
- Seating the student near the teacher
- Providing consistent structure
- Standing closer to the student when presenting a lesson or giving instructions
- Providing consistent and reasonable consequences for misbehavior
- Seating the student near a positive role model
- Keeping rules simple and clear
- Developing strategies for transition periods (cafeteria, P.E., and so forth)
- Alerting the bus driver and playground monitors concerning a possible behavior problem

Concentration Deficits
- Allowing the student a short break between tasks
- Clearly defining behavioral limits

- Minimizing distractions
- Allowing time out of the seat
- Providing additional structure to reduce inattentiveness
- Increasing space between desks
- Using nonverbal signals to help the student stay on task
- Using nonembarrassing time-out procedures

Grading
- Deemphasizing handwriting as a grading criterion
- Allowing extra credit for student-initiated projects and for in-class participation
- Reducing the number of correct answers required to achieve a decent grade

Homework
- Reducing the number of problems required for homework
- Breaking down large assignments into smaller projects
- Encouraging the student to keep track of performance on tests and homework assignments
- Making certain the student records accurately and understands the homework assignment
- Modifying the homework so that the student can complete the assignments

Learning Strategies
- Helping the student identify his perferred learning style (how he learns most effectively and efficiently)
- Encouraging the student to experiment with different ways of learning assigned material

Motivation
- Emphasizing rewards for achievement rather than negative consequences for mistakes and poor judgment
- Using a reward system for completing homework and in-class schoolwork
- Providing more immediate rewards for accomplishments
- Making performance and behavior contracts with the student

Organization and Time Management
- Urging the student to define realistic short-term and long-term goals
- Showing the student how to plan and execute long-range projects

Parent Instruction
- Providing workshops that teach parents effective at-home instructional methods (tutoring, review, and drilling)
- Modeling how parents can provide effective emotional and educational support and guidance at home
- Examining appropriate versus inappropriate parent intervention methods
- Teaching parents how to motivate children to learn
- Demonstrating how to provide the most effective support for the efforts of the teacher and resource specialist

Peer Assistance
- Encouraging peer help with planning, organization, and time management
- Providing peer note taking
- Providing peer tutoring
- Assigning a volunteer homework buddy
- Forming study groups in which superior students help struggling classmates
- Pairing students to check each other's work for errors

Psychological Support
- Ignoring certain inappropriate behaviors
- Encouraging self-monitoring of behavior and performance
- Providing group and individual counseling
- Helping the student acquire better socialization skills
- Encouraging all students to be sensitive, understanding, and supportive of classmates with special needs

Study Skills
- Providing instruction in how to study, take notes, and identify important information
- Helping the student develop personalized learning strategies that work with his individual learning style

- Teaching the student how to prepare for and take tests
- Teaching the student memorization techniques

Teacher Training
- Providing in-service training for teachers to help them understand learning deficits and manage associated behavior problems
- Creating a team of master teachers and resource specialists in each district to advise and counsel classroom teachers on ways to maximize the learning of struggling children

Testing
- Allowing the student to answer test questions on tape
- Highlighting test-taking instructions (verbally, in writing, or with a highlighting marker)
- Making certain that the student understands test questions
- Marking the student's correct answers as opposed to mistakes
- Using frequent short quizzes as opposed to long exams
- Allowing open-book tests
- Reading the test items to the student
- Using multiple-choice questions rather than essays to assess mastery
- Giving take-home tests

The preceding list of accommodations is designed to help struggling students compensate for a wide range of educational deficits. Even if the teacher is able to implement only three or four of the described modifications, it could have a dramatic impact on your child's ability to function effectively in the classroom and can be instrumental in reducing her anxiety and feelings of inadequacy.

Be reasonable in requesting accommodations, and focus on those that are most important and most urgent. You cannot realistically expect a teacher to make forty accommodations for your child! Be prepared to negotiate and make every effort to be diplomatic. If appropriate, help the teacher understand why certain accommodations can be beneficial and how they can be implemented without causing an undue burden or hardship for her or the other students. If the teacher is resistant, ask that the principal, school psychologist, or resource specialist participate in the discussion. Although federal law requires that reasonable accommodations be made for students with disabilities, voluntary cooperation is certainly preferable to a confrontation. If you cannot reach agreement, ask to speak with the school district's Section 504 compliance/grievance officer. All school districts are legally required to have one.

The modifications are intended to create an educational context that allows struggling students to demonstrate their talents and abilities. It is important to realize, however, that before a request from parents for accommodation in a child's curriculum, class instruction, and testing can be considered, there must be documentation of a disability and clear justification that the modifications are appropriate. This documentation is based on achievement and diagnostic test scores and on observations by the classroom teacher, resource specialist, or other special education personnel (see chapters 4–6).

Section 504 accommodations are intended for the regular classroom, and, as previously stated, children may be eligible for these adjustments without necessarily qualifying for the resource program. Of course, most students in the resource program would benefit from appropriate Section 504 accommodations. Recommendations about modifications should be discussed at the IEP conference. If your child is not eligible for a formal IEP, make an appointment to discuss Section 504 accommodations with the classroom teacher, school psychologist, and/or resource specialist.

Translating the Law into a Plan of Action

If you find yourself in dispute with your child's school about testing, eligibility for special education, or eligibility for accommodations, read the foregoing summary of the provisions of federal law again carefully. These laws are your ammunition. They spell out your child's rights. The more you know about these rights, the more formidable you will be if forced into a confrontation with school personnel. Ideally, you'll be able to reach an amicable agreement without having to resort to legal remedies. If not, you must be prepared to go to "war."

You are not alone in this battle. You have powerful allies that include federal law and legal precedent. The first step in asserting your position is to let the school authorities know that you mean business and that you're not going to be easily deterred. Begin by requesting the school district's Parents' Rights Manual. All schools are required by law to make this manual available to parents upon request.

If you cannot come to an agreement, you're entitled to request a hearing before an impartial referee who is not employed by your local school district. Upon being notified of your request, the district is obligated to schedule this hearing. If you haven't done so already, it would be advisable at this point to hire a knowledgeable and forceful advocate to represent you in your interaction with the school district (see chapter 6).

If you believe the district is unwilling to implement reasonable accommodations, you should consult with the Section 504 compliance official. If the situation cannot be rectified to your satisfaction, you can file a formal grievance and argue that the district is in noncompliance with Section 504.

Should your advocate not be able to work out an agreement with the school district before the hearing, or if the hearing before the impartial referee goes against you, an attorney may be able to negotiate a settlement with the school district. Your last resort is to exercise your right of due process and bring a lawsuit against the district.

Under the provisions of Section 504, you may also claim damages in court. This can be a major deterrent to abuses. School districts do not want to become involved in expensive and time-consuming lawsuits if they can avoid them, and they certainly don't want to be held responsible for damages. The cost of litigation can be a major deterrent for financially strapped school districts, and the negative publicity can be very unpleasant for the district, and politically unwise for school board members. No one can ever be certain how a jury will rule, and the risks to the school district if it allows the case to go to trial can be significant. For these reasons, most school districts would prefer to negotiate a settlement rather than defend themselves in court. Sometimes just the threat of legal action will get the school district to acknowledge its obligation to provide learning assistance for a student.

If you believe that you might be forced into litigation with your school district, you should make an appointment for a consultation with a private educational psychologist, educational therapist, or neuropsychologist. This person can help you assess the situation objectively, evaluate the results of school-administered tests, and advise you about the reasonableness of your position.

Be forewarned that the educational psychologist or therapist you select will probably want to do independent testing, especially if it's likely that his or her testimony might be required in court. Although an educational therapist or psychologist might agree to represent you as an advocate, this person may decline your request. Educational therapists and psychologists generally prefer to remain on good terms with school districts, because they can be a source of referrals. Becoming involved in a protracted, unpleasant dispute can roil the waters and negatively affect their income. Because of this potential conflict of interest, it might be advisable to choose someone who does not practice in the local community to represent your child at meetings and hearings. The ideal person will be familiar with educational codes and have experience dealing with similar cases. His or her insights can be invaluable in helping you avoid pitfalls and missteps.

At the hearing you and/or your representative would present your case and substantiate your position with test scores, report cards, teacher comments, and reports from private practitioners. If the hearing does not produce the results you want, you can file suit. At this point you'll require the services of a lawyer who is knowledgeable about education law and has experience in educational litigation. The attorney would want to consult with your educational expert or would hire her own expert.

Before hiring an attorney, there are several key questions you should ask. Since this is an important decision, you might want to interview several before selecting one. Hiring an attorney can be an intimidating prospect, but if your case is strong, an attorney may be willing to accept it on contingency (be willing to forgo payment from you in return for sharing in any award for actual and punitive damages levied against the school district).

Questions to Ask an Attorney

Have you had experience negotiating with school districts?

Have you been involved in litigation that has dealt with learning disabled students' rights?

Are you licensed to practice in federal court?

How many cases of this type have you won?

What percentage of cases have you been able to resolve through a negotiated settlement?

Would you be willing to request permission from previous clients for me to contact them?

How good is this case? Do you believe it can be won?

Do you believe that the case can be settled without having to go to court?

What are your hourly fees?

Can you estimate how much this case might cost?

Will we require expert witnesses, and, if so, will their services be very costly?

Will my child need additional testing, or can you use previous test results?

If we go to court, will my child be required to testify?

Would you take this case on a contingency basis in lieu of charging me an hourly fee? If so, what would the percentage be?

If we settle and there are no monetary damages, would I then be expected to reimburse you for your fees?

In preparation for litigation, you can procure additional information about Section 504 regulations from the federal government by contacting the Equal Employment Opportunity Commission (1-800-669-EEOC) and the President's Commission on the Employment of Persons with Disabilities (202-376-6200). Your state may also provide specific literature about IDEA and Section 504, and about the compliance requirements for local school districts.

Many states, counties, and school districts have their own supplemental codes, guidelines, and localized policies that amplify federal requirements mandated in the Individuals with Disabilities Act, Section 504 of the Rehabilitation Act, and Americans with Disabilities Act. These state and local policies, however, do not supersede federal law. For example, the state of California requires the following time line for testing a child and developing an IEP, but many local districts flagrantly disregard it:

Procedure	Deadline for Completion
Written referral	15 days
Assessment plan and informed consent	At least 15 days
Assessment team meeting	50 days (not to include days in July and August)
Development and implementation of IEP review	Immediately Annually or by request

If you are forced to bring a lawsuit, being able to substantiate blatant noncompliance by your child's school with federal, state, or county mandated guidelines can strengthen your legal position.

Kids Who Don't Qualify for Help

Tens of thousands of academically deficient children each year are denied learning assistance. Some don't meet the eligibility criteria for enrollment in a resource program as defined by IDEA or don't conform to the school district's interpretation of these criteria. Others have problems that are not perceived as a disability under Section 504. For instance, a child whose IQ is in the low-average range and who is reading two years below grade level might not qualify for help because his performance is considered congruent with his ability. That this child's school performance might be significantly enhanced by learning assistance and that he might actually be able to learn how to read and comprehend at grade level are issues that the school district may conveniently disregard.

Conversely, a gifted child with an IQ of 150 who is testing slightly below grade level might also be denied help because he does not meet the eligibility criteria for placement in a resource program. Despite his superior intelligence, the child may be struggling with subtle to moderate *nonspecific* learning deficits that are preventing him from working at a level commensurate with his ability. For those not familiar with "edubabble," the term "nonspecific" means: We don't know precisely what's causing the problem, but whatever it is, your child doesn't qualify for help.

As previously stated, the basic criteria that qualify children for learning assistance include a discrepancy between ability and achievement (for example, a child with an above-average IQ who is performing significantly below his potential ability in one or more subjects) and specific, measurable perceptual processing deficits. In practice, the eligibility criteria vary from state to state and from school district to school district. Local economics plays a key role in how districts perceive their obligations under federal law. As a general rule, wealthier districts provide the most services. These districts are also more predisposed to providing help for marginally performing students with less severe learning disabilities.

It is clear that some school districts are interpreting federal laws "creatively." Some of these districts may unwittingly be in noncompliance or questionable compliance. Some may selectively disregard aspects of the laws, and others may exploit administrative loopholes that allow them to deny or reduce services to children who are clearly in need of assistance.

Even being in compliance with federal law is no guarantee that every struggling student's educational needs are being met. Some districts offer programs that are of marginal quality; others have programs that are abysmal. Students enrolled in these programs will receive virtually no meaningful remediation during the entire course of their elementary education. The situation may deteriorate even more in high school where students are sometimes herded like cattle into the equivalent of an educational stockyard. Teenagers mark time in these "feedlots," oblivious to the harsh realities that await them. Because they acquire minimal skills, these students will be qualified, at best, for marginal employment at the minimum wage or, at worst, for no employment at all.

Whether these unconscionable educational policies reflect misplaced priorities, administrative incompetence, insufficient school board oversight, inadequate staffing, or poorly trained, unqualified personnel, the explanation offers little comfort to concerned parents. The current policies and practices in many school districts are seriously flawed, and the situation requires fundamental changes. Informed, proactive parents can make these changes happen.

There are splendid national and local organizations and agencies that lobby for the rights of struggling children and provide parents with information about their rights and about issues relating to learning problems. These organizations may also be able to refer you to qualified advocates and attorneys. The advice is often free and in many cases is provided by parents who have themselves fought for their children. The list includes, among others: Children and Adults with Attention Deficit Disorder (CHADD), the International Dyslexia Association (formerly Orton Dyslexia Society), and Parents' Educational Resource Center (PERC). Many of these organizations also sponsor support groups where parents can share their experiences and brainstorm strategies. In the appendix you will find a more complete list of agencies and organizations that provide assistance to parents and children.

Parents must bear the responsibility for challenging schools that are not in compliance with federal law. This can be a disconcerting and unpleasant prospect, especially for people who are not adversarial by nature. It can be an even more unpleasant prospect when parents conclude that they require legal counsel. There is no question that lawyers are expensive, but in the long run, hiring a lawyer may actually be the far less expensive alternative. If your child is being emotionally and educationally damaged because her school is not in compliance, her earning potential over the course of her life may be reduced dramatically. If you don't fight now, you will find that psychiatrists and psychologists are also expensive, and there's no guarantee that they can repair the damage that has been done to your child's self-concept.

No one wants to go to court. If you're forced to do so and you win the case, you'll probably recover your legal expenses and perhaps damages as well. For this reason, most school districts are usually advised by their counsel to make reasonable settlements with disgruntled parents who have legitimate complaints.

Avoid confrontation if possible. Be diplomatic at first. Escalate in stages. Be prepared to go the distance if need be. Your child may not realize it, but she's counting on you to be resolute, to fight for her, and to protect her interests.

Part III
Finding the Right Person to Make an Evaluation

Chapter 8
Diagnosticians

Pediatricians, Developmental Pediatricians, Pediatric
Neurologists, Educational Psychologists, and
Neuropsychologists

Y ou can see that your child is struggling in school. Perhaps you've
been told that he doesn't meet the eligibility requirements for the
resource program despite his obvious difficulties. Perhaps your
child's teacher has expressed concern about his chronic inattentiveness,
and you're wondering whether he might have ADD and be a candidate
for medication. Perhaps you lack faith in the educational workup done
by the school psychologist or have misgivings about the proposed remediation strategy. You may question the efficacy of the resource program
or the methods being used by your child's private educational therapist.
Or you may fear that your child's learning problems are somehow linked
to a difficult pregnancy or complications during delivery. You want to
know what's going on, what the prognosis is, and what types of interventions are needed. You also want to feel assured that you're doing all you
can to assist your child. How do you find someone who can assess
the situation, help you evaluate your options, and point you in the right
direction?

If you had similar concerns about the accuracy of a medical diagnosis,
the appropriateness of a recommended treatment, or the explanation
about what is causing the problem, you would undoubtedly seek a second
opinion from a specialist. This physician would either confirm what
you've been told or would offer a different explanation and recommendation.

This same procedure of seeking an independent diagnosis from a specialist is as applicable in education as it is in medicine. When you are
unclear about the nature of your child's learning problems, perplexed

about the causes, and skeptical about the recommended treatment, you need a second opinion.

An Accurate Diagnosis

The newest high-tech diagnostic tools have made possible exciting research into cerebral physiology and metabolism. Laboratory testing procedures and diagnostic instruments can now explain the origins and neurological mechanics of many complex and perplexing learning dysfunctions. Cerebral areas that process specific types of information are being pinpointed with increasing precision, and anomalies in the brain associated with disabilities such as dyslexia have been identified. Using high-tech imaging equipment called functional magnetic resonance imaging (fMRI), scientists have found, for example, that dyslexic people show little activity in areas known to be critically important in linking written words with phonic components.

Neurologists also have a more comprehensive understanding of how neurotransmitters (cerebral messagers) function and how they affect learning. This has led to a better grasp of the underlying physiological and metabolic factors that can cause learning problems. It has also led to greater insight into how different types of medication affect neurological functioning.

Although the highly sophisticated diagnostic equipment used for research is not found in a neurologist's office, the insights derived from the new technology are being disseminated to physicians, university professors, and clinicians. Many of these professionals are using this latest research to develop effective and useful methods for treating the learning disabled.

Not all the diagnostic instruments used to identify the sources of neurological dysfunctions represent cutting-edge technology. The EEG (electroencephalogram) has been used for decades by neurologists to identify seizures and electric abnormalities that might represent brain dysfunction or brain damage. Tools such as the MRI and CAT scan that can evaluate brain structure have also been available for many years.

In addition to the diagnostic methods described above, educational psychologists, neuropsychologists, clinical psychologists, and educational therapists have their own diagnostic resources in the form of tests that typically require only a pencil, paper, verbal and pictorial cues, and, in some cases, a computer. These tests have proven highly effective in predicting and explaining learning and behavioral patterns and in designing effective intervention strategies.

The data derived from a comprehensive diagnostic assessment can be of critical importance in understanding the dynamics of a child's perceptual processing deficits and in providing guidance for the therapist who is treating the child. The assessment can be especially useful when the symptoms and origins of the learning problem are complex and confusing, and involve multiple, overlapping deficits and causal factors.

Although extensive diagnostic testing can be invaluable in certain cases, parents should guard against overtesting. A comprehensive assessment is not necessary for every child. The cost of an extensive evaluation can be prohibitive, and the financial burden can be heavy if your insurance company refuses to pay any of the fees. Spending thousands of dollars on an assessment when your child has an easily identifiable problem could be an extravagant indulgence.

The most complete diagnostic evaluations are typically offered at medical school–affiliated hospitals. The workup usually includes an evaluation by an educational psychologist, clinical psychologist, child psychiatrist, developmental pediatrician, pediatric neurologist, speech and language therapist, educational therapist, and social worker. This interdisciplinary assessment might be appropriate under the following circumstances:

- your child's problems are severe and complex
- an accurate diagnosis has been elusive
- your child is falling further and further behind, and no one knows what to do
- your child is becoming increasingly frustrated and discouraged.

An assessment by a private diagnostician or by specialists at a university-affiliated hospital can provide you with a different interpretation of your child's problems. The independent workup might reveal issues that were not uncovered in the school evaluation. It might indicate that the current school remediation strategy is adequately addressing your child's educational needs and that patience is required, or it might indicate that the plan needs to be reformulated to accelerate progress and prevent demoralization, academic shutdown, and self-concept damage.

Before suggesting a major educational course correction, the diagnostician would want to examine your child's learning difficulties from both a micro (highly specific) or macro (broad) perspective. If appropriate, the diagnostician might recommend that educational therapy, occupational therapy, vision therapy, speech and language therapy, family counseling, psychotherapy, or medication be added to the remediation equation (see chapters 10 and 11). Having this diagnostic input can play an instrumental role in allaying your concerns and getting your child on track.

The following summary describes a logical sequence for having your child independently evaluated. Your child may not require all these diagnostic resources, but the summary lists your options for procuring the information you need to understand and remediate your child's learning problems.

Out-of-School Assessment Options for Learning Disabilities

- physical exam and medical history by a pediatrician
- diagnostic assessment by an educational psychologist, clinical psychologist, or educational therapist
- diagnostic assessment of sensory processing by a neuropsychologist
- comprehensive physiological and developmental workup by a developmental pediatrician
- neurological exam by a pediatric neurologist
- comprehensive, multidiscipline evaluation at a university-affiliated medical program.

Pediatricians

Traditionally, the starting point in the process of understanding your child's learning difficulties has been an examination by and consultation with his pediatrician. This input is especially critical when parents suspect that there might be physiological, metabolic, or neurological factors affecting a child's performance in school.

Most pediatricians are aware of the symptoms of learning disabilities and understand their academic and emotional implications. If the pediatrician believes that your child's learning deficits might reflect an organic impairment—actual measurable physiological damage or metabolic imbalance—she will most likely direct you to a specialist for further testing. This specialist might be a developmental pediatrician, pediatric neurologist, allergist, or child psychiatrist. If the pediatrician believes your child is manifesting symptoms of ADD or ADHD, she may prescribe medication or refer your child to someone who specializes in treating these conditions. If your child is manifesting symptoms of a possible psychological problem, the pediatrician would refer him to a child psychiatrist or child psychologist, and if she believes that further educational testing is required, she would refer your child to an educational psychologist, neuropsychologist, or educational therapist.

It should be noted that pediatricians are under the same intense pressure to see as many patients as possible each day as are physicians in other specialties. Thus, they may not be able to spend the time required to compile an extensive medical history, collect and organize the pertinent data, carefully assess the information, and advise you about your options. Doing a comprehensive physical exam, checking for soft neurological signs (motor coordination and balance deficits that might indicate a neurological problem warranting a referral to a pediatric neurologist), and carefully correlating the input from the school psychologist, resource specialist, tutor, and/or educational therapist invariably require more than a fifteen-minute office visit.

Most pediatricians do the best they can under less than ideal conditions, but the result of their assessment may be disappointing. Because of the economically imposed time constraints, the evaluation may be brief, incomplete, or inconclusive. Medical offices are designed to treat medical problems. These facilities do not lend themselves to the evaluation of a learning dysfunction. Despite the best of intentions, some hard-pressed physicians may fail to appreciate the seriousness of the problem or may be unable to respond adequately to your concerns and questions. If the pediatrician is not particularly knowledgeable about learning disabilities, she may provide few if any substantive suggestions about how to help your child with his problems.

The pediatrician is usually the first person parents consult when their child is having difficulty concentrating and/or controlling impulsive, frenetic behavior. Based on the parents' and teacher's observations and the physician's observations in the examining room, the pediatrician may make a tentative diagnosis of ADD or ADHD. To placate desperate parents, some pediatricians may suggest a trial with medication to help a child focus and concentrate better in school. This suggestion might be appropriate if the child has a problem with concentration or hyperactivity. Medication might not be indicated, however, if the child has only subtle focusing deficits, and medication is certainly not a cure-all for learning problems such as dyslexia. The child taking medication may be more compliant and less distractible, but he may still reverse letters or be unable to follow verbal and written directions, and recall the information that he reads in textbooks or hears in class. An exclusive reliance on medication as a cure could delay identification of underlying problems that need to be treated by an educational therapist, clinical psychologist, or child psychiatrist.

Ritalin (generic name methylphenidate) is one of the most commonly prescribed medications in the pediatrician's arsenal. This medication is usually prescribed when there are clear indications of chronic inattentiveness or hyperactivity and a pattern of school-related difficulties.

Before prescribing drugs such as Ritalin or its generic counterpart, many pediatricians ask parents to complete a diagnostic behavioral inventory called the Conner's Rating Scale. This scale describes behaviors that are considered symptomatic of ADD and ADHD. The Test of Variables of Attention (TOVA) is another diagnostic tool for ADD and ADHD that may be used as part of a battery of diagnostic instruments that include a development history, checklist rating inventories completed by teachers and parents, and a neuropsychological screening. Because the TOVA is generally not administered by pediatricians, the physician would refer the child to a clinical psychologist or a neuropsychologist.

Some pediatricians recommend medication with the following caveat: "We'll know very quickly if the medication is appropriate. If there's improvement in focusing and schoolwork, the medication is indicated. If not, we can adjust the dosage or possibly change the medication. If there is still no improvement or if there are significant negative side effects, such as sleeplessness, significantly diminished appetite, and/or wide mood swings, we'll know that medication is not appropriate."

This "let's take a shot at it" approach to medicating a child can be disquieting for parents who are apprehensive about drug therapy. Parents who are reluctant to try such an experiment may feel more assured and supportive if the pediatrician orders additional diagnostic tests to confirm the tentative diagnosis of ADD or ADHD.

If the pediatrician concludes that more extensive testing is appropriate before making a diagnosis or recommending treatment, she may refer a child to a developmental pediatrician, child psychiatrist, pediatric neurologist, clinical psychologist, neuropsychologist, educational psychologist, or educational therapist (see entries later in this chapter). Such referrals may be discouraged by certain health insurance plans, however, even though the advice of a specialist could be instrumental in designing the most effective intervention program. A child who might not otherwise be eligible for enrollment in a resource program would probably be admitted into the program if ADD or ADHD is diagnosed by an expert. Even if the child isn't admitted, he would undoubtedly qualify for in-class accommodations under Section 504 of the Rehabilitation Act (see chapter 7).

The decision to place a child on medication can be unsettling for parents who are concerned about side effects or fear that their child will become physiologically or psychologically dependent on the medication. Most pediatricians would dismiss this concern as unwarranted, but some parents remain convinced that children receiving psychotropic medication are at greater risk for "graduating" to hard drugs. Physicians typically respond that more than two decades of extensive clinical experience and research have established no direct link between medication such as Ritalin and physiological or psychological addiction.

Many physicians contend that adults and young adults with chronic ADD who never received doctor-prescribed medication as children may actually be at greater risk for medicating themselves later with street drugs such as marijuana and cocaine. Not being in control of one's own mental process can be profoundly disturbing, and the desire to achieve self-regulation can be compelling. Of course, people resorting to street drugs to reduce their distractibility are not cured, nor have they gained sustained control of their focusing capacity. Any improvement in concentration achieved through self-medication is at best temporary. For a few hours they may no longer be frenetic, impulsive, or inattentive, but they must pay a terrible price for the temporary tranquility the drugs produce.

Concerns about medication are legitimate issues to raise with your child's pediatrician. If you are skeptical about the answers you are given, review the research yourself or consult another physician for a second opinion.

Although the time you and your child spend with the pediatrician may be quite limited, you should be prepared to ask incisive questions and to solicit concrete suggestions and recommendations about how best to help your child. If the doctor has other patients waiting and you feel rushed or pressured, suggest that you set up another appointment to discuss your concerns in greater depth.

Questions for Your Child's Pediatrician

Do you believe that after your physical exam and learning my child's medical history you have enough information to make an accurate diagnosis and recommend what needs to be done to help my child with his learning problems?

Would you be willing to write a brief summary of your findings and recommendations that could be discussed at the next IEP conference?

Do you recommend any dietary changes?

Have you detected any soft signs of a possible neurological problem?

Is further testing by other specialists advisable?

If you believe further testing is needed, will my medical plan pay for these services?

Do you establish contact with the school personnel who are working with my child?

If you recommend medication, how will we know if it's working?

After prescribing medication, will you be responsible for medical management? How often will you want to see my child?

How should I explain to my child why he is taking medication?

Would you recommend that my child continue to take medication during vacations and during the summer?

Is there any downside to taking this medication?

How should I inform you about possible side effects?

If the medication is effective in helping my child in school, how long do you anticipate he will need to be on this drug?

Are you finding any indications of a brain dysfunction or possible brain damage?

Do you think that we need to supplement the remediation help my child is receiving in school with private tutoring or educational therapy?

Could you refer me to a good educational therapist?

Would you be willing to have a brief telephone discussion with my child's educational therapist?

Do you have any specific issues that you think I should discuss with the school personnel at the next IEP conference?

Developmental Pediatricians

After completing their residency in pediatrics, developmental pediatricians (also referred to as developmental and behavioral pediatricians) are required to complete an intensive two-year fellowship that trains them to recognize conditions that indicate abnormal development in children. They are also trained to assess learning problems, coordinate intervention, and treat related medical conditions such as ADD and ADHD. In addition to diagnosing and managing the treatment of learning dysfunctions, developmental pediatricians treat conditions such as autism, mental retardation, and cerebral palsy.

Developmental pediatricians receive referrals from other pediatricians, family physicians, clinical psychologists, educational psychologists, neuropsychologists, classroom teachers, resource specialists, and educational therapists. The learning disabled children typically referred are floundering in school and tend to have significant deficits. Their problems are either puzzling or have proven unresponsive to intervention. One of the developmental pediatrician's primary objectives is to determine if the underlying problems are of organic (brain damage) or nonorganic origin. Another equally important objective is to advise parents about how their child's problems should be treated.

A comprehensive evaluation by a developmental pediatrician usually consists of four sessions. The initial session is for parents and might last ninety minutes. During this meeting the pediatrician takes an in-depth medical, developmental, and academic history, and reviews any testing that has been done in school or privately. During the second session, the child is medically and developmentally assessed. This session typically lasts thirty minutes. Another thirty-minute session is scheduled to complete the evaluation. (With older children, the two thirty-minute sessions might be combined.) The final session is a conference with the child's parents to discuss the results of the assessment and make recommendations about treatment.

With the parents' permission the developmental pediatrician might invite the child's resource specialist or educational therapist to participate in this conference. If not, the physician would certainly want input from these professionals and would incorporate this data into the diagnosis and recommendations. At the final session, the developmental pediatrician might recommend further testing by a neuropsychologist or pediatric neurologist, although this would be the exception rather than the rule because developmental pediatricians are well trained in neurology. The number of children referred to pediatric neurologists is generally no more than five percent.

The fee for an assessment by a developmental pediatrician generally ranges from $1,200 to $1,400. Insurance may cover the entire cost or only a portion of the fees. In some instances the assessment may not be covered by medical insurance, and parents are advised to check in advance with their insurance company.

Since psychoeducational testing is an important component in the accurate diagnosis of learning problems, many developmental pediatricians have an educational diagnostician on staff. If they do not, they refer their patients to a neuropsychologist, educational psychologist, or educational therapist for any testing that needs to be done.

Developmental pediatricians usually work closely with school personnel, and some even attend IEP meetings. Many use the Anser System in their assessment. These in-depth questionnaires for parents and teachers pinpoint academic deficits and behavioral issues that can interfere with learning.

A developmental pediatrician's recommendations generally have great credibility with school personnel, and her insights are usually factored into the remediation strategy developed at the IEP conference. The developmental pediatrician can also play an instrumental role in making certain that a child is properly placed in a resource program or special day class.

The developmental pediatrician may recommend medication for children showing symptoms of ADD and ADHD. After prescribing medication, some developmental pediatricians provide ongoing medical management. Others refer the child to the family pediatrician once the proper dosage is determined. In this case the child would be periodically reevaluated by the developmental pediatrician.

When appropriate, a developmental pediatrician will refer children with special needs to other specialists such as occupational therapists, educational therapists, social workers, child psychiatrists, clinical psychologists, marriage and family therapists, and developmental optometrists. The physician and the specialist would then coordinate their interventions.

Some developmental pediatricians offer more comprehensive treatment and management programs than others. These physicians may personally provide family and individual counseling. They may also make specific recommendations about appropriate remediation methodologies, and they may even have an educational therapist on staff to treat the child's learning deficits. In some cases, the developmental pediatrician may actually attend the IEP conference. Such comprehensive case management services are the exception, however, and when offered, are obviously costly.

The developmental pediatrician's answers to the following questions may help you understand the issues. These physicians are usually on a very tight schedule, so you'll need to select those questions that are of greatest concern to you.

Questions for the Developmental Pediatrician

In what ways does your assessment differ from that of a pediatric neurologist or a neuropsychologist?

What kinds of problems are you looking for?

To make a diagnosis do you need to do extensive psychoeducational testing? If so, will you refer us to the appropriate person?

Will our child need a neurological assessment or additional lab tests?

Once you identify our child's problems, will you then develop a plan for addressing these problems?

If you recommend medication, will you monitor our child, or will you refer us to another physician to do this?

Do you provide individual and/or family counseling as a component of medical management, or do you refer out for this service?

If we have questions about the advisability or the effects of medication, can you recommend some nontechnical books or articles that we might read to become better informed?

Will you assess the current school remediation program and suggest modifications?

Will you have any contact with school personnel?

Do you believe dietary factors may be affecting our child's performance and concentration? If so, will you make nutritional recommendations?

Do you believe our child requires psychological counseling?

Do you believe our child would benefit from private educational therapy or tutoring? If so, can you refer us to a provider?

Does our child need to be in a special school? If so, will you make a formal recommendation to this effect that we can give to the school district?

Will you send us a written summary of your assessment?

What is the prognosis for our child?

Will you want to schedule periodic visits to assess our child's progress?

Have you found any symptoms of organic neurological problems (brain damage)?

Are a portion of your fees usually covered by medical insurance?

Educational Psychologists

Virtually all educational psychologists began their careers as school psychologists. In most states educational psychologists must be licensed, credentialed, or certified, and must pass qualifying boards before they can establish a private practice. Because the number of licensed educational psychologists in the United States is quite small, parents from rural areas who seek their services may need to travel to larger towns or cities.

Educational psychologists are concerned about learning efficiency and sensory processing as it relates to academic performance. Many also deal with adult issues relating to career development, job performance, and general cognitive functioning. Trained in learning theory, measurement, and appraisal of individual learning differences, educational psychologists have expertise in assessing, understanding, and designing programs that will optimize learning.

Many major universities offer graduate degrees in educational psychology. The minimum requirement for licensing in most states is an M.A. degree, although most licensed educational psychologists have doctorates (Ed.D., Ph.D., or Psy.D.).

Educational psychologists must be well versed in educational and psychological instruments that measure learning and educational functioning. They are extensively trained in how to interpret educational and aptitude tests, and are knowledgeable about ways to treat learning differences. Although some educational psychologists may do limited educational therapy, most refer children with learning disabilities to educational therapists or tutors. The educational psychologist usually consults with the educational therapist and participates in the process of defining educational objectives and recommending specific remediation strategies.

As an integral part of the evaluation process, the educational psychologist will undoubtedly solicit input from a child's teacher and resource specialist. This information is usually obtained by having school personnel fill out an inventory. The educational psychologist would factor this important information into any recommendations that are offered for making modifications in the resource program or in the instructional methods being used in mainstream classes.

The diagnostic tests given by an educational psychologist are designed to measure and assess factors such as:

- mental ability and maturity (cognitive sophistication and IQ);
- academic strengths and weaknesses in relation to cognitive, visual motor, and psychomotor functioning;

- sensory and modality processing (input/output) and specifically how sensory modalities (auditory, visual, tactile, gross motor, fine motor, and kinesthetic) coordinate;
- academic achievement relative to ability level, developmental factors, and learning style;
- impact of psychosocial factors (environmental, societal, social, and emotional) on learning efficiency.

Children are typically referred to an educational psychologist by pediatricians, family physicians, developmental pediatricians, occupational therapists, speech and language pathologists, educational therapists, and pediatric neurologists. In some cases, a teacher, resource specialist, or another parent may be the source of the referral.

Parents who contact an educational psychologist are typically perplexed by their child's learning problems and dissatisfied with the resource or private remediation program. These parents want an independent evaluation. Although some of the components of this evaluation might replicate testing that has been done in school, it's likely that the private assessment will be more comprehensive. In effect, parents are paying for the educational psychologist's interpretation of the testing data and his recommendations about how best to address their child's learning needs.

In some instances, evaluations by a licensed educational psychologist may be covered in full or in part by your medical insurance, especially when your child is referred by a pediatrician. If you believe your child would benefit from an evaluation by an educational psychologist, you should request a referral from your child's physician. It should be noted, however, that your medical insurance plan may discourage such referrals. If this is the case, you may need to be more insistent in requesting a referral, and, in a worst-case scenario, you should be prepared to pay for the diagnostic evaluation yourself.

Depending on the comprehensiveness of the assessment, the fee generally ranges from $800 to $1,200 or more. The evaluation includes a written report and a conference with the parents to discuss the results of the tests. At this conference the educational psychologist would help parents understand the underlying issues responsible for their child's learning difficulties and would make specific recommendations about how to design the most effective in-school and after-school remediation strategy.

Many educational psychologists have students participate in a portion of the conference so that the students can better understand their learning strengths and weaknesses and the proposed remediation strategy. Although the psychologist's explanation must be geared to the child's maturity level, even nine-year-olds can be guided to important insights about their learning problems. Involving older students in the discussion can be vital. Resolving the learning deficits of these students often hinges on their assuming an active role in the remediation process.

Another important reason for involving students in a discussion of the test results and the proposed intervention plan is to help them realize they must become advocates for themselves. If they have difficulty following verbal directions, they need to feel okay about asking their teachers to explain something again. If they have reading problems, they need to feel okay about telling the teacher that they need time to prepare in advance the section that they'll be asked to read aloud in class.

This self-advocacy will be especially important in college, where they can no longer rely on their parents to speak up for them. Those with documented learning problems can request special compensations such as untimed tests, tutors, or someone to take notes for them. They can also use the resources of the learning assistance program. These accommodations and programs are mandated by federal law.

The educational psychologist's answers to the following questions may help you understand his or her role in the remediation equation and the function of the educational assessment that is being proposed. These questions should be asked prior to the assessment.

Questions for the Educational Psychologist

Am I correct in assuming that you were once a school psychologist?

After testing my child, would you then communicate with the school psychologists and resource specialists at his school?

Have you had any personal dealings with my child's school and specifically with the school psychologist and his resource specialist? If so, what were your reactions?

Are you proposing to administer tests that are different from the ones already given in school?

Which additional tests will you be giving, and why do you believe these particular tests would be beneficial?

Can you use the results of recently administered tests from school in making your assessment?

Why would you want to readminister tests that have already been given?

In what ways might your interpretation of the test results differ from those of the school psychologist?

Will you establish contact with my child's teacher?

Will you be contacting my child's pediatrician?

If your tests indicate significant learning problems, will you design a remediation strategy?

Will you refer us to an education therapist or tutor?

Will you be monitoring the remediation program?

Do school resource specialists generally accept your recommendations?

Are you available to attend the next IEP conference if your services are needed?

In what ways does your assessment differ from that of a neuropsychologist?

If our child requires psychotherapy, can you refer us to someone?

What is the fee for the testing battery you are proposing?

How many hours of testing are required?

Will we have a conference with you so that you can explain the result and make recommendations?

Will we be given the written report prior to this conference?

If you believe that our child requires medication for ADD, will you refer us to a physician who can prescribe the medication and monitor our child?

Neuropsychologists

Neuropsychologists focus on the relationship between brain function, brain metabolism, and behavior. Their evaluations search for the neuropsychological indicators that explain a child's performance level in class and on standardized tests.

Neuropsychology is a subspecialty of clinical psychology. The American Board of Professional Psychology offers certification in neuropsychology to professionals who have practiced for five years and who have passed written and oral exams. Although clinical psychologists may call themselves neuropsychologists, there are relatively few certified child neuropsychologists. Parents seeking the services of a neuropsychologist should inquire abut what internships and experience the psychologist has had and whether she is board certified.

A neuropsychologist might administer many of the same tests that an educational psychologist would use but would interpret the test results from a different perspective. In perplexing and complex cases, the neuropsychologist would also use specialized diagnostic tests that educational psychologists are not trained to administer. Some of these tests are given on a computer and then scored and interpreted with highly sophisticated software programs.

The neuropsychologist wants to understand what is happening functionally in the child's brain. To explain a child's school-related behavior and performance, she would examine the functional efficiency of different brain regions. Right and left brain functions would also be factored into the interpretation of performance and behavior.

A neuropsychologist would analyze scores on an intelligence test differently from other diagnosticians. If a child is given a Wechsler Intelligence Test (WISC III) and receives a verbal IQ score of 113 and a performance IQ score of 90, a school psychologist would note this discrepancy of 23 points and explain that it might indicate a learning disability. This is valuable information, but simply providing the scores and saying the child may be learning disabled does not indicate the specific brain function factors responsible for the disparity.*

A neuropsychologist would want to delve more deeply into the issues that might be causing the score difference. These might include deficits in motor speed, perceptual analysis, visual discrimination, sequencing, and/or spatial organization. Because any of these could have a negative impact on specific areas of academic functioning, the process of systematically identifying and understanding the causal elements could provide invaluable insight and guidance when designing the most effective remediation plan. If appropriate, the neuropsychologist may also use other diagnostic tools, such as the Tactual Performance Test, that might suggest strategies for improving and maximizing the child's level of cognitive and academic functioning.

Neuropsychologists can administer a number of tests to examine the brain processes that underlie learning. These diagnosticians are specifically interested in assessing language, sensory and motor functions, perceptual decoding, attention, memory, and learning style. Because the left

---

*Clinical psychologists who have been well-trained in administering intelligence tests would also examine the scores analytically. When interpreting the Wechsler Intelligence Score for Children (WISC-R), most clinical psychologists look at the scaled scores and how the child processed information on each subtest. These scaled scores provide a "signature" of the child's processing style and indicate areas that might need attention. An educational psychologist would go through the same analytical process. Because of specialized training in educational theory and instruction, an educational psychologist would be able to propose specific remediation strategies that address the identified deficits.

and right cerebral hemispheres process information differently, with the left hemisphere usually being dominant for verbal, sequential, and logical processing, and the right being dominant for visual-spatial functions and emotions—a child's hemispheric modes of learning are assessed as an integral component of a neuropsychological workup.

Any neuropsychological evaluation would include a clinical interview with the child's parents. The neuropsychologist would also consider information from other professionals and, if appropriate, administer psychological tests to identify emotional factors that could be affecting the child's capacity to learn. The neuropsychologist would include in the assessment specific information about the child's daily activity. Input and observations from the parents, teacher, resource specialist, tutor, and educational therapist also provide important data about factors that are hampering the child's academic progress. For example, the neuropsychologist might note that the child does well orally in class but has poor follow-through and is highly distractible. The child may do his homework but fail to submit it. These behaviors could be symptomatic of ADD or could indicate deficiencies in right cerebral functioning.

Neuropsychologists can play a key role in designing an optimum remediation program. They might suggest to a resource specialist or educational therapist that specific interventions be used to enhance brain function and make the academic remediation program more effective. These might include visualization techniques to improve memory or tactile/kinesthetic manipulatives to improve understanding of abstract concepts in math or science.

Developmental pediatricians and neuropsychologists often work together on specific cases. Developmental pediatricians want as much data as possible about a child's level of cognitive functioning and sensory processing, and they will, when appropriate, refer some children to a neuropsychologist for further testing.

Some neuropsychologists and clinical psychologists are now using highly specialized biofeedback equipment to treat ADD and ADHD. This biofeedback training, which is considered controversial by many medical and mental health professionals, is based on the belief that children can learn to control the brain waves that cause impulsivity and inattentiveness. Parents may want a second opinion before their child begins such a program.*

---

*Other innovative diagnostic and treatment methods include thought field therapy, which uses highly focused learning strategies to remediate thinking deficits, and the quantitative electroencephalograph

The proposed questions for an educational psychologist are also appropriate for a neuropsychologist. You might, however, add the following questions to the list:

How does your assessment differ from that of a school psychologist or an educational psychologist?

If you find neurological components to our child's learning difficulties, will you be able to design strategies that will resolve these issues? If so, who will implement them?

Will your report be comprehensible to us and to the school personnel?

Pediatric Neurologists

Pediatric neurologists, also referred to as child neurologists, diagnose and treat disorders of the nervous system. The training of these physicians includes a residency in general pediatrics as well as neurology. Those eligible for board certification as pediatric neurologists must also be certified in both pediatrics and neurology with special competence in child neurology. Any neurologist may evaluate children, but the special competencies required for board certification in pediatric neurology differentiate these physicians from neurologists who primarily treat adults.

Parents are usually referred to a pediatric neurologist by a family physician, a pediatrician, or occasionally a developmental pediatrician who suspects that organic components may be involved in a child's school struggle (see chapter 11 for information about the distinction between a dysfunction and an organic impairment). Because there are relatively few board-certified pediatric neurologists in the United States, parents living in nonurban areas may need to take their child to a major medical center.

Pediatric neurologists deal specifically with the peripheral nervous system (muscles) and with the central nervous system (diseases and organic impairments of the brain and spinal cord). Organic impairments might involve such conditions as seizures and brain tumors. Pediatric neurologists also treat nonorganic problems such as Tourette's syndrome and other behavioral and developmental problems associated with brain function. Although some pediatric neurologists treat ADD and ADHD, many refer patients with these conditions to developmental pediatricians and child psychiatrists if there are no indications of organic (physiological) damage. The psychiatrist or pediatrician would monitor any medication that is prescribed.

(QEEG) which uses computer technology to analyze electrical patterns in the brain. The latter method is not widely used.

Behavioral and developmental pediatric neurologists represent another diagnostic and treatment option. This medical subspecialty focuses primarily on diagnosing and treating ADD, ADHD, learning disabilities, and developmental delays.

In seeking a pediatric neurologist, you may want to consider having your child evaluated at a university-affiliated diagnostic program that is affiliated with a major medical center. These programs offer multidisciplinary resources that include an assessment by a pediatrician, developmental pediatrician, licensed social worker, clinical psychologist, educational psychologist, child psychiatrist, occupational therapist, speech and language pathologist, and educational therapist. Certainly such extensive professional resources offer diagnostic advantages if your child's problem is multifaceted or puzzling.

The alternative to a university-affiliated program is to seek the services of a pediatric neurologist in private practice. There are two advantages to this. First, you'll be dealing exclusively with a fully trained specialist, not medical students and residents. The second advantage involves cost. Multidiscipline assessments are very expensive, and they are not always necessary. A pediatric neurologist in private practice can often supply the information you need.

A typical evaluation by a pediatric neurologist might take one hour, although the physician may recommend additional testing that could include blood tests and an MRI. The neurologist will take a history of both the child and the family. Some conditions such as ADD tend to run in families. The information-gathering component of the assessment might last twenty minutes. The neurologist would then do a complete neurological exam that requires approximately fifteen minutes. This exam would focus on the spine, head size, skin, extremities, language ability, mental or emotional state, memory, cognitive capabilities, ability to follow commands, and general affect (facial expression and reactions). The neurologist would also do a cranial nerve exam, checking for hearing, vision, and facial symptoms, as well as a motor exam that would evaluate the strength of extremities, motor coordination, balance, gait, and reflexes. Because the neurological exam does not involve highly intrusive procedures involving needles, MRIs, or X rays, children should be reassured by their parents in advance to reduce their apprehensions.

After the neurological exam, the physician would meet with the child's parents. During this conference, which typically lasts twenty-five minutes, the pediatric neurologist would discuss his findings, make recommendations, and explore treatment recommendations. After making a diagnosis, the pediatric neurologist might prescribe medication or refer the child for specialized services, such as occupational therapy, educational therapy, speech and language therapy, psychotherapy, or family therapy.

ADD and ADHD are conditions frequently addressed by pediatric neurologists. Some neurologists use the Conner's Rating Scale as a diagnostic tool, but this is not the only way to diagnose ADD and ADHD. Another way is to use the eighteen symptoms of ADD described in the *Diagnostic Statistical Manual (DSM IV)*. This comprehensive reference book describes virtually every conceivable illness, disorder, or pathology, and it provides codes used by physicians, psychologists, and other health care providers to classify specific conditions. The procedure of using DSM IV descriptions as diagnostic criteria is called a standardized diagnosis. (The term standardized has a different meaning in this context than it does in an educational context. A standardized score on an educational test is a normed, statistically derived correlation.) If the neurologist identifies one or more described symptoms, he or she would consider this indicative of ADD or ADHD.

Some pediatric neurologists who treat ADD and ADHD prescribe medication and continue to monitor their patients themselves. As previously noted, the most commonly prescribed medication for ADD and ADHD is Ritalin (the brand name for methyphenidate). Other less commonly prescribed medications include Cylert and Dexedrine. When a child is also showing symptoms of depression, a neurologist might prescribe tricyclic drugs such as Norpramine, Disopramine, or Imipramine. Every medication has side effects, and tricyclics can in some cases affect heart function. Consequently, any child using these drugs must be monitored very closely.

A pediatric neurologist would refer a child who appears to have significant psychological overlay or psychological problems to either a child psychiatrist or a child psychologist. If the neurologist believes there may be a family dysfunction, he would probably make a referral to either a licensed social worker or a licensed marriage and family counselor. If vision problems are detected, the neurologist would refer the child to a pediatric ophthalmologist. When further educational diagnostic testing is required, the neurologist would refer the patient to either an educational psychologist or a neuropsychologist.

Pediatric neurologists do not automatically perform an electroencephalogram on a learning disabled child who is referred for a neurological assessment. An EEG is done only when there are underlying concerns about seizures. Any neurologist who automatically administers an EEG to all children manifesting learning problems should be viewed with some suspicion.

Although parents may expect a high-tech evaluation when they go to a pediatric neurologist, the most sophisticated assessment equipment is used primarily for research. Functional studies (mapping of brain activity), specialized brain scans, and functional MRIs (a more technologically advance type of MRI) are not performed in a neurologist's office.

Some neurologists may resent being questioned about their training and credentials, but raising these issues is certainly justifiable. The following questions may be of value. Use your own judgment about the appropriateness of the inquiries.

Questions for a Pediatric Neurologist

Is there any relationship between the problem you have diagnosed and previous medical problems our child has had?

On a scale of one to ten, how serious is our child's problem?

Can you refer us to specialists who can treat the specific deficits you've diagnosed?

Do you believe our child requires an EEG?

Do you recommend further lab tests?

Will you personally monitor our child, or will you refer us to someone else to prescribe medication and oversee the treatment?

Do you suggest that we come back for periodic reassessments?

Will you have any direct contact with school personnel?

Will you be making verbal or written recommendations that we can present at the IEP conference?

Will we get a summary of your findings to keep in our child's medical file?

What is the prognosis?

Do you believe our child can overcome his learning problem, or will he have to learn how to compensate for it?

How long do you think our child will need to be in treatment and/or remain on medication?

How likely is it that our child's younger siblings will have similar problems?

Could the conditions you've diagnosed affect our child's performance on an IQ test? Should we consider his current scores valid?

How do we explain the results of the assessment to our child?

Part IV

Finding the Right Person to Treat the Emotional Fallout

Chapter 9
Mental Health Professionals

Psychiatrists and Child Psychiatrists, Clinical Psychologists, Child Psychologists, Marriage and Family Counselors, and Clinical Social Workers

My heart breaks when I see my child's frustration and unhappiness. I feel her pain and I want to cry, but worst of all, I don't know how to help her.

C hildren who struggle in school invariably suffer emotional pain. Some experience more than others, and some handle it better than others. Others are crushed by it.

The parents of a child who is experiencing significant psychological distress because of school failure have two compelling responsibilities: to get the learning problem fixed and to get the psychological suffering reduced. To sit back and hope the pain will go away of its own accord is risky and potentially disastrous. If the situation is not quickly rectified, the child's distress could cause profound and irreversible self-concept damage.

In most urban areas there are many available treatment options when a child is hurting emotionally. In fact, the choices can be overwhelming. As parents attempt to evaluate the different treatment philosophies, training, and methods of the mental health professionals who specialize in working with children, they should be guided by a basic principle: The more you know about the issues, the easier it is to find what you're seeking.

The "I'm Dumb!" Syndrome
When the struggling child looks around the classroom and sees that most of her classmates are "getting it" while she's confused and unable to do

the assigned work, she's going to deduce, consciously or unconsciously, that she's in some way defective. From her vantage point the very fact that she must struggle while other children appear to be learning effortlessly is proof of her inadequacy.

Having a child who is convinced she's "dumb" can be one of parenting's most heartrending experiences. The anguish is all the more intense when you're forced to watch the day-by-day deterioration in your child's self-image and feel powerless to prevent the damage.

Although a steady diet of failure, frustration, and discouragement can chip away at a child's emotional resources, learning disabled children can be remarkably resourceful as they instinctively attempt to protect themselves. Unfortunately, the defenses these children typically choose—blaming, denial, procrastination, irresponsibility, laziness, acting out, and resistance—offer little protection. The self-defeating behaviors only magnify and exacerbate the problem.

On the surface, a child's counterproductive attitudes and actions may appear quite willful, which is misleading. Most children don't consciously consider how they're going to compensate for their feelings of inadequacy. They don't say to themselves, "I'm doing poorly in school, and I feel frustrated and demoralized. I think I'll misbehave and slug this kid sitting next to me or talk back to my teacher to let everyone know how unhappy I am." Decisions about how to evade feeling worthless and vulnerable are unconsciously driven. One child may shut down and refuse to study or complete his assignments. Another may escape into a fantasy world. And another may compensate by focusing on athletics or developing video game skills.

Pushed to despair by the struggling child's conduct, teachers and parents may conclude that the child is acting out to get attention when it's actually far more likely that the child is resorting to the behavior to deflect attention from his inadequacies. He may become the class clown or class bully. He may sabotage himself by continually getting into trouble, or he may sabotage others by causing them to get into trouble. These actions are a smoke screen designed to hide feelings of inferiority. If the child's unconscious gave voice to the underlying feelings that drive his behavior, it would probably say, "I feel so stupid! If I act this way, you won't see how dumb I really am and how much I dislike myself. If I act this way, I won't have to deal with my pain."

The struggling child's unconscious mind will automatically assess the situation, identify the weaknesses and vulnerabilities, and decide how to cope. The child will then act accordingly without understanding the forces that are driving his behavior. In some respects the process is akin to dreaming. Just as the child doesn't consciously select his dreams, he also doesn't consciously select the psychological armor that he uses to protect himself.

Frustration, anger, fear, insecurity, and feelings of incompetence may implode and manifest as depression, or explode and manifest as hostility, aggression, rebellion, antisocial behavior, and/or conduct disorders. Between these two extremes are countless possibilities for a child to express his pain, resentment, demoralization, sadness, and anger.

The signs of children's emotional distress are sometimes blatant and sometimes subtle and difficult to detect. The evidence may be so inconspicuous that it might be overlooked by teachers, parents, and even mental health professionals. The effects of this oversight can be grave. Internal conflict that might have been resolved with relative ease in first or second grade can become far more challenging to treat by the time a child is in eighth or ninth grade.

Not all children resort to acting out in their attempt to protect themselves. Some may appear to be coping quite well with their learning problems and their frustration and demoralization. Rather than compensate with misbehavior, aggressiveness, disrespect, or resistance, these children may become funny, charming, or cute. Their more socially acceptable coping mechanisms can be a double-edged sword, however. Because behaving children don't cause problems in the classroom, their teachers may be more tolerant of their learning deficits and may rationalize the potential risks ("He's such a nice child. He tries so hard and never acts out. I'm sure everything will work out.") Although well intentioned, the teacher may not recognize or may discount the significance of the problem and may unwittingly be doing the child a grave disservice.

Other factors can also influence a child's coping mechanisms. The effectiveness of the resource program, special day class, or after-school remedial program can have a significant impact on how the child deals with his learning problems. If he can see progress, he may not feel compelled to put on self-protective armor.

Struggling children who have talents and interests in nonacademic areas clearly have an advantage over those who don't. A child may be a good athlete, artist, musician, or mechanic. He may decide in second grade that when he finishes high school he wants to drive heavy equipment and build roads, or he may know that he wants to be an electrician like his dad or an airplane mechanic like his uncle. He may know that he wants to program computers, design video games, play professional golf, drive race cars, be a dancer, or be a police officer. He may possess natural leadership abilities and may aspire to become a politician. For such a child, school is a required and unpleasant rite of passage that he must somehow endure. His learning difficulties are an inconvenience, but he realizes that he has appealing options after he completes formal education.

When a child appears to be successfully handling his learning problems, everyone usually breathes a sigh of relief. The child's teachers and parents may conclude that the situation is under control and they don't need to be as vigilant. The resource program may be first-rate, and the child may appear to be making great strides. He may do everything expected and demanded of him. He may dutifully attempt to complete his in-class assignments, obligingly go to the resource room every day, and conscientiously do his homework every evening.

Despite appearances, the child may be painfully aware of his inadequacies, and his fantasy about one day becoming a veterinarian, an attorney, a pilot, or a filmmaker may begin to fade. The lowering of expectations may proceed in barely perceptible increments, and all the while the child may continue to plug away at school. The child himself may not even be consciously aware that he's abandoning his goals, and those closest to him may not recognize the psychological toll his negative school experiences are exacting. Once the child accepts his "fate", he will expect and demand less from himself, from school, and, perhaps, from life.

With some children the emotional impact of the academic battle is very evident. These youngsters are angry and resistant, withdrawn and alienated, or rebellious and antisocial. Some are disruptive in class, and others join gangs, become addicted to drugs, disfigure themselves with grotesque tattoos, or pierce their bodies with pins and other objects. Although these youngsters are crying for help, their cries may not be heard because everyone is so repulsed by their outward behavior.

An alienated child would be the last to admit that he wants or needs help. Entangled in his own web of distorted behavior, he may conclude that his only recourse is to act out his unhappiness. In his search for an identity, he will seek out others who share his feelings of alienation and despair, and this subculture of kindred spirits will reinforce the antisocial values and attitudes that bind the group together.

Handling the Emotional Fallout

If your child has learning problems and has acquired a pattern of counter-productive coping mechanisms such as procrastination, irresponsibility, or refusing to study or complete homework, it would be reasonable to assume that the behaviors are linked to the school dilemma. If the behaviors persist despite intensive learning assistance and if your child appears to be depressed, angry, self-sabotaging, rebellious, or withdrawn, the need for an objective psychological assessment is clearly indicated. Your child may require short-term counseling to deal with the psychological overlay (see chapter 3). If the behavior is attributable to a psychological problem (see chapter 3), then more extended psychotherapy, and perhaps medication, may be required.

Untreated psychological problems can cause festering wounds and deep scars, especially when these problems are overlaid with guilt and distortions in perception: "My parents got divorced because I was a bad boy" or "I'm a bad person because I caused him to touch me." The unconscious mind can become intent on defending itself and hiding its pain, fear, vulnerability, anger, and insecurity, and it does not easily give up its secrets. Nor does the unconscious easily repair its wounds and find equilibrium. The healing process requires skillful professional intervention.

Children with deep-seated psychological problems who do not receive help usually continue to have these problems as adults. The angry child who expresses his hostility by being a bully is likely to become an angry adult bully. He may abuse his wife or his children. He may become a criminal, or he may gravitate to an authoritarian career in which he is given great power and can act out his bullying with relative impunity. So, too, will the fearful, insecure child typically become a fearful, insecure adult. The antidote for this negative programming is to help the child examine and resolve the underlying issues that are causing the feelings and driving the behavior. The bully who is helped to recognize that he is abusive, who gains insight into the source of his conduct, and who wants to handle his anger differently can transform himself. And the child who hates himself can learn to accept and appreciate who he is and begin to relinquish the fear, insecurity, and pain that are running his life.

Phases and Stages

As children go through developmental stages, they experience predictable, age-appropriate emotions. A two-year-old is occasionally going to be oppositional and challenging. An eight-year-old is sometimes going to disobey the family rules about being home on time for dinner. A ten-year-old is likely to feel unpopular if not invited to a birthday party. A twelve-year-old is probably going to resent parental efforts to establish limits or monitor schoolwork, and he's likely to express his desire for independence through minor acts of disobedience. A fourteen-year-old is going to feel embarrassed by virtually everything her parents say and do, and a sixteen-year-old is likely to be self-preoccupied and frequently uncommunicative and secretive. The emotional reactions associated with a particular developmental stage usually diminish when the child emerges from the phase. During the phase, however, children will occasionally feel sadness, self-doubt, and insecurity. These transitory emotions do not necessarily signal a psychological problem or psychological overlay.

Chronic despondency or oppositional behavior is another matter. Persistant emotional distress should trigger an alarm that alerts parents to the need for skilled counseling is vital. Children who are withdrawn and despondent or who show symptoms of anorexia, bulimia, or a conduct disorder are crying out for help. *These conditions must be treated before serious and perhaps irreparable physical or psychological damage occurs.*

The dilemma that parents face is deciding when to be alarmed by their child's behavior and when to be patient and vigilant. Should you interpret your child's counterproductive attitudes and behavior as symptoms of a transitory developmental stage, or should you interpret them as reflecting serious inner turmoil that you must address? Does a child say "No one likes me!" because he's had a temporary falling out with his pals or because fear, tenuous self-esteem, or guilt are causing him to become depressed? Does the statement "I don't want to live anymore" indicate suicidal tendencies, or is it a melodramatic reaction to a minor problem or disappointment? Should you be mildly concerned or very concerned? Should you react by gently saying, "Tell me what's happening," or should you turn to the listings in the yellow pages for child psychiatrists? As is the case so often in parenting, you must rely on your intuition and informed judgment to help you recognize red flags that might signal a serious emotional crisis or a pattern of self-defeating or self-destructive behavior.

Certain behaviors and attitudes should trigger legitimate concern. For example, you may observe that your child is chronically tired. This behavior might indicate a physiological problem or depression. You may notice that a seemingly innocuous event can trigger explosive anger. You may observe that your daughter has gravitated to a peer group of non-achievers who are angry, nihilistic, and alienated. She has dyed her hair orange and wants to wear rings in her nose or eyebrows. You may observe that your son has shut down in school, refuses to study, is rebellious and highly resentful of authority figures, or has become totally enmeshed in Dungeons and Dragons. You may smell the aroma of marijuana on his clothes or notice that his eyes are often dilated. Your observations along with your judgment and parental intuition should tell you whether your child is simply going through a stage or is in trouble psychologically.

If you conclude the problem is serious, *and especially if there are threats of suicide,* you have a compelling obligation to seek help from a mental health expert. If you're unsure about how to interpret the behavior, you need to consult with a trained professional who can help you decide if counseling is required.

Emotional problems rarely go away of their own accord. The symptoms may change somewhat over time, but if the underlying issues are not resolved, they will continue to exert their control in one form or another. Constant unhappiness, acting out, depression, manipulation, or hostility are danger signals that cannot be disregarded. If you observe this behavior or intuitively sense your child is experiencing significant emotional turmoil, ask the teacher if he has noticed anything. If so, express your concerns to the school psychologist. Ask whether a psychological assessment (as distinguished from the educational assessment) is recommended. If the school psychologist agrees that there is a potential problem, request a referral to a first-rate mental health professional. You might also request a referral from your child's pediatrician.

Is Anyone Listening? Is Anyone Seeing?

When a two-year-old cries out in the night, he expects someone to come and comfort him. He assumes his parents will understand why he's crying and make everything all right. He may need a diaper change or a bottle. He may need cough syrup or medicine to lower his fever. If he has been frightened by a bad dream, he may need to cuddle until he feels secure and peaceful, and can go back to sleep.

The someone your child expects to be there for him is you. You are his first line of defense against illness, danger, depression, self-destructive behavior, flawed choices, and chronic failure. Your eyes, ears, and intuition must be fully attuned. The alternative is to be oblivious. This negligence sets the stage for a potential tragedy.

The following list profiles behaviors and feelings that could indicate a psychological problem. As you assess your child, you'll want to differentiate between *occasional* and *chronic* episodes of particular behaviors such as fearfulness or sleeplessness. An infrequent temper tantrum may not indicate an emotional problem, but recurring tantrums should trigger legitimate concern about the child's level of anger and frustration and his lack of reasonable emotional control.

Red Flags of a Possible Emotional Problem

Disorganized Thinking:
    Disorientation (time, place)
    Delusions (persecution, imaginary voices)
    Sensory distortions (visual or auditory hallucinations)
Nonadaptive Behavior:
    Withdrawal (seclusion, detachment, excessive sensitivity, inability to form friendships)
    Chronic tantrums
    Excessive superstitious rituals that must be performed before doing a task
    Extreme mood changes
    Excessive fantasizing
    Phobias (fear of people, germs)
    Fixations (excessive and exclusive interests)
    Expressed or implied suicidal tendencies
Physical Dysfunctions:
    Age-inappropriate bedwetting
    Age-inappropriate incontinence
    Chronic stomachaches or headaches (could also be caused by a potentially serious physical illness)
    Chronic sleep disturbances
Other Symptoms:
    Explosive anger or hostility
    Excessive fearfulness
    Chronic bullying
    Chronic lying
    Depression
    Excessive anxiety
    Excessive need to control others and situations
    Continual manipulative behavior

Unwillingness to communicate
Chronic stealing
Continual self-sabotaging behavior

Finding Help Within the System

Just as academic problems can trigger emotional turmoil, so, too, can emotional problems trigger academic problems. Because teachers are not formally trained to diagnose emotional problems, you cannot expect them to recognize the warning signs. You also cannot count on the school district to diagnose and treat your child's psychological problems. Yes, there are districts that offer limited counseling services. These districts may have social workers on staff and may employ part-time private therapists to work with children who have conduct problems. Yes, there are also competent and alert school psychologists who can identify emotional problems. Ironically, these school psychologists may not be allowed to refer families to private mental health providers because their school districts may fear that by doing so they may be exposing the district to potential financial liability.

Most school districts offer, at best, limited counseling services for children with subtle to moderate emotional problems. Counseling programs funded by the county and severely emotionally disturbed (SED) programs are usually reserved for children who have more serious psychological difficulties, have been identified as special education students, and have had a formal IEP (see nonpublic schools, chapter 10). Children with less incapacitating psychological problems are usually left to fend for themselves.

Some financially strapped districts have actually eliminated or severely restricted their guidance counseling services. Although guidance counselors have been trained primarily to provide help with academic issues, they may also provide limited crisis counseling. It should be noted, however, that a school guidance counselor is not the equivalent of a licensed mental health professional. A school counselor who identifies symptoms of emotional distress will usually refer the child to a school social worker (if the district provides these services), a county mental health program, or, if permitted by school district policy, a qualified mental health professional in the private sector. In some districts, counselors can also recommend that children with emotional problems attend a magnet school that has mental health professionals on staff and offers more extensive counseling services.

School psychologists are also not generally considered mental health professionals. They have been trained to test children, interpret the test results, and help design remediation programs. Some have had additional training in recognizing psychological problems, and certain of the diagnostic tests they are qualified to administer could indicate signs of emotional distress. As is the case with guidance counselors, school psychologists might do limited crisis intervention counseling.

It would certainly be comforting if you could count on your school district to identify and treat your child's psychological issues, but most school districts do not consider themselves responsible for providing these services. If your child needs help, your options are to avail yourself of programs offered by the county mental health department or seek a qualified private therapist.

Psychiatrists and Child Psychiatrists

Psychiatrists and child psychiatrists are medical doctors who are trained to treat mental conditions. They are allowed to prescribe medication and treat patients in the hospital. Although any psychiatrist may treat children, preteenagers, and teenagers, most refer younger patients to child psychiatrists who have received specialized training in treating this population.

Parents seeking a psychiatrist should solicit a referral from someone whose judgment they trust. Family pediatricians, family physicians, school psychologists, and school counselors are excellent sources, especially if they've had positive experiences with a particular psychiatrist. Perhaps the best source of a referral to a child psychiatrist is another parent whose child has worked successfully with a particular therapist. The local medical association also makes referrals, but it makes no judgment about the skills of the psychiatrist.

Psychiatrists typically meet with a child's parents for all or part of the initial session. The child is not present during this discussion. Before the session begins, the psychiatrist usually asks the parents to complete a written questionnaire that addresses the child's behavior, background, and medical history. During the session, the parents' concerns are discussed and any significant events that might have occurred in the child's life are described. School-related issues that might affect the child emotionally are also discussed. Parents then have an opportunity to ask questions about the psychiatrist's methods and treatment philosophy.

The psychiatrist might meet with the parents and child for a portion of the second session. From this point on, the sessions are exclusively with the child. It's possible for parents to be asked to participate at some point in one or more family sessions, and they may request a private meeting to discuss parenting issues. Confidential information provided by the child cannot be revealed by the psychiatrist. A firmly established code of professional ethics prevents psychiatrists from doing so.

It shocks some parents when their child's psychiatrist is unwilling to share with them what has been discussed in the sessions. They argue, "It's our child, and we have a right to know what's going on!" Parents must realize that for the therapist to relay what is discussed in the sesions would be a violation of trust. The psychiatrist might ask the child's permission to talk about a particular issue with his parents, but the child may refuse this request, and the psychiatrist would honor this. The exception to this policy of confidentiality is when children are at risk for hurting themselves or others. In such cases, the psychiatrist will be guided by her assessment of the risk.

Since many children are not thrilled initially about the prospect of being in therapy, child psychiatrists must use ingenious methods to establish trust and rapport. Children in emotional turmoil can be very defended. They are often frightened by their repressed or suppressed feelings, and they may be reluctant to delve into them. Patience and the ability to establish trust are requisites to overcoming this resistance.

Although some psychiatrists still practice "talk therapy," traditional psychotherapy is undergoing a radical transformation. Psychiatrists who provide fifty-minute psychotherapy sessions are becoming an endangered species. In many cases, patients must pay out of pocket for this therapy.

More and more psychiatrists are restricting their counseling sessions to fifteen or twenty minutes and are prescribing medication to treat a wide range of psychological problems. This new treatment model reflects economic realities and pressure from health maintenance organizations (HMOs) and preferred provider organizations (PPOs) to restrict costs. Psychiatrists can see more patients each day if their sessions are shorter, and the need for expensive long-term psychotherapy can be reduced by managing emotional problems with psychotropic (mood altering) drugs. This makes the psychiatrists happy because they can earn more money (seeing three or four patients per hour at $65 per visit versus earning $150 per hour for psychotherapy), and it makes the medical insurance companies happy because they save money by eliminating the cost associated with extended traditional therapy.

The value of prescribing medication to treat a range of mental conditions is not at issue. What is at issue is whether a deep-seated problem can actually be resolved with drugs. Certainly, the symptoms of depression, aggression, anxiety, or attention deficit disorder can be significantly reduced with drug therapy. And these mood-altering drugs are frequently a godsend. Patients who might otherwise be emotionally immobilized by their problems can now function in the world. Black clouds of depression and profound feelings of alienation and anxiety can be lifted.

This is well and good. But if a child has been molested or shows extreme hostility toward authority figures, can drug therapy solve what is causing the feelings and the behavior? Will the child be able to function only as long as he continues to take medication? Does the "disease" still exist when medication has eliminated or dulled the symptoms? Some medical doctors will respond yes to this question, and others will respond no. At the core of these questions are three basic issues that should be addressed:

1. Is curing my child the goal, or is maintenance the goal?
2. If my child takes medication for ADD, ADHD, or depression, will he still make poor choices, have flawed judgment, and act impulsively?
3. When my child discontinues medication, will he revert to his previous behavior?

You may want to explore these issues with the psychiatrist you are considering for your child.

Most medical insurance providers severely restrict the number of sessions that are covered. After the allowed sessions are used, the therapist must request authorization for additional sessions. The person to whom they must appeal is often not a licensed therapist but a bureaucrat with limited training in psychology. This person, who may have a B.A. or M.A. degree, is guided as much by economics and company guidelines as by patient needs. The ultimate approval of additional sessions often hinges on the persuasiveness and assertiveness of the therapist making the request. The policy of many insurance companies may be stated as: "Deal with the immediate crisis. Long-term psychotherapy is not authorized under this patient's plan."

The following questions may be useful, although you certainly don't need to ask them. You may intuitively know from the first moments you spend with a particular psychiatrist that this is the person you want to work with your child. If you're uncertain, the questions may help you get a better read on the psychiatrist's modus operandi. His answers will either allay your concerns or convince you that it would be best to seek someone else.

Questions for a Psychiatrist

In light of what we've told you about our child's difficulties in school, do you believe our child will require an evaluation by a developmental pediatrician or pediatric neurologist?

Do you believe our child will require psychoeducational testing by an educational psychologist, educational therapist, or neuropsychologist? If so, will you coordinate this testing?

If our child refuses to come in for a session, how do you recommend that we handle it?

As our child goes through the therapy process, will we experience periods when his behavior will change for the worse? If so, how should we handle it?

If our family goes through a difficult period while our child is in therapy, would it be appropriate for us to make an appointment to see you as a family?

How can we tell if our child is making progress in therapy?

What are the criteria for determining when our child has successfully completed therapy?

Would you be willing to advise our child's teacher about how he might better handle his acting out in the classroom?

How do you determine if resistance to studying and completing assignments reflects psychological overlay or a psychological problem?

What are your criteria for prescribing antidepressants?

Will you have fifty-minute psychotherapy sessions with our child, or do you believe that fifteen- or twenty-minute sessions will allow you to get to the bottom of the issues that are troubling our child?

How do you determine if a child has ADD?

If you decide to recommend medication, would you be willing to meet with us to explain the pros and cons of the treatment?

Do you usually prescribe Ritalin (Cylert, Dexadrine) for most of your patients who have ADD?

How long do children with ADD remain on medication?

Are there any potential side effects to the medication—sleeplessness, mood changes when the drug wears off, loss of appetite, diminished growth?

What does research indicate about children on Ritalin becoming at
risk for addiction to other drugs such as alcohol, marijuana, cocaine,
or prescription drugs?

If you prescribe medication, should our child continue using it during
weekends and vacations?

Does our medical insurance limit the number of sessions that are covered?

If more sessions are required, can you request extended coverage?

Clinical Psychologists and Child Psychologists

Licensed clinical psychologists and child psychologists represent another
treatment option for many children experiencing emotional distress. Unlike psychiatrists, who are MDs, psychologists have either a Ph.D. (doctor
of philosophy), Psy.D. (doctor of psychology), or Ed.D. (doctor of education). Upon finishing graduate school, psychologists must spend a prescribed number of clinical hours in supervised training. They are then
required to pass comprehensive written and oral state licensing exams
before they can begin treating clients. Some states have reciprocal licensing agreements that permit psychologists licensed in one state to apply
for a license to practice in another without having to retake licensing
exams.

The initial session with a psychologist parallels the initial session with
a psychiatrist. Part or all of the first session is usually spent exclusively
with the parents. The parents usually complete forms that provide a history of the child. During this initial session, the concerns of the parents
are discussed (without the child present), and the parents' questions about
the psychologist's methods and treatment objectives are answered.

Some clinical psychologists work exclusively with adults, and others
also treat teenagers and preteenagers. Most psychologists, however, generally refer younger clients to child psychologists who have received specialized postdoctoral training.

Psychologists can avail themselves of a wide range of treatment options. Some specialize in a particular method and use it exclusively with
all their clients. Although there are Freudian, neo-Freudian, Jungian, Gestalt, and behavioral psychologists, many psychologists are eclectic and
will use any methods that prove to be appropriate and effective in helping
children examine the feelings that are causing the emotional conflict.

Behavioral psychologists have a different orientation. These therapists
are primarily interested in modifying counterproductive behavior, and

they do not believe it is necessary to delve into the underlying issues that may be causing the child to act in a particular way. Behavioral therapy uses positive reinforcement to reward acceptable conduct and negative reinforcement to discourage unacceptable conduct.

Other psychologists may use a range of new and innovative methods such as Eye Movement Desensitization and Reprocessing (EMDR) and Neurolinguistic Programming (NLP). Psychologists using these neurologically based techniques believe that the procedures facilitate and expedite the identification and treatment of certain types of emotional problems.

Recently there has been a movement to allow psychologists who receive additional training to prescribe medication for such problems as depression and anxiety. Although some psychologists are in favor of this expanded treatment option, others are opposed because of potential malpractice liability.

As with psychiatrists, medical insurance providers are exerting intense pressure on psychologists to limit the number of sessions spent with clients. These health organizations are, in effect, defining how the new therapeutic model is going to work. They want psychologists to get their client through the immediate crisis and nothing more. By establishing arbitrary limits on the number of therapy sessions, the HMOs and PPOs are clearly stating that they aren't willing to pay for long-term therapy even if extended therapy might uncover and resolve the child's underlying problems. When the allotted number of therapy sessions is exhausted, the psychologist may request additional sessions. This request may be approved or denied depending on how the insurance company's guidelines are interpreted by an often unqualified person who is empowered to make the decision. In many cases the psychologist must literally plead to have additional sessions approved. Clearly, the decisions to authorize additional sessions are going to be closely scrutinized by supervisors. Too many treatment extensions mean that the insurance company is going to make less money. Because economics are of paramount importance to medical insurers, there's a basic conflict of interest: Is what's best for the patient best for the insurer? It doesn't take a rocket scientist to realize that the answer to this question is often no.

The objective of psychotherapy is to help a child examine feelings and behavior that are working at cross purposes with his emotional well-being. With gentle prodding a skilled psychologist can help the child uncover and examine his fears, insecurities, guilt, hostility, and anxieties. As the child establishes rapport and trust with the therapist, he will begin to let down the defenses that prevent him from confronting and dealing with the underlying issues. The ultimate goal is to help the child free himself from the negative forces that are causing his pain, sadness, and diminished self-esteem.

Crisis intervention therapy, on the other hand, has a very different and more immediate objective. The goal here is restore a semblance of emotional stability, reduce the symptoms, and help the child become more functional in school and at home. Neither the insurance company nor the therapist expects the underlying issues to be resolved with this type of expedient, cost-driven therapy.

Parents whose child requires more extensive therapy than their medical insurance covers are faced with a dilemma. Do they embark on a restricted crisis intervention path, or do they seek a more extensive treatment plan from the outset? In either scenario, there will be a cutoff point at which the sessions will be terminated, and this cutoff point will most likely be determined by the insurance company, whether or not the child has completed the psychotherapeutic process. The parents must then decide whether they are prepared to fund the additional therapy sessions themselves.

Family economics must certainly be factored into the equation. It may be difficult if not impossible for many families to afford extended psychotherapy, and parents may therefore be forced to put their child in crisis intervention therapy. Other parents may weigh the prospect of going into debt against that of having a dysfunctional child who may be permanently damaged, and they may choose to find the money somehow to pay for the additional therapy. The financial burdens imposed by this choice can be significant. Depending on geographical area, the fees charged by a licensed clinical psychologist can range from $85 to $140 or more per hour. Therapists in metropolitan areas, where expenses are higher, generally charge the highest rates.

Any major family expenses must be evaluated in terms of need, urgency, and anticipated results. There are no guarantees that psychotherapy will resolve a child's emotional problems, but there may be no viable alternative other than using medication to obtain societal conformity and to dull the emotions that are causing the child's unhappiness and counterproductive behavior.

Self-esteem and emotional health play vital roles in the way children see and experience life. Youngsters who like themselves appreciate their own abilities and feel that they deserve success. They consistently act in ways that reinforce their positive feelings about themselves. They establish goals, acknowledge their responsibilities, and meet their obligations. They also generally make astute judgments and wise choices. When they miscalculate, they are able to learn from their mistakes. Their emotional resilience allows them to handle most of the glitches and setbacks. These children delight in challenges, push themselves to the limit of their abilities, take pride in their accomplishments, and have a distinctive zest for life. Because they like and respect themselves, they are capable of loving others and can accept being loved by others.

The self-concept of emotionally conflicted children is very different. Many of these youngsters make chronically flawed choices, and they rarely, if ever, learn from their mistakes. Those who lack emotional resilience crumble when they experience a defeat, or withdraw into a protective cocoon. Those who don't respect themselves frequently show disrespect for others. Those who are angry reject their family's rules and society's rules. Those who feel undeserving of success avoid challenges, deny responsibility for their choices and behavior, run away from their obligations, and unconsciously engineer their own failures. As adults, many are incapable of experiencing love unless their relationships are overlaid with dependency, anger, and degradation. That these children and their adult counterparts derive little joy from life should come as no surprise.

The preceding profile is, of course, a generalization, and many emotionally distressed children exhibit less severe symptoms. These youngsters may be passive, codependent, tentative, and insecure, but because they do not make obvious waves, their problems may be overlooked. Although not overtly self-sabotaging, they are nevertheless in need of assistance.

Wise parents recognize the critical importance of self-esteem in the self-actualization equation. They realize that seeking professional help for a child at psychological risk is their only real option.

As you go through the process of selecting a therapist for your child, the following questions may be of help. Any therapist who refuses to respond to your legitimate questions during the interviewing stage should be eliminated from consideration. As with psychiatrists, you must accept that once therapy begins, the psychologist cannot discuss your child's therapy without your child's approval. To do so would be a violation of confidentiality and would undermine trust. Confidentiality can be broken only when a child is at risk of hurting himself or others. If the psychologist feels it appropriate to make specific suggestions about how you can better handle your child's behavior and emotions at home, he must do so in a way that does not violate confidentiality. There may also be occasions when the therapist will want to work privately with you or perhaps the entire family. A skilled therapist can do so without damaging your child's trust.

Questions for a Clinical Psychologist

Do you believe my child should be treated by a psychologist, a child psychologist, or a child psychiatrist? Can you explain why?

How long have you been in practice, and what training have you had working with children?

What specific technique or combination of techniques will you be using to treat my child?

If your method involves a combination of treatment techniques, can you describe how it works?

Can you explain why you believe this approach will be effective in addressing our child's problem?

If you ultimately conclude that you aren't the right person to treat our child, will you refer us elsewhere?

If our child refuses to come in for a session, how do you recommend that we handle it?

How can we tell if our child is making progress in therapy?

Because of his problems, our child gets far more attention than his siblings. Do you have any suggestions about how we should handle this?

What type of support should we expect to provide at home?

Our child often says that he feels singled out. He doesn't want to be in therapy because he thinks it means he's crazy. How should we deal with this?

Our child gets very angry and throws things and hits his younger sister. How should we respond?

Do you believe in time-outs and in sending a child to his room?

How should we handle blatant disobedience?

As our child goes through the process, will there be periods when his behavior changes for the worse? If so, how should we deal with this?

What are the criteria for determining when our child has successfully completed the therapeutic process?

If our family goes through a difficult period while our child is in therapy, would it be appropriate for us to make an apointment to see you?

How do you determine if a child has ADD?

Are you permitted to prescribe medication for our child?

Do you recommend that we consult a medical doctor about medication? If so, would you be willing to explain the pros and cons and your criteria for making this recommendation?

Would you refer us to a psychiatrist, neurologist, or pediatrician who can evaluate our child and address our concerns about medication?

How do you determine if our child's resistance to studying and completing his assignments reflects psychological overlay or a psychological problem?

Would you be willing to advise our child's teacher about how she might better handle his acting out in the classroom?

If appropriate, would you be willing to make written recommendations about handling relevant emotional issues that could be incorporated into our child's IEP?

Do you know what percentage of your fees will be covered by our particular medical insurance?

Do you know if our medical insurance limits the number of covered sessions?

If more sessions are required than generally authorized by an insurance company, can you request an extension? If so, how likely is it that this request will be honored?

We realize that it's impossible to estimate precisely, but can you give us some idea as to how long our child will need to be in therapy?

What are your fees when there is copayment from the insurance company, and what are your fees when copayment expires?

Do you have a sliding scale?

Can a balance accrue that we can pay off after our child finishes therapy?

Marriage and Family Counselors

The model of individual psychotherapy is not the only "talk therapy" method that can effectively address a child's emotional problems. In many states, licensed marriage, family, and child counselors (LMFCCs) treat psychological issues by examining the family dynamics and pinpointing specific factors that are contributing to the emotional discord of the family and individual family members. The premise of this therapeutic approach is that the emotional problems of any one family member are intertwined in the family system of interaction.

Parents who go to a family therapist because of their child's emotional problems may discover that they are in some way contributing to their child's problem. They may also discover that their family dynamic must be realigned before their child's counterproductive behavior and attitudes can be expected to change. The parents of the child manifesting emotional distress (in family therapy this person is called the identified patient, or IP) may believe that the child is the exclusive source of the family's unhappiness when actually the child's behavior is being either caused or exacerbated by the family's problems. The family dysfunction may be attributable to poor communication, marital discord, inconsistent application of rules, unreasonable or unfair expectations, double messages, codependency, and/or poorly defined guidelines and standards of acceptable and unacceptable behavior.

Although family therapists may have private sessions with an individual family member, some prefer to work with the entire family. It is actually quite common for an M.F.C.C. to work privately with a child and to invite siblings and parents to participate when appropriate. It's also possible that during a family session the therapist may want to work with one person exclusively and may request that other family members wait in the reception area. The therapist may also schedule sessions with specific family members (for example, all the children without the parents or one parent and one child).

After analyzing the family interaction, the therapist's goal might be to help Dad realize that he's excessively autocratic or critical. She may want to help Mom realize how her frustration at work is causing her to lose her temper at home. She may want to help a teenager realize that his rebelliousness and irresponsibility are angry reactions to his feeling unloved or unappreciated. She may want to help a ten-year-old realize that she's jealous of her older sister, resentful of her younger brother, and angry at her father for making repeated business trips and being away from home for weeks on end. At the same time, the therapist may want to help the entire family realize how frustration, stress, and misunderstandings are negatively affecting the quality of life for everyone in the family.

A struggling child can certainly generate major stress, and parents may not understand or accept that a child with ADD, dyslexia, or auditory processing deficits could require different rules and expectations. One of the objectives of an astute family therapist who has had experience working with special needs children might be to help family members become more tolerant and empathetic. The therapist might help the parents realize that specific accommodations are necessary, and she might help the child's siblings understand the reasons for these accommodations so that they are not resentful and jealous.

Mothers are particularly vulnerable to the demands that the special needs child can impose. Such a child often requires extra energy, attention, nurturing, and discipline from the primary caregiver, especially if he becomes helpless, manipulative, or resistant. The attention that the mother must devote to the child can take away from the attention she gives the rest of the family. A phenomenon called triangulation could result in which two family members pit themselves against a third family member.

A mother and father may also see different behavior from the child. Returning home from work at seven o'clock, the father may say to the mother, "He behaves fine for me. It must be something you're doing that's setting him off." This type of statement is guaranteed to trigger upset and resentment.

Although children may be unfairly blamed for causing the family's problems (the identified patient phenomenon), in the case of a struggling child, this attribution could be accurate. How the family handles the child's unique needs will determine whether or not the family becomes or remains dysfunctional.

Family therapists often do nonverbal play therapy with children who have language-based learning disabilities. Sand play has proven to be one of the most effective forms of therapy for children with learning disabilities and ADD. The interaction of the small human figures, animals, and objects that the child selects to play with in the sandbox provide symbolic "language" that the child uses to express feelings and thoughts that he cannot communicate in words. Sand play also provides a safe place where the child can work out his psychological overlay and act out his frustration and anger without hurting himself or others.

By enhancing communication, suggesting ways to interact more effectively, and encouraging family members to accept responsibility for their part in the family's problems, the therapist can alter the dynamics of the family system. If the therapy is successful, the child will no longer be perceived (or perceive himself) as the one who is causing all the unhappiness in the family, and he can begin to relinquish his defenses and counterproductive behavior and attitudes.

Although family therapy can be an effective treatment tool, some emotional problems are not directly attributable to a dysfunction in the family system, and resolving these problems may necessitate individual psychotherapy. For example, a child who has been molested by a caregiver will need the support of a skillful therapist as he processes his pain and trauma. Family counseling may be appropriate at some point to help the child's parents and siblings learn how to respond and provide support. In this case, both a psychologist and a family therapist may be needed, although many psychologists can fulfill both functions.

When a family therapist concludes that a child has profound emotional problems that require highly specialized psychotherapeutic skills or possibly drug management, he has a professional responsibility to refer the family to a child psychologist or child psychiatrist. The procedure is analogous to a family physician referring a child to a pediatric neurologist.

The following questions should help you assess the qualifications of the family therapist you are considering for your family. The therapist's answers should allay any concerns you might have about the appropriateness of the family therapy model in addressing the particular issues affecting your child and your family.

Questions for a Licensed Marriage and Family Counselor

Why do you believe that family counseling would be appropriate in treating the problems we've described?

Why do you believe that it's a family problem rather than our child's problem?

Will we always meet as a family, or will there be private sessions for us and for our child?

What do we do if some family members refuse to participate?

Is it possible that family therapy would turn up issues that might cause problems in our marriage?

Will we be made to feel responsible for causing our child's problems?

Is it possible you'll discover that our child's emotional distress is not being caused or exacerbated by a family problem? What would you do in this situation?

Are your fees covered by our medical insurance?

If more sessions are required, are you optimistic that you can get approval for payment from our insurance company?

Your model for how a family should ideally interact may not be the same as our model, which is strongly influenced by our religious beliefs and cultural practices. Will you factor our religious beliefs into the family equation?

Licensed Clinical Social Workers

Licensed clinical social workers ascribe to a therapeutic model that is similar to that of licensed marriage, family, and child therapists. Although LCSWs do individual therapy, they also frequently work with the entire family and provide insight about how to handle shared family problems. Another primary goal of an LCSW is to help clients make appropriate and reasonable accommodations to society and the community. A social worker often focuses on communication problems, counterproductive and socially inappropriate behavior, inconsistent child-rearing practices, and school problems that reflect family issues, emotional distress, and/or psychological overlay.

Many school districts have social workers on staff whose function is to help students and their families resolve school, family, and peer issues that are having an impact on deportment, attitude, and academic performance. A social worker might meet with a child and his parents to help them analyze problems, reconcile differences, and address peer issues with behavioral implications, such as wearing gang colors or using gang signals. A primary objective is to help clients create a home environment that is conducive to emotional stability and productive behavior.

Licensed clinical social workers in private practice perform the same functions as social workers in a local school. Their primary functions include providing case management, crisis intervention, therapy, and, when appropriate, home visits. These visits allow the social worker to observe the family dynamics and develop effective interventions. When they are operating in a private capacity, however, LCSWs can usually delve more extensively into family and societal factors and can provide more in-depth treatment.

Whereas some states do not license marriage, family, and child counselors, all states license social workers. The supervised clinical training required for a LCSW license exceeds that of the MFCC license, although the extra requirements do not necessarily guarantee that one type of therapist is more competent than the other.

Since the philosophy, orientation, and therapeutic techniques of social workers and marriage, family, and child counselors are similar, the questions suggested on the previous page are equally appropriate when interviewing both. You deserve to know the LCSW's answers to these questions before you commit your family to therapy with this person. Any therapist who refuses to answer your legitimate questions should not be considered.

Part V
Finding the Right Person to Provide Specialized Services

Chapter 10
Learning Assistance Providers

Tutors, Educational Therapists, Learning and Reading
Centers, Privately Funded Specialized Private Schools, and
Publicly Funded Nonpublic Schools

After monitoring your child's progress in school, you conclude
that she needs more assistance than what is being provided in
the resource program. Worried that your child might never
catch up, you hire a tutor. But according to your child's teacher, the improvement the tutor claims your daughter is making is not transferring to
the classroom. Your anxiety mounts, and troubling questions arise. Are
your child's problems being adequately addressed in her tutorial program? Does the tutor really know what she is doing? Is she charging a
fair price? Should you look for someone else?

Why Seek Private Learning Assistance?

There are six basic reasons for seeking private supplemental learning assistance for your child:

1. Your child doesn't qualify for in-school remedial help.
2. Your child has qualified for the resource program but is not responding positively to the assistance.
3. You believe your child's learning deficits haven't been accurately identified and/or aren't being adequately treated.
4. You want to see greater progress.
5. You want to accelerate the speed of progress.
6. You want to make certain your child resolves her deficits, or learns how to compensate successfully for them.

There are many highly competent private tutors who know how to
"fix" learning problems. Unfortunately, there are also many marginally

competent ones who hang out a professional shingle and pose as highly qualified remediation experts.

This posturing is not limited to individual practitioners. Locally owned, nationally owned, and franchised learning centers may also be staffed with putative "specialists" who have had little professional training and possess few, if any, specialized skills. Some of these centers may lead you to believe they have professionals on staff who are trained to remediate learning disabilities when their specialists are simply credentialed or certified teachers who have received perhaps one week of formal training in the company's methods.

If you have concluded that your child requires private learning assistance, you want her to be helped by the most competent person you can find. You want someone with exceptional skills, and you want to avoid those who are incompetent or unscrupulous. To do so you must be able to evaluate critically the claims that are made and make an informed judgment about the skills and methods of the person who will be doing the remediation. The less informed you are, the greater the risk of your being misled, exploited, and disillusioned.

Smart consumers do their homework before hiring someone to provide a service they can't or don't want to perform themselves. They seek a second opinion They are cautious and, when appropriate, skeptical. They realize that helping a struggling child requires the skills of an experienced, knowledgeable, and comprehensively trained specialist.

Commonsense Procedures Before Hiring an Academic Specialist

- Solicit a referral from someone whose judgment you trust.
- Request the provider's background, credentials, and experience.
- Ask the provider to describe the methods he will use.
- Ask approximately how much time the remediation will require.
- Ask how much the service will cost.
- Verify the provider's reputation with the Better Business Bureau, an appropriate professional accrediting association, or a trusted professional.
- Ask for references from previous clients.

You want to find an academic specialist who can accruately identify and effectively remediate your child's learning problems. You want someone with excellent teaching skills who has the ability to motivate your child and build her confidence. And, of course, you want someone you can afford. If you're earning $20 an hour, you're probably not in a position to pay an educational therapist $65 an hour unless you can reduce your expenses, create a new income source, tap into your savings, or borrow money. None of these options is pleasant, but making a financial sacrifice to resolve your child's learning problems can be one of your wisest investments. If the remediation helps your child *before* she is psychologically damaged and *before* she imprints indelible negative associations with learning and with school, you and the academic specialist have literally changed the course of her life. After completing her education, your daughter might earn far more during her first month of employment than your entire investment in her remediation program.

Finding Top-Notch Help

Geography plays a key role in your being able to find superior learning assistance for your child. Families living in urban communities generally have a greater selection of educational support resources, while those living in small towns and rural areas may be fortunate to find one qualified person in their community.

Your educational sophistication can also play an important role. The more you understand about your child's deficits and needs, and the more you know about different instructional techniques, the better your chances of finding an exceptional academic specialist. For example, if you conclude after doing research that a remediation program based on phonics would be more effective in helping your child overcome a serious reading problem than a sight word or whole language method, you can then ask the provider incisive questions about his remediation methods.

If you've heard about remediation methods such as Orton-Gillingham, Slingerland, Lindamood Auditory Discrimination in Depth, and Visualizing Verbalizing, and the tutor or therapist is not familiar with these techniques, this might be an important warning signal about the person's knowledge and training. If the academic specialist insists on using a whole language approach, you may decide to give her the benefit of the doubt for a reasonable period of time while carefully monitoring the results, or you may decide to hire someone else.

In seeking private assistance for your child, your options are to go to a tutor, an educational therapist, an independently owned learning clinic, a learning center owned or franchised by a national chain, or a specialized private school. All these providers may claim they can resolve your child's learning problems, and they may use different methods. The challenge is to decide which person or which program is best for your child.

Let's examine your options. We'll begin with the most common form of educational assistance: tutoring.

Tutors

Tutors are typically teachers who work privately with students after school in their own homes or at the students' homes. Some tutors teach school during the day and supplement their income by tutoring. Others are retired from the classroom.

There are two types of tutors: content area specialists who teach one or two subjects exclusively, such as Spanish or biology, and generalists who focus on developing basic skills in reading, math, spelling, or language arts. Generalists tend to work primarily with younger children, while content area specialists usually assist students who are in middle school and high school. Most tutors have a B.A. or M.A. in their teaching specialty and a teaching credential or certificate.

A tutor typically reviews what has been taught in class, explains confusing material, and focuses on helping students "catch up." She goes over material that has been presented, explains concepts and applications, and has students practice until they have achieved mastery. Tutors also help students complete homework assignments and review for tests.

Although good tutors individualize their instruction, most employ the same instructional methods they use in teaching class. If a child is having difficulty reading fluently, the tutor would first identify the child's *comfort reading level.* She would then methodically help the child sound out words phonetically and recognize nonphonetic words by sight. She might use flash cards to facilitate memorization of nonphonetic words and encourage the child to use her finger as she needs to help her track words more efficiently.* The tutor's goal is to help the child read at grade level, keep up with the class, and be able to complete class work and homework independently. If the student is also struggling to memorize the multiplication tables or align her number columns properly, the tutor might drill the tables and have the child practice lining up the number columns. She

---

*Some classroom teachers and tutors discourage this practice, arguing that the child's finger becomes a crutch and discourages fluency. Those taking this position know little about teaching reading skills to children with visual tracking and blending deficits. These children have deficient ocular muscle control, and their finger or a cardboard cutout can help them compensate for their tracking deficits. The finger tracking method will not correct the underlying problem, but it will help students read accurately and allow them to develop more positive associations with reading.

might use graph paper to facilitate column alignment and flash cards to drill number facts.

Tutors typically use the teaching techniques with which they're comfortable. If they believe that flash cards are effective, they may use them with all students. Many tutors do not realize that their own preferred learning and teaching style is not necessarily the best style for the student. This is especially true in the case of tutors who have been teaching for many years and have become set in their ways and attitudes. If the tutor's preferred instructional style fails to make inroads, there is a risk that he might erroneously conclude that the student lacks ability when the child may simply be unresponsive to the tutor's teaching methods.

Tutors who insist on teaching struggling students the way they themselves learn best are destined to be ineffectual with certain children. It's common for tutors who are visual learners (understand and retain written information best) to use a visually loaded teaching method. Those who are auditory learners tend to use a verbally loaded teaching method.

Good tutors are pragmatists who have mastered the art of making expedient tactical adjustments in their teaching methodology. Realizing that they'll have limited success if they rely exclusively on one teaching strategy, they attempt to identify the struggling student's preferred learning style and modify their teaching so that it capitalizes on the student's strengths and preferences. They also help the child identify how she learns best so that she can create her own individualized learning strategies.

A first-rate tutor might be working with a student who cannot seem to grasp the concept of fractions. To help her comprehend part/whole relationships, the tutor might use hands-on materials called manipulatives to demonstrate tangibly what fractions are and how they work. A one-inch strip of plastic sitting on top of a four-inch square piece of plastic represents in concrete terms the fraction $1/4$. Two one-inch strips sitting on top of a four-inch square represent $1/2$. The child can feel it, see it, and manipulate it. If the tutor is helping a child in American history, she might have the child act out a difficult concept, such as how the system of checks and balances was built into the U.S. Constitution. The student might assume different roles: president, congressman, senator, and Supreme Court justice. A hypothetical new law might be written, passed by Congress, submitted for signature or veto by the president, and reviewed by the Supreme Court to determine its constitutionality.

One of the more traditional functions of tutoring is to help students with challenging homework assignments. As she works with the student, the tutor can gauge what deficits need to be addressed. For example, in helping a child with a writing assignment, the tutor may observe run-on sentences, mixed tenses, and nonparallel construction. Although she must be careful not to correct every mistake in the student's essay, she could use the writing assignment as a springboard for remediating the student's errors in grammar and syntax.

Most tutors do not administer a battery of formal diagnostic or academic tests before beginning to work with a child. They usually do a brief informal assessment of the student's academic strengths and weaknesses, and review the results of standardized tests that have been administered in school. Tutors would then typically focus on improving basic comprehension, vocabulary, math, spelling skills, and study skills.

Although relatively few tutors have had formal training in working with seriously learning disabled students, some are clearly more qualified than others. They may have taken graduate courses in specialized reading methods and/or in identifying and treating learning disabilities. Most tutors, however, are not credentialed or certified resource or reading specialists.

A scrupulous tutor would not attempt to remediate the underlying perceptual decoding deficits of a seriously dyslexic child unless she has had special training in this area. Just as a family physician will refer a seriously ill patient to a specialist, the wise tutor will recognize her limitations and refer the child with special needs to an educational therapist (see following section) who has more extensive training. Unfortunately, in many communities there may not be a qualified educational therapist, and the tutor may have no recourse but to work with the learning disabled child as best she can.

Tutors can be highly effective in helping students who have fallen behind. A content area tutor may be precisely what the student who is struggling in chemistry requires. Help from a competent English tutor may do wonders for the student whose book reports and essays are poorly written and disorganized. But if this student appears unable to master writing skills, a conscientious English tutor would want to refer the child to a specialist who could determine if underlying perceptually based language deficits are causing the writing difficulties.

The student who has profound reading comprehension and retention deficits, chronic spelling problems, difficulty understanding and following instructions, or persistent letter and number reversals would also require specialized instruction. Although some tutors may be able to assist with these problems, the ideal person to address them is an educational therapist.

There are tutors who have a phenomenal track record for helping struggling students. Possessing first-rate teaching skills, these tutors intuitively figure out how to get the job done. At issue is what happens when a child doesn't respond to the instructional methods being used and the tutor can't figure out how to resolve the problem. At this juncture a specialist can be invaluable.

Questions for a Tutor

How long have you been tutoring children?

Have you taught or are you currently teaching school?

What is your educational background?

Are you a credentialed or certified teacher?

What are your fees?

Do you prefer working with children in a specific age range?

Do you plan to do any sort of formal or informal assessment? If so, what tests will you do and what is the charge for this?

Do you maintain contact with my child's teacher and/or resource specialist? If so, how often?

How long is each session, and how many sessions per week do you recommend?

Do you assign additional homework?

Do you expect me to help my child with homework assignments and/ or with material you assign?

Do you plan to have periodic conferences with me, and will you provide verbal or written progress updates? If so, will there be a charge for these conferences?

Have you had training in working with children with learning disabilities? If so, what kind and how much?

How do you propose to build my child's academic self-confidence?

What methods would you use to motivate my child?

When children don't respond to your help, what do you do?

How do you handle children with concentration problems?

How do you handle children who have difficulty following and understanding instructions?

How do you handle resistance?

Will you be making recommendations about specific in-class accommodations that should be made for my child?

Do you believe you are qualified to help my child in all the deficit areas that have been identified, including science and language arts?

Do you teach study skills? If so, do you use a particular program?

Do you provide help with recording assignment, time management, organization, planning, and goal setting?

Have you had training in specialized programs such as Lindamood or Slingerland that are designed to help children with learning problems?

Are you willing to attend IEP conferences? If so, what is your fee?

Do you focus primarily on actually correcting problems or on teaching children how to compensate for their problems?

Do you believe in working individually with children or in small groups? If children work in groups, are the children grouped by chronological age or by the nature of their learning deficits?

What are your criteria for deciding that the tutoring has been successfully completed?

May I talk with the parents of some of the students you've tutored?

Would it be okay if I speak with a teacher and a resource specialist who have referred students to you?

Educational Therapists

The term "educational therapist" is of relatively recent origin. It evolved because many credentialed or certified school resource specialists began developing private practices to work with struggling students. These resource specialists had one or two years of additional formal training in graduate school, and many possessed advanced degrees. Wanting to distinguish themselves from tutors with less specialized training, they coined the term educational therapist.

An organization called the Association of Educational Therapists (AET), founded in 1979, has developed a set of rigorous eligibility requirements for professional membership. These requirements include verification of graduate-level coursework and supervised training in educational therapy. There are three types of professional memberships:

1. *Certified Educational Therapist (ET),* the highest level.
Requirements:
• a comprehensive application which includes an in-depth description of a case study that follows AET guidelines and the testing and treatment protocols used

- minimum of an M.A. degree earned in special education or areas related to special education
- professional membership in good standing for a minimum of one year
- additional direct service hours (beyond the basic fifteen hundred hours required for professional membership—see below) using psycho-educational interventions
- forty hours of continuing education every two years

2. *Professional Certification*
Requirements:
- verified graduate-level coursework as prescribed by AET
- fifteen hundred direct service hours, five hundred of which have been supervised
- forty hours of continuing education every two years

3. *Associate Professional Certification*
These individuals have completed formal casework in educational therapy but have not yet fulfilled the requirements of fifteen hundred direct service hours and/or five hundred supervised hours to gain professional standing.
Requirements:
- verified graduate-level coursework as prescribed by the AET
- internship that meets the training institution's required hours of supervision

The Association of Educational Therapists requires all members to adhere to a code of ethics. This code, which covers such issues as confidentiality, conflict of interest, and misconduct, is designed to assure a high standard of professionalism and accountability.

As previously stated, many educational therapists were once resource specialists. Because of their school teaching experience and training in a wide range of treatment and testing protocols, they are qualified to diagnose learning problems and develop highly individualized remediation strategies. This process is referred to as prescriptive teaching.

As is the case with tutors, educational therapists sometimes provide help with homework and/or review class work, but most do not see this as their primary role. They consider themselves specialists who have been trained to identify complex learning deficits, design effective educational prescriptions, and implement them with skill and professionalism.

Parents may be referred directly to an educational therapist by their child's pediatrician, teacher, resource specialist, or family friend. Although an educational therapist cannot administer all the tests that a licensed clinical psychologist, school psychologist, or educational psychologist is authorized to administer (see chapters 4 and 9), they can administer an extensive battery of diagnostic tests that can usually pinpoint a student's specific areas of dysfunction and deficiency. Some of these tests may duplicate tests done in school, but most educational therapists insist on administering their own battery because of concerns about the accuracy and comprehensiveness of the school workup or about the conclusions reached. Independent diagnostic testing is especially important when a child has not been previously assessed or when the child's parents question the validity or interpretation of a previous evaluation. The downside is that the assessment can cost from $500 to $1,000 or more, depending on how extensive it is. Basic tests, such as the Woodcock Johnson Psycho-Educational Battery of Academic Achievement, rarely need to be duplicated if the test was recently administered in school. (See chapter 5 for a description of commonly given diagnostic and achievement tests.) Parents should discuss the issue of test duplication with the educational therapist during the initial conference.

Many educational therapists work closely with educational and clinical psychologists (see chapter 9). A psychologist may administer the WISC III (a test restricted to psychologists) and the Bender-Gestalt, and conclude that a child is showing symptoms of a learning dysfunction. At this juncture the psychologist might do additional diagnostic testing or refer the child to an educational therapist for further assessment.

Once the educational therapist identifies a child's specific deficits, the next step is to develop an effective treatment plan. If the child is also receiving counseling, the educational therapist and the clinical psychologist would coordinate their efforts and consult when appropriate.

Educational therapists generally work one-on-one with students, but in some cases a therapist may work with small homogeneous groups consisting of two to four children of the same age and having similar learning problems. Small-group instruction can be quite effective when the therapist is addressing such issues as study skills, time management, or organization. In the proper context, a group format can actually be more effective than private instruction because of the dynamics of group interaction. If skillfully handled, small-group instruction can produce positive synergy that energizes less motivated students. There are two additional advantages: Students are trained to function efficiently in a real-world context that includes other students, and the cost of the remediation is reduced.

In addition to providing specialized academic remediation, educational therapists also furnish context-appropriate educational counseling and emotional support for children who have been scarred by negative school experiences. This counseling is not intended to be a substitute for psychotherapy or family therapy. Rather, it focuses on motivation, goal setting, time management, getting along with the teacher, homework completion, accepting responsibility, and attention to detail.

Another common function of an educational therapist is to represent a student at the IEP conference. He can discuss the scores the child received on the privately administered diagnostic assessment and achievement tests, compare these scores with those obtained by the school psychologist and resource specialist, provide an update about the child's progress, and participate in planning in-school interventions and educational objectives.

If there is disagreement about the interpretation of test results or about the proposed remediation strategy, the educational therapist might serve as an advocate for the struggling child. As previously noted, many educational therapists do not want to assume the role of advocate because of a conflict of interest. If a therapist relies primarily on referrals from teachers in the district, he might be reluctant to assume an adversarial role. In this case, the therapist would probably refer the family to an advocate who specializes in mediating conflicts and, when necessary, representing families involved in disputes, hearings, and possible litigation.

Because the success of any remediation program often hinges on the student's attitude, motivation, and effort, the insightful educational therapist realizes that she cannot focus exclusively on developing academic skills and learning efficiency. She must also build her student's academic self-confidence by carefully orchestrating repeated opportunities for him to experience meaningful victories. She must demand more from the child than anyone has previously, but not more than the child is capable of doing. This delicate balancing act requires structuring the remediation so that the student can prevail over challenges as they become more difficult. In this way the educational therapist allows the child to prove to *himself* that he is capable. This is much more effective than simply telling the child he is capable.

Intentionally engineering success is a vital component in any strategy designed to enhance a struggling student's self-concept. The educational therapist must also be prepared to nudge the child from his comfort zone and encourage him to take reasonable risks, make sustained effort, and stretch for defined goals. This can be a scary proposition for a child whose negative school experiences have convinced him that he's incompetent. Transforming a defeated learner into an empowered learner is a process that must be managed with consummate skill.

An experienced educational therapist knows that struggling children are often frustrated, demoralized, and angry, and that these feelings affect their attitude toward school and studying. In seeking antidotes to procrastination, laziness, sloppiness, and disorganization, the educational therapist will use a process of trial and error until she finds the most effective methods for helping a student. She realizes that these methods must address the child's deficits but also capitalize on his learning strengths and natural aptitude. She also realizes that focusing exclusively on the deficits during a remediation session is likely to trigger demoralization and resistance.

To be effective the remediation strategy must address not only the student's academic and perceptual decoding problems (how sensory data is processed by the brain), but also the child's self-defeating coping mechanisms (see psychological overlay, chapter 3). This self-defeating school behavior often dissipates as the learning problem becomes less debilitating. If the behavior persists, the educational therapist would undoubtedly recommend professional counseling (see chapters 10 and 11).

Finding a first-rate educational therapist may require intensive detective work. If you're fortunate, you may be referred to one by your child's pediatrician or neurologist. If your child has been tested privately, the clinical or educational psychologist may make a referral. The school psychologist or resource specialist may also recommend someone. Many school districts, however, discourage such referrals for legal reasons; they're afraid that if school personnel make referrals to private practitioners, they are admitting the school cannot handle the problem. This might lead to the district's being sued and held responsible for funding the private services.

Two organizations might be able to help you find a local qualified educational therapist in your community. The previously mentioned Association of Educational Therapists and the Parents' Educational Resource Center maintain referral lists but do not recommend particular therapists. Parents' Educational Resource Center, a nonprofit organization funded by the Charles Schwab Foundation, also provides a lending library of relevant books and tapes, and members of the organization can talk in person or by phone with a resource specialist about issues that concern them (see Appendix).

The following questions may help you select an educational therapist and get a better read on her methods.

Questions for an Educational Therapist

In what way do your services differ from those of a tutor?

What is your educational background and professional training?

How long have you been an educational therapist?

Are you a member of the Association of Educational Therapists?

Have you taught school? If so, where and for how long?

Were you a credentialed or certified resource specialist before becoming an educational therapist?

What are your fees?

What are the sources of your referrals?

Do you have an age range with which you prefer to work?

Do you plan on doing a formal or informal assessment? How much will this cost?

Do you maintain contact with my child's teacher and/or resource specialist? If so, how often?

How long is each remedial session, and how many per week do you recommend?

Do you assign additional homework?

Do you expect me to help my child with homework assignments and/or academic material you might assign?

What methods would you use to motivate my child?

How do you handle children with concentration and focusing problems?

Do you plan to have periodic conferences with me, and will you provide periodic verbal or written progress updates? If so, will there be a charge for these conferences?

What do you do when children don't respond to your help?

How do you propose to build my child's self-confidence?

Are you willing to attend IEP conferences. If so, what is your fee?

Do you teach study skills?

Do you think my child should receive private instruction or small-group instruction? If you propose group instruction, what criteria do you use to group children—age or the nature of the students' learning deficits?

How do you handle children who have difficulty following and understanding instructions?

Do you make recommendations about at-home and in-class accommodations?

Do you teach children time-management, assignment recording, planning, organizational, and goal-setting skills?

Do you believe that significant learning deficits can be corrected, or do you believe that the goal should be to teach a child how to compensate for the deficits? What are your criteria for making this determination?

What percentage of students who complete your program require further assistance later?

What are your criteria for terminating your work with a child?

What might cause you to be unable to resolve a child's learning problems? If this happens, what would you then recommend?

Do you ever work together with a content area tutor in a specific subject?

May I talk with the parents of some students with whom you have worked?

May I contact teachers and resource specialists who have referred students to you?

Learning Centers

There are three major types of learning centers: university-affiliated graduate student training programs, independently owned and operated, and national or franchised, which are operated by private or publicly traded corporations. The philosophy and methodologies of these three types of centers are quite distinct.

University-Affiliated Learning Centers

The primary function of university-affiliated learning centers* is to train graduate students in remedial methodologies and diagnostic procedures.

*These learning centers should not be confused with the educational support services offered by universities and colleges to their own learning disabled students. Federal law requires that college students with documented disabilities be provided with tutorial support and learning assistance. Any learning disabled student admitted to a college or university automatically qualifies for these free services. If a student can't take adequate notes in class, the educational support program will send someone to take notes for him. The student may also ask for permission to take untimed tests. Special

The programs offer graduate students an opportunity for hands-on, as opposed to theoretical, testing and teaching experience, and participation in these labs is a requirement for graduation and for receiving state credentials.

Struggling elementary, middle, and high school students admitted into these lab programs are usually evaluated extensively and then provided with tutoring, educational therapy, and, in some cases, counseling services. The graduate students offer these services under the supervision of university instructors and professors. In some programs the services are videotaped and then systematically critiqued and evaluated by the supervising instructors. Frequently, the services provided are offered free or at a significantly reduced rate.

University-affiliated programs represent a win-win situation for everyone. Graduate students receive training and are provided with an invaluable opportunity to get hands-on experience. At the same time, struggling children get help at no cost or at a reduced rate. The only potential downside is that the graduate students providing the assistance are not seasoned resource specialists and may lack the skills and experience a veteran tutor or educational therapist possesses. It should be noted, however, that many graduate students have already had extensive classroom experience. Some are returning to school to pursue an advanced degree, and others are making the transition from teacher to resource specialist.

Graduate students frequently make up for any lack of extensive front-line experience with raw enthusiasm and an intense desire to help the children they're tutoring. Because they're affiliated with a university, they have access to some of the newest, most innovative remedial tools and teaching methods available. They can brainstorm with professors and lab instructors about the most effective techniques for dealing with their students' problems and can capitalize on the experience and knowledge of the clinic supervisor.

Not all universities offer graduate programs in learning disabilities. In those that have affiliated learning centers, the admission criteria for enrolling children vary. It may be a particular university's policy to accept referrals only from local school districts or exclusively from inner-city schools. Other universities may have "open enrollment" and accept any qualified child whose parents take the initiative to apply. Parent income

admission criteria are also used for students with disabilities, and they may ask to take the SAT untimed. Parents and learning disabled high school students should request more information about these programs from their child's school counselor.

may be an admission criterion and could affect the fee structure if a fee is charged for the services. Some universities may accept only those children whose families cannot afford private learning assistance.

In most cases, university-affiliated learning assistance programs are linked to the university calendar. A child may work with a graduate student instructor for an entire semester or perhaps two semesters. The timetable for beginning and ending the program and the policies about assigning instructors vary from university to university.

If you live near a university or teaching college that has an affiliated learning disabilities lab, and you're interested in having your child participate in a graduate student training program, ask the principal or resource specialist at your child's school about eligibility requirements. You should also request information directly from the university about enrollment deadlines, fees, and schedules. Start by contacting the department of special education or educational psychology at the university. You may be able to bypass your child's school and apply for admission directly to the university.

Since the diagnostic and remediation services at a university-affiliated learning center are often free or provided at a significantly reduced rate, it makes sense for you to be careful not to pose questions that might be considered provocative. Wanting information about any program in which you are considering enrolling your child is certainly justifiable, but you must use discretion. If hundreds of families are applying for admission and the university can accept only thirty-five children, you certainly don't want to make waves with questions that might be misconstrued as hostile or confrontative. When you pay full fare for a service, you clearly have more prerogatives.

Despite the foregoing admonition, the following questions address issues that could justifiably concern you. The answers may help you decide if the university learning lab is the right program for your child.

Questions for the Director of a University-Affiliated Learning Center

Will someone share the results of the diagnostic evaluation with me?

Will the results of my child's assessment be in writing and presented in a report that I can use at the IEP conference and refer to later?

Will my child's program be under the supervision of a professor or university instructor?

If I have concerns, am I allowed to consult with the supervising professor or instructor?

Will the graduate student establish contact with my child's teacher and/or resource specialist?

Will my child work with the same instructor each session?

Do children work privately with the instructor or in small groups?

If children work in groups, are they grouped according to age or the nature of their disabilities?

Will I be provided with periodic updates about progress, and will these updates be in writing?

If the methods being used do not appear to be successful, will alternative techniques be employed? Who will make this decision?

Will the graduate student who works with my child have any teaching experience?

If my child requires additional help after the semester ends, can she continue in the program the next semester?

Are individual and family counseling services available?

Does the program involve a specific number of sessions?

If my child requires additional help after this program is completed, will you make a referral to a private therapist or learning center?

Will there be testing after the program is completed to determine progress and if there are still residual learning problems?

Independently Owned and Operated Learning Centers

In many communities, nonprofit or for-profit learning centers have been established by entrepreneurial teachers, resource specialists, educational therapists, or educational psychologists to test and treat children with academic problems. Depending on the size of the center, enrollment may range from ten to several hundred students.

Learning centers typically employ credentialed (or certified) tutors and/or educational therapists and offer both individual and small-group remedial services. The academic specialists usually have university training and previous classroom teaching experience. Many are part-time employees who teach school during the day and work at the center in the late afternoon or early evening.

Some centers train their staff in their own proprietary methods; others hire trained personnel with extensive backgrounds in remediation and encourage them to design their own strategies when working with students. In most well-run centers, the tutors and educational therapists are supervised by the center director, who is usually a seasoned educator with frontline experience and an advanced degree.

In some cases a program may be oriented exclusively toward tutoring, and the center may do only limited diagnostic testing. The center may rely on tests administered in school or may give basic standardized achievement tests such as the Woodcock Johnson or the CTBS to determine a student's current level of skills. Criteria-referenced instruments (material selected from different grade levels) may also be used to assess a student's approximate skill level.

Those centers that offer specialized educational therapy in addition to content area tutoring usually require that children be given an extensive diagnostic testing battery. These tests, which may be administered by an educational therapist, clinical psychologist, or educational psychologist, can cost from $500 to $1,000 or more depending on the extensiveness of the battery, the affluence of the community in which the center is located, and the credentials of the person doing the evaluation. The test results and recommendations are summarized in a more or less standardized written report. The format, content, and tone of this summary will be essentially the same whether it is presented to parents in Chicago or Dallas, although the actual diagnostic tests administered may vary somewhat.

As previously stated, a comprehensive assessment by a private diagnostician may be redundant, expensive, and unnecessary if school-adminstered evaluation was sufficiently comprehensive, provided accurate information, and were properly interpreted. In fact, to readminister the *same form* of a test within one year actually *invalidates* the results.

If the test results are in doubt or are no longer current, additional testing would certainly be advisable. To design an effective remediation strategy, the therapist must have accurate, up-to-date information. The issue of redundant testing may be a moot point, however, as some private learning centers insist on doing their own evaluation and will not enroll a child in their program without having done so.

Learning centers may also offer additional services. There may be an occupational therapist (see chapter 11) and/or an adaptive physical education specialist on staff to work with children who have significant coordination, vestibular (balance), and central nervous system deficits. The center may also provide limited or extensive individual and group counseling services. Some centers have adjunct physicians to advise parents and, when appropriate, to recommend and prescribe medication.

The fees charged by learning centers are usually competitive with those charged by private educational therapists. Private tutoring from a credentialed or certified teacher might range from $25 to $45 per hour, and educational therapy might range from $40 to $70 or more per hour. Centers in urban areas and more affluent communities generally charge top dollar.

Many learning centers prefer to work with small groups of two to four children. The children are usually grouped according to age and type of learning deficits. The rationale for group remediation is that struggling children must learn how to function efficiently in a classroom of twenty-five or more students and must be able to work independently while other students are being helped by the teacher. Children may make substantive progress in a one-on-one situation, but these gains may not transfer to the classroom where there are distractions and where they won't have their teacher's exclusive attention. This problem of gains transferring to the classroom is especially relevant in the case of students with ADD who struggle to pay attention, control their impulses, and follow and recall instructions.

The contention that group instruction is an effective strategy for helping students with focusing problems may be quite reasonable, but it assumes that the tutor or educational therapist is adroit at working with groups of inattentive children and can individualize the instruction so that each child's remedial needs are met. Working effectively with a group of ADD students requires very special skills that many academic specialists do not possess.

There is also an obvious financial incentive for learning centers to recommend group tutoring. Four students paying $35 an hour generates more than twice the income as one child paying $65 an hour for a private session.

The nature and severity of your child's learning deficits should be a primary consideration in determining the instructional format. Two hours of group tutoring at $35 per hour may be not only a better bargain but also a better educational strategy for your child than one hour of private instruction at $65 per hour. This assumes, of course, that you agree with the argument that group instruction could be beneficial for children with focusing problems. Your decision about group versus private remediation should be based on your child's needs and your own financial resources, not on what is most expedient or profitable for the learning center.

The answers to the following questions may help you decide if the learning center you are considering is appropriate for your child.

Questions for the Director
of a Locally Owned and Operated Learning Center

What are your credentials?

What are the credentials of your instructors?

Are any instructors on your staff credentialed resource specialists or certified educational therapists?

How many years have you been in business?

Do you require comprehensive testing, or are you willing to use the results of the school's assessment?

Could you describe your diagnostic testing battery?

Who administers this battery, and what are the credentials of this person?

Will we be given a written summary of the results?

What is the fee for testing?

Do you personally oversee each child's remedial program?

Is the educational therapist who will work with my child a member of the Association of Educational Therapists?

Do you have criteria for assigning a child to a particular tutor or educational therapist?

Will my child be working exclusively with this person until she completes the remedial program?

Do you achieve success with most of the children with whom you work, and how do you define and determine success?

What approximate percentage of the children need to return for additional assistance after completing the program?

Do you provide any specialized proprietary training (unique methods developed at the center) for your tutors and educational therapists?

Is there a charge for conferences to discuss progress and problems?

Are there any contractual obligations? If so, could you clearly define these obligations?

Am I charged if my child misses a session because of illness or other compelling reasons? If advance notice is required, how many hours in advance must I inform you?

What are your goals for my child and the general time frame you project for attaining these goals?

Could you describe the types of intervention strategies you might use with my child?

Why would your program be more successful than that offered at another center?

What are the criteria for determining that my child has successfully completed the program?

Do you offer study skills instruction, and do you have a particular program that you use?

Do you ever recommend that a child receive educational therapy while also receiving content area tutoring in subjects such as science, language arts, or math?

If we cannot afford more than one intervention at the same time, how do you prioritize one type of assistance over another?

National and Franchised Learning Centers

There are several corporations that offer educational services in company-owned and franchised learning centers throughout the United States. Although the teaching curricula and methods used at these centers are often purported to be proprietary and developed exclusively for use at the corporations' centers, much of the actual instructional material is generic and similar to that used in a typical school classroom.

Instructors are usually credentialed or certified teachers who go through a brief on-site training program. This training may involve one or two weeks of instruction in how to implement the company's methods and curriculum. The instructors at these centers are rarely certified or credentialed resource specialists, and it's highly unusual for a national learning center to have a licensed educational psychologist or certified educational therapist on staff. Limited academic testing is administered and in some cases additional company-developed tests are given, but children are not comprehensively assessed for learning disabilities.

Franchised and company-owned learning centers typically work on a ratio of three or four students per instructor. Some centers require that parents sign a contract committing a child to a specific number of hours of instruction. If the child does not attain the defined objectives, these centers may provide as many as twelve additional hours of instruction at no additional cost.

Many national learning centers advertise that their proprietary curricula and methods can improve by several grade levels the reading or math skills of most children who are struggling in school. They also assert that they can document significant gains in academic skills. Although the executives of these educational corporations may deny that their programs are intended for learning disabled students, on-site directors of local franchises may imply or claim outright that the programs will improve the skills of learning disabled children.

There is little doubt that programs at national learning centers can be highly effective when children have fallen behind in school because of poor instruction, illness, or relocation from another district. But if a child has significant specific perceptual processing deficits, basic tutoring in reading or math will not address the underlying causes, irrespective of the corporation's proprietary curricula and instructional methods. The staff at most franchised learning centers is not trained to remediate dyslexia or a profound auditory discrimination problem, and the limited academic (as opposed to diagnostic) testing that is done is not designed to identify these dysfunctions. The parents of a learning disabled child are likely to be dissatisfied and disappointed with the outcome, and may end up taking their child to a qualified educational therapist after investing a great deal of money and achieving very little.

Educational corporations and franchised learning centers are in business to make money, and they are not averse to franchising centers to business people with no formal training in education. The franchise owner is then usually required to hire an educational director who is credentialed or certified and who has been trained by the parent corporation. In many cases the educational director is a former teacher but not necessarily a certified resource specialist. This person is responsible for training the staff, handling parent conferences, testing the children, "selling" the program to prospective clients, and "closing" contracts.

There is nothing intrinsically wrong with going into the educational business to make money. The downside occurs when children are enrolled in programs that do not adequately address the underlying causes of their academic problems. In a for-profit business, the directors have an economic incentive to enroll as many children as possible, and this may cloud their judgment.

Two weeks of training and periodic on-site visits by supervisors from the corporate office cannot transform a credentialed teacher into an educational therapist, and a proprietary program used for all struggling readers irrespective of their particular problems is not the equivalent of individualized educational therapy. A dyslexic child with auditory discrimination and visual sequencing problems requires specialized treatment from a fully trained expert who can select and implement the most effective remedial methods. A center that lacks this professional expertise and enrolls a seriously learning disabled child is acting unscrupulously.

Company-owned and franchised learning centers have assisted many children who have fallen behind. Some centers have excellent enrichment programs that can accelerate students' learning and improve their comprehension, math skills, and study skills. Scrupulous centers will refer the parents of learning disabled children elsewhere. Some may even have a qualified resource specialist on staff.

Let the buyer beware, however. You must ask the right questions, and you should be prepared to scout around until you find the educational program that addresses your child's needs. Catchy TV and newspaper ads do not necessarily translate into first-rate remediation.

The answers supplied by the director of the learning center to the following questions may help you evaluate the educational program.

Questions for the Director of a National or Franchised Learning Center

What are your credentials and background?

Were you ever a teacher, school psychologist, or resource specialist?

What type of testing do you do?

Do you do diagnostic assessments for learning disabilities?

Who does the testing, and what are this person's credentials?

Will the tutor assigned to my child have a degree in special education?

Do you have a credentialed or certified resource specialist on staff?

Do you have an educational therapist on staff who is a member of the Association of Educational Therapists?

Are all your tutors credentialed or certified in this state?

Do all your tutors have classroom experience?

How long does it take you to train tutors in your methods?

Are newly trained tutors supervised for a period of time, or do they immediately begin working with students? If they are supervised, how long does this supervision last?

What are the criteria for assigning students to a particular tutor?

How many children are in each group, and are the children grouped according to age and specific academic difficulty?

Will my child be integrated into a group that has been meeting for some time?

Do you accept children with learning disabilities such as dyslexia, and do you have staff trained to handle these types of problems?

Do you ever combine children with significant learning disabilities and those with subtle problems in the same group?

Do all the children in the group graduate at the same time?

Do you offer individual tutoring? If so, what is the fee for this service?

What methods do you use for building self-confidence?

What are your methods for motivating children?

How do you deal with resistance and counterproductive behavior?

What is your success rate in dealing with the types of learning problems my child is manifesting?

Do your instructors establish contact with my child's teacher and resource specialist, and, if so, how frequently?

Will I be provided with written progress reports?

May I have periodic conferences with our child's tutor, and is there a fee for this service?

If my child misses a session, am I charged? Can she make it up?

Do you require parents to sign a contract for a specified number of sessions? If so, why?

What do you do if a child does not respond to your teaching methods?

What are your criteria for determining that my child has successfully completed the program?

Privately Funded Schools for Special Needs Children

Some parents will conclude that their child's educational needs cannot be met by the programs offered by their local public school. If their child's deficits are severe, highly resistant to standard treatment protocols, or compounded by significant concentration problems (ADD or ADHD) or emotional issues such as chronic irresponsibility, self-sabotaging behavior, and/or learning phobias, they may also conclude that their child requires more than a supplemental after-school learning assistance program.

Some parents may decide to enroll their struggling child in a regular private school that doesn't specialize in providing services for learning disabled children but has smaller classes. Unfortunately, this strategy often backfires, especially when the private school has an accelerated curriculum. The child may become even more frustrated and demoralized as he struggles to keep up with his class. If the teachers in the private school are not trained to work with children with special needs, they will not be any more successful in helping the struggling child than a public school teacher. And if the teachers are used to gifted students and an accelerated program, they may actually be quite intolerant of the child who learns differently.

Some parents of children with learning problems opt for parochial schools. Many of these schools do not have resource specialists on staff or even on-site tutors; in addition, the class size may actually be *larger* than in the public school. Struggling children may be more damaged in such a school than if they remained in their local public school.

Other parents of children with entrenched and significant learning problems may decide that their child should be enrolled in a full-time private school that specializes in working with learning disabled students. This decision can pose many challenges. The first, of course, involves cost. Most full-time day-school programs are very expensive. The tuition may range from $8,000 to $20,000 or more per year, depending on the school and the number of additional services the child requires. Many private schools charge extra for private counseling or psychotherapy, occupational therapy, and speech therapy. Unless the school offers scholarships or a sliding scale, the tuition and associated fees can be prohibitive for many families.

Families that do have the resources to pay the tuition face another challenge: finding a first-rate school near where they live. Most private special education schools are located in larger cities or in the suburbs of such cities. Boarding schools (called "residential schools") offering special education services may be located in nonurban areas, but they are usually even more expensive than day schools and may be located far from the child's home.

Parents may decide that they have no viable alternative and that they must somehow find the money for a private school. They may figure out how to augment their income, tap into their savings, or borrow to pay the tuition. Parents can be quite creative when they're clear about their priorities. Some may offer to work part-time at the school in return for a reduced tuition, and others may look for a second job.

Parents can also request that their local school district pay the tuition for private schooling. This is clearly not an easy sell, but if parents can prove that the local school cannot meet a child's legitimate educational needs, they may prevail. To win the battle they may need to hire an advocate. New provisions in the IDEA act require states to provide a mediator and stipulate that parents must be part of any team that is making a placement decision for their child. If agreement cannot be reached, parents may decide to seek an attorney with experience in school litigation and take the district to court.

Enrolling a child in a specialized private school is no guarantee that a serious learning problem will be resolved, but it does increase the likelihood that a child will overcome his problem or at least learn how to compensate successfully for it. A school that specializes in teaching children with learning problems will adjust its program to the child's needs rather than make the child adjust to the programs being offered. A first-rate school will develop an individualized curriculum that takes into consideration the child's learning deficiencies and is based on his abilities.

Specialized private schools offer an oasis for students with significant deficits. These youngsters are surrounded by other children with similar learning problems. They are taught by teachers who are specialists and who are empathetic. The challenge is finding a good school with first-rate teachers, tutors, educational therapists, and counselors. Such a school will ideally also have a clinical psychologist, psychiatrist, family and child counselor, and/or social worker available to provide emotional support.

Many specialized private schools espouse a particular remediation methodology. Others are eclectic and will use a range of methods tailored to a child's particular deficits. The advantages of a top-notch school for children with significant learning problems are obvious. Classes are small. Teachers are well trained, empathetic, and nurturing. Skills and course content are taught methodically. The children's preferred learning styles are factored into the instructional equation. Supplemental academic and psychological support is often readily available.

Parents considering a particular private school might find it advisable to meet with an educational consultant who is an expert in fitting special needs children with the appropriate program. These consultants are usually very familiar with the curricula, orientation, fees, and educational philosophy of schools in the local community and throughout the nation. (See Independent Educational Consultants Association in the Appendix.) In many instances the consultant will actually have visited the schools being recommended. After meeting with you and your child and reviewing your child's background, test scores, and educational needs, the consultant should be able to suggest a list of appropriate schools. The session could save you a great deal of time and provide you with a wealth of information. The cost of the consultation could prove a very wise investment.

There is an alternative to hiring a private consultant. The National Association of Private Schools for Exceptional Children (NAPSEC) provides a free list of schools that may be appropriate based on age, sex, disability, type of program desired (day, residential, summer), and geographical location. They advise about what to look for when placing a child in a private special education school and inform you about rights as mandated by IDEA (Individuals with Disabilities Education Act). They also provide suggestions about the IEP and other useful information. NAPSEC recommends that parents call each school on the list and ask the questions listed in their booklet. (See appendix for more information.)

Ask the director of the school you're considering if you might speak with the parents of several currently enrolled students and the parents of some graduates. You might also request permission for your child to talk with students and spend a day on campus before actually enrolling. This would allow him to experience the ambiance at the school and allay any fears or misgivings he might have.

Although it would be ideal to have several options when considering a specialized private school, your choices may be limited, especially if you do not live near a city and are unwillng or unable to consider a residential school. If you live in a rural area, you may have no local options.

The responses to the following questions may help you evaluate the private school you're considering for your child.

Questions for the Headmaster or Admissions Director of a Specialized Private School

Could you explain how the program at your school would address my child's learning difficulties?

Do you use specific techniques or are your methods eclectic and generic? Do the methods have a name?

Will you do a comprehensive assessment prior to my child's beginning classes, or will you rely on previous tests to help you determine proper placement and appropriate educational support services?

Is there an additional charge for this testing?

How much is the tuition? Does this fee cover room, board, books, and other normal expenses?

Are there additional fees for services such as counseling, supplemental tutoring, and conferences?

Is there a social worker and/or clinical psychologist on staff?

What are the credentials and background of the teachers?

Have they received any specialized training?

What specialized supplemental support services do you offer, and is there an additional fee for these services?

Is your school accredited?

Are students with different learning problems taught together?

How do you deal with resistance and poor motivation?

What characteristics set your program apart from those of other private schools that specialize in helping struggling children?

If my child continues into your high school program, will she meet the course requirement for admission to college?

What percentage of your high school graduates go on to college?

Do you expect parents to help their child with homework and review material taught in class (questions relevant only for nonresidential schools)?

Do you use specific techniques for improving students' self-confidence?

Are teachers and educational therapists available for periodic conferences?

Does your enrollment include children with emotional and medical problems?

Are children with emotional problems separated in any manner from students who have primarily learning differences?

How is misbehavior handled?

Is your primary mission to remediate my child's learning problems so that she can be reintegrated into a public school program, or do you believe that my child will continue at your school for a protracted period of time?

Nonpublic Schools

A category of schools has been created to serve significantly disabled children with medical, learning, and adjustment problems who cannot be adequately educated in traditional public schools. Designated as nonpublic schools (NPS), these publicly funded private schools serve children with disabilities and special needs. The tuition for these programs is paid by the state and the local school district, and not by parents.

Because the needs of certain children with serious medical, academic, behavior, and attitude problems may not be adequately addressed or may not be responsive to the programs and environment in a public school classroom, school districts are required by law to offer an alternative that fulfills the federal mandate of providing all students with a "fair and appropriate public education" (FAPE). Children for whom it can be clearly demonstrated that public school placement is not appropriate are candidates for referral to an approved state and locally funded nonpublic school.

Generally, nonpublic schools are staffed by highly trained teachers, offer extensive counseling and, when appropriate, individualized medical services, and limit their class size so that behavior and academic problems can be addressed more intensively and more effectively. In actual practice the quality of services can vary from school to school. For this reason the parents of students who are candidates for placement in an NPS must make certain that the proposed program meets their child's needs. Once their child is enrolled in an NPS, parents must then closely monitor the school's educational procedures and social environment to make certain their child's requirements are being adequately addressed. Although it is the IEP team and Local Education Agency (LEA) that actually select and place children in approved special education private school, parents (as now mandated by provisions in the new Individuals with Disabilities Education Act [IDEA]) are considered part of this team and have the right to make their feelings and desires known.

Before a school district will fund the tuition for a child at a nonpublic school, it must be demonstrated at the IEP conference that the student has exceptional educational and emotional needs and that the local school district lacks the resources to address these needs. In some cases the school district will initiate placement in an NPS, and in other cases parents may need to advocate vigorously for their child's placement.

Because of the associated costs, some school districts are reluctant to authorize the enrollment of students in nonpublic schools unless there is compelling evidence that their own programs cannot meet the federal standard established by IDEA. Enrollment of a student in an NPS program represents a loss of income for the district. Money that would normally be sent to the local district for educating the special needs student is diverted to the nonpublic school. As the tuition for enrollment in a nonpublic school is significantly higher than the cost of educating a child in a local school or a magnet school,* the local district is required to make up the difference between state reimbursement and the NPS tuition. The tuition at such schools might exceed $25,000 per year. (The mathematics used to compare educational costs of public schools versus nonpublic schools is suspect. The actual cost of educating a disabled student with special needs at a public school is probably considerably higher than the "officially" cited figure.) The loss of income and the added expense explains the reluctance by some districts to recommend nonpublic school

---

*Some larger school districts designate certain schools for a particular population of students. Intellectually gifted students may be bused to one magnet school, while significantly learning disabled or intellectually challenged students are bused to other schools. The rationale for this practice is that these specialized schools can better serve the needs of students who share similar profiles.

enrollment despite the provision of federal law that mandates a *fair and appropriate public education.*

Children attending nonpublic schools generally have significant disabilities, and some may be highly resistant to learning. Many of these children are also struggling with emotional issues associated with their disability and learning problems.

Nonpublic schools that offer services to children with chronic oppositional behavior may be designated as 504 SED (Severely Emotionally Disturbed) Schools. The designation refers to Section 504 of the Rehabilitation Act of 1973. Changes in the SED classification were enacted in July 1997, and parents of students with emotional problems are advised to request updated literature describing the new criteria for this designation from their local school district.

Some parents may be apprehensive about sending their child to an SED school. These parents may be concerned about their child's being labeled and fearful that children with more serious emotional problems could negatively influence or even harm their child. These concerns and anxieties are understandable.

Unfortunately, there is no ideal solution to this dilemma. If a child is unable to function in a mainstream school because of significant emotional problems, there may be no alternative but to place the child in an SED school. All parents can do under the circumstance is provide emotional support and monitor the child's program closely to make certain it is meeting the child's needs. If it is not, the parents need to communicate their concerns to the school administration about the efficacy of the program.

If parents can afford to provide private supplemental psychotherapy, they should certainly do so. In the interim, parents must make sure that their child attends school, learns how to socializes with other children, acquires academic skills, and assimilates the rules of society. Making certain that the child consistently takes any prescribed medication is also vital to helping the child stabilize psychologically.

Many children with significant emotional problems can learn to function effectively in the world if they're provided with effective counseling; consistent, firm, and loving support from their parents and teachers; clearly defined behavior guidelines; and opportunities to experience success. A first-rate SED program can provide these critical ingredients. Parents must weigh any minuses of an SED program against the potential pluses. Ideally, the pluses will outweigh the minuses.

The director's answers to the following questions may allay some concerns. Ask only those questions that address the relevant issues.

Questions for the Director of a Nonpublic School

Will the school provide regularly scheduled counseling sessions, or will these sessions be scheduled only when there is a crisis?

Will my child participate in group therapy sessions?

What are the credentials of the counselors?

Is there a licensed social worker or marriage, family, and child counselor on staff?

Will I be alerted if there are any problems with my child?

On a scale from one to ten, with ten being severe, how serious are my child's emotional problems in your opinion?

Using the same scale, how serious are his learning problems?

Using the same scale, on average how serious are the emotional problems of the other children at the school? In other words, do their problems generally fall between four and six or between seven and ten?

How would you rate, on average, the severity of the other children's learning problems?

Are all the teaching staff credentialed or certified?

Will my child work exclusively with one resource specialist or one special day class instructor?

How many children are in each class on average? What is the maximum number in each class?

Do you believe my child can be successfully integrated at some point into mainstream classes or will he remain at this school for his entire education?

Will we have periodic conferences with you and the staff?

How often are these conferences scheduled?

Does the school district monitor what is happening in the programs at this school?

Is it possible that funding for the program could be cut off before our child has finished the program? If so, what would happen then?

Will we get any written reports from you other than standard report cards?

Do you recommend any additional after-school programs for our child other than the ones you offer?

Will we be responsible for any portion of the tuition?

Do any of the children at the school have drug problems? How would you handle a situation in which you discover children are taking drugs?

If a child has a problem with drugs, is confidentiality maintained, or are the police informed?

Are children ever expelled, and, if so, what are the criteria for expulsion?

Chapter 11
Specialized Clinicians

Speech and Language Pathologists, Occupational Therapists, and Developmental Optometrists

Coordination

My child has always been uncoordinated. When he was little, we used to find his clumsiness amusing, but we don't anymore. He has terrible balance and can't catch or hit a baseball. He is always chosen last when the kids play. They don't want him on their team, and they make fun of him. I know this humiliates him.

Speech

We thought her pronunciation was cute when she was five. Her funny way of saying her "r's" and her other little quirks seemed charming. She's seven now, and we know that her pronunciation mistakes embarrass her and make her feel self-conscious.

Receptive Language

When he was four, he seemed to understand words like hat and ball. But when I sent him to his room to get something, he would return without it. He couldn't repeat sentences and couldn't associate sounds and words with the objects they represent. I would say the word cow, *and he couldn't link it with moo or the word* dog *with bowwow. We finally figured out that his speech was delayed because he didn't understand what was being said.*

Expressive Language

He understands the concepts, but when he tries to express his ideas, he can't find the words. He stammers and struggles, and the content is often unintelligible. This frustrates him horribly. He is convinced that he's the dumbest kid in his class.

Visual Efficiency

My daughter dreads being asked to read aloud in class. She loses her place, misreads words, and struggles to sound out even familiar words. It is as if her eyes can't see the words properly. When the kids laugh at her mistakes, I know she wants to burrow into a hole and hide.

T he children described above are at risk academically, socially, and emotionally. They are struggling with deficits that require more than the basic services of a school resource specialist.

In an ideal educational system, the problems of these children would be identified in kindergarten or first grade, and special assistance would be provided before academic shutdown and psychological scarring occur. This is precisely what happens in better school districts where early diagnosis and intervention are standard operating procedure. Parents, kindergarten teachers, and first grade teachers may not understand what is causing a particular child to struggle, but they recognize that something is amiss and make certain the school psychologist or the Child Study Team is apprised of the problem. The child is quickly assessed, and deficits in decoding (deciphering spoken and written language), encoding (expressing information in spoken and written language), motor coordination, and/or visual efficiency (seeing letters and words accurately) are identified. An intervention strategy is developed, presented at the IEP conference, and approved. The child is then provided with the appropriate assistance from skilled, trained professionals. The help might involve occupational therapy, speech and language therapy, resource room remedial support, adaptive physical education, counseling, or a referral for vision therapy or psychotherapy.

Unfortunately, the services that struggling children require to prevail over their problems may be denied or offered only after serious academic and emotional damage has already occurred. This denial of services may happen despite federal laws which mandate that aid be furnished for all children with documented special needs (see chapter 7).

In addition to the obvious academic impact of failing to provide assistance for children with special needs, there are also psychological and social consequences. No child wants to be teased by his classmates for his deficiencies. No child wants to feel different or inadequate. No child wants to experience humiliation. Despite what parents may say and do to make things better, the embarrassment and shame can leave a lasting and sometimes indelible mark.

Some children react to feelings of inadequacy by becoming detached or by retreating into a world of daydreams and fantasies. Others respond by acting out aggressively or by acting "weird." These behaviors only exacerbate their social rejection and isolation.

There are also children who resourcefully compensate for their deficits by developing skills and talents in areas that circumvent their disabilities. They may become charming or funny, or they may become star athletes, computer wizards, cartoonists, bookworms, or chess masters. Unfortunately, the number of children who compensate counterproductively for their unresolved deficits far exceeds the number who compensate resourcefully.

Impairments and Dysfunctions

Two types of underlying problems can impede the sequential development of language, vision, motor, and learning skills. The first type is of organic origin and involves measurable deficiencies in brain function, metabolism, physiology, or visual acuity. This type of physiologically based problem is classified as an *impairment*. Hearing loss, poor vision, or cerebral palsy are examples of measurable organic impairments. A severe learning disability may be caused by an organic impairment when the disability is attributable to brain damage caused by oxygen deprivation, disease, trauma, or genetically based defects. In these cases, actual abnormalities in brain physiology and function can be identified by neurologists.

The second type of underlying problem that can affect language, vision, motor, and learning skills is of nonorganic origin and is called a *dysfunction*. Unlike impairments, dysfunctions do not involve neurological or physiological damage that can be measured by medical diagnostic instruments. Most learning problems are of nonorganic origin. The underlying perceptual processing dysfunctions frequently involve deficits in visual or auditory discrimination, memory, and sequencing. These deficits cause children to struggle in reading, math, spelling, handwriting, and language arts.

The diagnostic tools and procedures for analyzing the physiology and metabolism of the brain are becoming more sophisticated and precise, and the line that separates organic impairments from nonorganic dysfunctions is beginning to blur. Although neurologists claim they still know very little about how the brain works, it is clear that they know far more today than they did ten years ago. More refined and precise methods for pinpointing the cerebral origins of impairments and dysfunctions are being developed, and new research findings continually expand our knowledge about how particular areas of the brain function (see chapter 8).

Most common articulation problems (inaccurate pronunciation), gross and fine-motor problems (difficulty with large muscle and small muscle motor coordination), and expressive language problems (difficulty with communication) are of nonorganic origin. Visual efficiency problems (difficulty tracking letters and words accurately) straddle the organic/nonorganic classification, depending on who makes the diagnosis. Developmental optometrists who treat these deficits consider visual tracking and convergence problems to be organic. Ophthalmologists who do not agree that eye muscles can be trained to work more efficiently might debate this contention.

Whether a child's problem is considered organic and defined as an impairment or nonorganic and defined as a dysfunction begs the question. Whatever the origins of the problem, it can erect major academic obstacles and cause significant emotional distress. For children to overcome their difficulties, they must be provided with specialized help from trained specialists.

Speech and Language Pathologists

Children who have difficulty with articulation (a speech problem), decoding skills (a receptive language problem), and language skills (an expressive language problem) require the assistance of a speech and language pathologist. Every public school is required to provide help for children with documented speech and language deficits as an integral part of the special education program. By law, speech and language pathologists must be licensed, certified, or credentialed.

An articulation problem is the most common reason for a child to be referred for speech and language therapy. At specific developmental stages it is common for children to have minor difficulty pronouncing certain letters and words properly. These mispronunciations should not necessarily trigger concern, especially if a child responds to gentle feedback and is able to correct the pronunciation deficits. An important distinction must be made between mispronunciations that occur at specific, developmental stages and articulation problems that persist.

Articulation problems may involve omitting sounds (saying *it* instead of *sit*), substituting one sound for another (saying *pad* for *bad*), or distorting sounds (saying *furog* for *frog*). Other red flags of a speech problem include lisping (difficulty distinguishing the *s, sh,* and *th* sounds) and stuttering (repetition of sounds of words, prolongations, or blockage). When these disturbances in speech rhythm are attributable to physiological or genetic factors, the deficits would be considered organic. Although the origin of stuttering is unclear, the problem appears to be emotionally based, and, as such, is considered nonorganic.

Children born prematurely and those born of multiple births seem more predisposed to speech and language disorders. Most children with articulation and speech problems are physiologically normal, however, and their pronunciation difficulties are usually considered nonorganic.

A relatively small percentage of youngsters with speech problems have organic physiological or neurological abnormalities. Dysarthria is an example of an organically based disability. This condition, which is caused by a weakening in the sound-producing muscles of the face, can result in distortions in articulation. Young children with dysarthria often have difficulty chewing and managing food, and are typically described as sloppy eaters.

Another condition, called oral apraxia, is attributable to a sensory-motor control impairment. Because this control is a requisite to producing intelligible speech, apraxia can be a primary cause of delayed speech.

There is an overlap of neurological systems involved in speech production and motor skills, and articulation problems attributable to weak muscles in the face and mouth (an early symptom is difficulty nursing) are frequently linked to other muscle weaknesses throughout the body. For this reason, speech therapists who treat clients with such conditions often work in tandem with occupational therapists. Although subtle apraxia will not be revealed by neurological EEG testing, children who have speech and language problems attributable to chronic muscle weakness are considered to have an organically based impairment.

Highly effective techniques have been developed to treat persistent articulation problems. These techniques, which may involve several hours of therapy per week, can actually be fun for children. Innovative speech therapy often incorporates practical aspects of daily life and experiences. A child does not necessarily sit at a table; she may work with the speech and language therapist in a kitchen and receive therapy while practicing sequencing tasks such as preparing a snack.

A school assessment for speech and language problems can be formal (testing) or informal (observation), and the procedures vary from district to district. The eligibility criteria for a school speech therapy program may be very stringent, and some children may qualify only for large-group sessions that meet for thirty minutes per week. Parents may need to fight for even this meager assistance.

Some parents whose children qualify for speech therapy in school may decide to supplement this program with private speech and language therapy. They may conclude that the school-based program is not sufficiently comprehensive and effective, or they may want their child to make quicker improvement. Other parents may decide to take their child to a private therapist because they believe their child still requires assistance, despite having ostensibly completed the school-based program.

Private speech therapy has many advantages over in-school programs, including additional time with the therapist, individualized instruction, and an opportunity for intensive parent training. Parents who can work effectively with their child at home and who acquire tools for incorporating speech and language development into all aspects of their child's life can significantly accelerate progress.

The average age of children in speech and language therapy is two years and five months. Younger children are typically referred by a pediatrician for an assessment when they are not babbling, responding to their name, or imitating sounds. Recurring ear infections before age three can be a primary cause of speech and language delays. Parents of children with recurring infections should ask their pediatrician if a referral to a speech and language pathologist is advisable. Surgery to insert tubes into the ears may also be an option.

By age three and a half to four, a child should be able to make most of his verbal messages understood. His words should be minimally seventy to eighty percent intelligible. The following chart indicates the developmental age at which children are expected to articulate specific sounds with relative consistency.*

---

*Reprinted from *Improving Your Child's Schoolwork* by Lawrence J. Greene (Prima, 1996).

Developmental Milestones in Articulation

Age	Sounds
3 years and 5 months	b, p, m, w
4 years and 5 months	t, d, g, k, ng, y
5 years and 5 months	f, u, s, z
6 years and 5 months	sh, l, th, r

If your child cannot produce the sounds correctly at the ages indicated, consult with your pediatrician. If the pediatrician agrees that there may be a problem, request a referral to a qualified speech and language pathologist. If the pediatrician does not appear to be overly concerned and you're still apprehensive, request an evaluation at your local school. Your school district should be able to refer you to a competent private speech and language pathologist if your child is in preschool. You might also look in the phone book. Parents can contact the American Speech and Hearing Association Hotline (see Appendix) and request informative literature and general guidance for selecting a therapist.

Receptive language, or the ability to distinguish particular sounds, is another area addressed by speech and language pathologists. Problems in receptive language are indicated by difficulty assimilating and accurately deciphering the sounds and meaning of spoken language.

When a child's auditory discrimination difficulties are linked to an articulation problem, the need for speech therapy is all the more vital. Serious auditory discrimination deficits, such as not being able to discriminate between sounds *a* and *e* or *p* and *b,* require specialized remediation. If not corrected, these deficits can result in phonics, spelling, and reading problems.

It should be noted that educational therapists also treat auditory discrimination problems using methods such as the Lindamood Auditory Discrimination in Depth Program (ADD). This program can be an effective alternative to speech therapy for children who are not decoding sounds properly. The person teaching the ADD program must be trained, but he doesn't need to be a certified speech pathologist. The Lindamood program, however, is not a substitute for speech therapy when a child has significant speech or language problems and requires highly specialized help with articulation or expressive language.

Language disorders are distinct from speech disorders, although it's possible for a child to struggle with both conditions. To communcate (encode) ideas, emotions, information, and perceptions, a child's brain must be able to process (decode) instantaneously sensory stimuli transmitted as spoken or written words, symbols, pictures, and events. His brain must also be able to process internal sensations such as joy, pain, hunger, happiness, and unhappiness. Once this sensory data is deciphered, the brain retrieves the words needed to communicate reactions to the stimuli. Expressive language is the end product of this complex neurological process.

Children who have difficulty retrieving the words they need to express themselves require language therapy. The less extreme form of this communication disorder is called *dysphasia,* but this term is rarely used. The more extreme form is called *aphasia.* This term is generally used to describe all types of language disorders irrespective of the severity.

Aphasia is often caused by damage in the temporal area of the brain and is considered an organic impairment. A child may have receptive aphasia, expressive aphasia, or both forms of the disorder. It should be noted that school districts often use the term *aphasia* exclusively to describe expressive language disorder. In many districts oral apraxia is included in this classification.

Children whose expressive language difficulties are directly attributable to deficiencies in receptive language struggle to communicate because they don't understand what is being said to them. They also have difficulty comprehending and responding to verbal cues such as "open the door."

Parents usually become aware of expressive language problems when they notice that their child has difficulty interacting with peers or describing what is happening or becomes frustrated when answering questions. Children who struggle with these problems are typically very self-conscious, and their confidence and social skills may be seriously undermined if they are not helped.

Most school districts place children with communication disorders in special programs, which are often in specialized magnet schools that serve the entire school district or the entire county. The resource specialists in classes for children with severe expressive language problems are specially trained, and intensive therapy from speech and language pathologists is an integral part of the intervention program.

Speech and language pathologists are licensed in most states and must have an M.A. degree and a certificate of clinical competence (CCC), which requires one year of clinical fellowship under supervision. Since there are different specialties, it's advisable to ask the therapist if he has specialized in working with children or with adults who suffer from stroke, brain trauma, or other conditions. It's also a good idea to interview the person you're considering and request permission to observe a therapy session before making any commitments.

If you are considering having a private speech and language pathologist evaluate and possibly treat your child, the following questions may help select the most qualified person. The answers to these questions may also help you understand the issues.

Questions for a Speech and Language Pathologist

Have you ever worked as a speech and language pathologist in a public school?

How will the program you are recommending differ from the program in school?

If my child begins to work with you, do you recommend that she discontinue the school program?

Will you establish contact with my child's resource specialist or in-school speech and language pathologist? If so, will you coordinate your efforts?

If I need your help, would you attend my child's IEP conference or IEP review? If so, what is your fee?

How many sessions per week do you recommend, and how long will the sessions last?

If your methods are different from the ones used in school, will this create confusion for my child?

Do you ever recommend small group sessions?

What are the advantages and disadvantages of small group versus private instruction?

Do you expect me to reinforce what you are teaching at home?

How do you suggest I handle resistance to receiving speech therapy?

Can you give me an idea of how long the program will last?

May I periodically observe one of my child's therapy sessions?

How will I be able to gauge the effectiveness of the therapy?

Do you believe my child can completely overcome her speech and language deficits, or will she simply learn how to compensate for them?

What are your fees?

Are any contracts required?

Is it possible that my medical insurance will cover all or part of your fees? If so, will you help me complete the necessary paperwork, and is there a charge for doing so?

Will we have periodic conferences, and is there a charge for these conferences?

Will you provide a written report summarizing any testing you've done, and will you provide subsequent progress reports?

Occupational Therapists

Children with significant gross motor, fine motor, and balance problems are at risk for being teased and ostracized by their classmates. A child with poor motor and eye-hand coordination are typically unable to catch or hit a softball or kick a soccer ball without tripping. Their clumsiness and poor athletic skill can cause them profound embarrassment.

Children are acutely aware of how athletically competent they are and how other children feel about them. They want to fit in, be popular, do what the other kids do, and be respected. The child who is invariably chosen last, who hears kids moan when they have no alternative but to have him on their team, and who knows that his errors on the playing field could cause his team to lose the game is going to feel terrible.

Unless the child with chronically poor coordination is evaluated and treated by a specialist (that is, an occupational therapist who has been trained to diagnose and treat motor and balance problems), he could develop an aversion to all activities that require motor coordination. He may become convinced that he's a hopeless klutz and decide that he can't learn how to swim, ski, ride a bicycle, or play baseball. This conclusion could cause him to avoid many potentially pleasurable experiences.

Difficulty crossing the midline is one of the primary indications of a motor coordination problem. This line separates the right and left hemispheres of the brain and bisects the corpus callosum, the bridge of nerve fibers that connect the two hemispheres. Being able to cross the midline describes the capacity to coordinate both sides of the body efficiently. The term *midline* is somewhat contrived, however, because there is no actual physiological midline in the body. Rather, the term is used as a functional description. Children with a midline problem have difficulty skipping and often crawl homolaterally (pushing forward the arm and leg on the same side of the body) as opposed to bilaterally (pushing forward the opposite arm and leg). A child with a midline problem might actually transfer the chalk from one hand to another when she crosses the midline while writing a sentence on the chalkboard. Visual efficiency deficits (decoding words accurately when reading and writing) are also frequently linked to mid-line problems.

Other indications of a coordination deficit include difficulty riding a bicycle or pumping one's legs on a swing. These symptoms are red flags of a possible *sensory integrative dysfunction*. Children with sensory integrative deficits may also be under- or over-responsive to movement and/or touch. In severe cases they may be *tactilely* defensive (hypersensitive to being touched). Toddlers manifesting this hypersensitivity may have difficulty making the transition from baby food to solid food because of the new sensations involved in chewing.

Children diagnosed with significant motor coordination problems attributable to an underlying sensory integrative dysfunction are candidates for occupational therapy. The term occupational therapy is somewhat misleading because it suggests a rehabilitation program for someone who has had an accident and is being retrained to return to work. Although some OTs work with patients who have sustained trauma, others specialize in working with children who have coordination deficits. The goal of this therapy is to improve central nervous system processing so that a child can use sensory data more efficiently and effectively.

The first premise of sensory integration therapy is that children who have an irregularity or disorder in brain function will experience varying degrees of difficulty in development, behavior, and learning. The second premise is that this condition is treatable with highly focused, systematic training.

Some children with coordination deficits and sensory integrative dysfunction have trouble with timing and sequencing of motor tasks, such as catching the ball in the glove with both hands and then taking the ball out of the glove and throwing it. Others have poor muscle tone in the upper, lower, or entire body. They may compensate for this lack of tone by locking their body into a position or wrapping their legs around the legs of a chair. Some become toe walkers or have problems pushing and pulling. Others rush through tasks because they lack the motor control to go slowly. And others have problems with rhythm or with timing, ordering, and organizing their behavior.

Conditions directly linked to motor coordination deficits and sensory integrative dysfunction include the following:

Dyspraxia: difficulty planning and making purposeful motor movements (a child playing hopscotch may remain poised in one square trying to make his muscles work correctly in order to hop to the next square)

Apraxia: profound difficulty making purposeful motor movement; this is a more extreme form of dyspraxia

Dystaxia: difficulty coordinating muscles (a child who knows what his muscles should do when he tries to do a jumping jack but whose muscles cannot function in a smooth, coordinated fashion)

Ataxia: profound muscle coordination deficits; this is a more extreme form of dystaxia.

The effects of fine-motor deficits can be seen in poor muscle control in the hands and fingers. Children with these deficits typically have poor handwriting. They frequently grasp a pencil incorrectly, and their letters, numbers, and words are misshapen. When drawing a picture of a person, these children often leave the fingers off in much the same way that children with listening problems often leave the ears off their pictures. By so doing, the children are unconsciously signaling that fingers or ears are not important parts of their anatomy and are only marginally functional.

Children with significant motor deficits also frequently have problems with proprioception. The proprioceptors are located in muscles, joints, and ligaments throughout the body and send signals to the brain about where the body is in space. When the proprioception system is not functioning efficiently, children become disoriented and have difficulty with motor tasks. A child who cannot close his eyes and bring his hands together so that they are aligned or walk a straight line has a proprioception problem.

Listed below are some symptoms that may indicate a sensory motor integration dysfunction. If your child is showing these symptoms, make an appointment to speak with a school administrator, school psychologist, school OT, or someone in the special education department. The school personnel may also have observed the same symptoms. If not or if the school is reluctant to acknowledge that your child might have a problem that needs to be identified and treated, request and, if necessary, insist that your child be scheduled for an OT assessment.

Symptoms of a Possible Sensory Integration Deficiency

- high sensitivity to movement, touch, sights, or sounds
- reduced reaction to movement, touch, sights, or sounds

- clumsiness
- poor posture
- stiff and awkward movement
- carelessness
- high distractibility
- overactivity (hyperactivity) or underactivity (hypoactivity)
- high impulsiveness and lack of self-control
- difficulty making transitions
- speech, language, or motor skill delays
- academic delays
- physical weakness
- difficulty manipulating objects such as scissors
- inability to tie shoes (age 5 and above)
- continually dropping things
- difficulty using eating utensils
- uses furniture or other people for support
- holds head in hands
- poor grasp of pencil (stiffness, tenseness, awkwardness, or unusual style)
- writing is off the line
- fear tasks involving motor movement

Carelessness, distractibility, hyperactivity, hypoactivity, impulsiveness, academic delays, and lack of control may also be attributable to attention deficit disorder, specific learning disabilities, or speech and language deficits. This overlap of symptoms underscores the need for a diagnostic assessment.

The preferred diagnostic test for children ages 4.0 to 8.11 (fourth grade, zero month, to eighth grade, eleventh month) is the Sensory Integration and Praxis Test (SIPT) developed by the late Dr. A. Jean Ayres, an occupational therapist trained in neuroscience. Occupational therapists who administer this standardized, nationally normed test must be certified by an association called Sensory Integration International. The assessment which consists of seventeen subtests, evaluates how children possess sensory information. The subtests can identify deficits in the following areas: tactile function (touch), proprioception (awareness of body in space), vestibular function (balance), bilateral integration (using both sides of the body), sequencing (doing tasks in order), motor planning (planning how to do unfamiliar motor tasks), motor-free visual perception (perceiving objects in space without moving them), and visual construction (copying a block pattern). Many OTs who administer the SIPT schedule two one-hour testing sessions, especially in the case of younger children.

Occupational therapists have different levels of training. Some have a basic B.A. degree in occupational therapy, others have an M.A., and a few have a Ph.D. Occupational therapists and occupational therapy assistants are certified by the National Board Certification of Occupational Therapists (NBCOT). All states have some form of regulation of occupational therapists, but this varies from state to state. Consequently, parents seeking these services should verify the educational background, clinical training, and experience of the person they are considering and should ask this key question: "Have you received advanced training in sensory integrative therapy?" Not all OTs have received this training.

In some school districts occupational therapy is offered as an educational service under the aegis of the special education program. These districts may employ a full-time OT who provides services in several schools, or they may have several part-time OTs on staff. Some districts contract with agencies to provide OT services on an as-needed basis.

Most districts will not pay for a SIPT because this two-hour-long computer-scored test can be expensive. Depending on the geographical area, the fees can range from $400 to $600, which includes a written report and a conference with the parents to explain the results.

To reduce costs, most school districts use a more informal method for identifying children who require occupational therapy services. The OT typically makes a classroom observation and discusses the child's performance and needs with the teacher. The OT might then administer a standardized test such as the Beery-Butenika Developmental Test of Visual Motor Integration to confirm if there are substantive deficits. The results of the OT's assessment would be presented at the IEP conference, and the school administrators, school psychologist, parents, occupational therapist, and special education personnel would then determine if the child qualifies for occupational therapy services.

Private occupational therapy services can be expensive. Depending on your geographical area, the fees may range from $70 to $110 for a fifty-minute private session. Although the potential return on this investment may be excellent, many families cannot afford these fees. Some medical insurance programs cover a portion of the occupational therapy assessment and treatment fee when a child is referred by a physician. Parents should check their health services manual or ask the medical benefits department about guidelines and procedures for reimbursement.

Certain HMO- and PPO-affiliated physicians may be reluctant to make a referral for occupational therapy, especially when the medical insurance company discourages these referrals. Some pediatricians, family physicians, and pediatric neurologists may also be skeptical about the value of sensory integrative therapy, but these doctors are the exception rather than the rule.

If you decide to hire a private occupational therapist to evaluate and possibly treat your child, the following questions may help select the most qualified person. The OT's answers may also help you understand the issues.

Questions for an Occupational Therapist

Before Scheduling Assessment

Are you certified to administer the SIPT (Sensory Integration and Praxis Test)?

Are you certified as an OT?

What degrees do you hold?

How many hours of clinical training did you have before you began working with children without supervision?

Have you had advanced training in pediatric neurodevelopment and sensory integration therapy?

What is the fee for the assessment?

During Conference After SIPT Has Been Administered

How many sessions do you believe will be required before we see improvement?

Will occupational therapy eliminate my child's coordination problems, or is the goal to help my child compensate for these problems?

How many sessions do you believe will be required before the sensory integration deficiencies are resolved?

Will the gains transfer to the classroom? To the playing field?

How does balance affect learning?

What does central nervous system processing mean? How do deficits in this area affect learning?

Can sensory integration therapy improve reading, auditory processing, and visual tracking skills? If so, how does the therapy achieve this?

Do you see any relationship between sensory motor deficiency and inattentiveness and poor concentration?

Do you believe that this therapy will help my child focus better in school and resolve his attention deficit disorder?

How will I know if the program is working?

Will you establish contact with my child's teacher?

Will I receive written updates from you?

Will we have periodic conferences to discuss progress? If so, do you charge a fee for these conferences?

What are the fees for the program?

Are we required to sign a contract?

Is the testing and the treatment ever covered by medical insurance? Is there a copayment?

Do I need a referral from a pediatrician to qualify for reimbursement?

Does insurance cover a certain number of sessions?

Developmental Optometrists

Children who have difficulty using their eyes effectively usually struggle to read with accuracy. This can make reading a nightmare and cause children to become frustrated, demoralized, and reading phobic.

To read with precision a child must be able to gather visual information quickly, efficiently, and comfortably. The skills required to do visual tasks include tracking (accuracy when reading), focusing (clarity when shifting focus to different distances), eye-teaming (comfort and stamina when using both eyes to perform a visual task), and proper reaction to light. In order to read, a child must be able to move his eyes smoothly from left to right. The eyes must also be able to converge and focus. Muscles behind the eyes control the lateral or horizontal movement as well as the convergence or teaming of the eyes.

Developmental and behavioral optometrists specialize in treating children who have visual inefficiency. Using a procedure called vision therapy, they systematically train the child's eyes to function more effectively. The premise of vision therapy is that the skills needed for gathering and using visual information are sequentially developed during childhood. Although children are not born with these skills, most naturally acquire the visual efficiency needed for reading with fluency. Unfortunately, some do not; their reading is labored, inaccurate, and uncomfortable, and their visual problems often lead to a reading disability.

When the muscles that control the movement of the eyes are not working efficiently, children make repeated mistakes as they read. Because their eyes move erratically, they may skip over words and omit letters, syllables, words, and even entire phrases. They may also make word transpositions (*was* may be perceived as *saw*) and reversals (*b* may be perceived as *d*, and *p* may be perceived as *q* or *g*). Word transpositions are classified as a kinetic tracking deficit, and letter reversals are classified as a static tracking deficit. These deficits, which are considered symptoms of dyslexia, can have a devastating effect on a self-conscious, emotionally fragile first grader who is learning to read. As the child struggles to perceive the words accurately, he will probably be aware that the other children are waiting impatiently for their turn to read. They may laugh or even groan at his mistakes and impulsively attempt to correct him. The net result is shame, humiliation, and negative associations with reading.

It is relatively common for teachers and resource specialists to refer dyslexic children for vision therapy. In fact, some school districts have a policy of referring all children who have symptoms of visual inefficiency and/or dyslexia for an evaluation by a developmental optometrist. Nevertheless, there is still great controversy among professionals about the causes, diagnosis, and treatments for dyslexia.

Although developmental optometrists treat dyslexia, they are certainly not the only professionals who specialize in dealing with this disorder. Resource specialists and educational therapists have their own treatment protocols. Their methods might incorporate programs such as Slingerland, Orton Gillingham, and Lindamood.

Despite the popular usage of the term, dyslexia affects only between three and nine percent of the school population, depending on the criteria being used to diagnose the condition. Some professionals contend that fifteen percent of the school population is learning disabled and that eighty percent of these l.d. students have dyslexia. This means that twelve percent of all students are dyslexic.*

Dyslexia has traditionally been considered a disorder in the brain's language center that interferes with the ability to isolate and manipulate sounds. Developmental optometrists have argued for some time, however, that dyslexia is linked to visual inefficiency, and recent research appears to confirm that there is a visual component in the disorder. Using a functional MRI to take a picture of the brain while people are thinking,

---

Learning Disabilities, Lifelong Issues (Cramer, Shirley, Brooks Publishing Co., Baltimore, 1996) page xxvii.

Stanford University scientists have been able to measure brain activity in dyslexics and nondyslexics. The fMRI was able to sense the ratio of oxygen-rich and oxygen-depleted blood in different regions of the brain, thus providing a map of neural activity. Heightened neural activity increased the amount of oxygen-rich blood flowing to the region where it occurred. By having dyslexic and nondyslexic subjects respond to visual stimuli, the researchers were able to record differences in the activity level of the brain's primary visual center.

The population in the Stanford study was small, and the preliminary research leaves many questions unanswered. It does provide a window into the actual neural mechanics of dyslexia, however, and this may ultimately lead to earlier diagnosis and more effective intervention methods.

Many developmental optometrists contend that letter reversals associated with deficits in directionality (knowing right from left), laterality (utilizing both sides of the body efficiently), spatial organization (perceiving relationships between objects that are seen), and concentration can be dramatically improved with methodical vision training. Although some ophthalmologists are skeptical about these claims and believe the muscles that control the eyes cannot be trained, more and more physicians are now acknowledging the evidence of gains in reading accuracy after children receive vision therapy.

The first step in determining whether your child is a possible candidate for developmental optometry is to question her teacher and make your own observations about her reading efficiency. Is she reversing numbers and letters, flipping over words (*was* becomes *saw*), omitting syllables, leaving out words or phrases, and/or continually losing her place when reading? Does she complain that the words are dancing around or flowing like a river across the page? The inventory below gives additional symptoms. Many of the symptoms in this inventory were derived from the *Educator's Checklist of Observable Clues to Classroom Vision Problems* published by the Optometric Extension Program Foundation of Santa Ana, California.

Symptoms of Visual Inefficiency

Complaints When Using Eyes While Seated at a Desk
- red, watery eyes
- eyestrain
- eyes become quickly fatigued

- headaches
- print blurs after reading for a short time
- words move, jump around, run together

Eye Movement (Ocular Motility)
- head turns when reading across page
- loses place often when reading
- needs finger or marker to keep place
- frequently omits words, especially small ones
- slopes words and sentences up or down when writing
- rereads or skips lines

Eye Teaming Ability
- omits letters, numbers, or phrases
- misaligns digits in number columns
- squints, closes, or covers one eye
- tires quickly when reading
- reading starts out strong, then fades
- tilts head to extreme while working at desk
- consistently poor posture while sitting at desk

Eye-Hand Coordination
- poor orientation in placement of words or drawing on paper
- writes crookedly, has difficulty spacing, cannot stay on ruled lines
- misaligns horizontal and vertical series of numbers

Visual Perception
- mistakes words with same or similar beginnings
- has difficulty with right and left directions
- fails to recognize the same word in the same or next sentence
- fails to visualize what is read silently or orally
- subvocalizes while reading silently

Refractive Status (Nearsightedness, Farsightedness, Focus Problems)
- comprehension and interest when reading quickly diminishes
- blinks excessively at desk or when reading but not elsewhere
- holds book too closely
- closes or covers one eye when reading or doing desk work

- makes errors in copying from chalkboard
- makes errors in copying from textbook to notebook
- squints to see chalkboard or asks to move nearer
- rubs eyes during or after short periods of visual activity
- blinks to make writing on chalkboard clearer after desk task

Physiological Changes While Reading
- vision worsens
- posture changes (tilts head, turns, or eyes are positioned closer to the paper)
- behavior changes (stress-related emotional changes)

If the words dance or flow, your child may have scotopic sensitivity syndrome, a unique and relatively rare condition in which the brain has difficulty decoding words printed in black on a white background. Some vision therapists claim that this sensitivity to black/white contrast can be overcome by use of pastel-colored lenses or colored overlays.

The Irlin Test, developed by the Irlin Institute, is designed to identify scotopic sensitivity. If the text detects the condition, it will also indicate what color is the most effective visual antidote for the problem. Pink lenses may be the best tint for one child, while blue lenses work best for another. Other environmental interventions for the disorder include reducing light levels, using natural lighting whenever possible, avoiding fluorescent light, using indirect lighting, printing on colored paper, and using colored acetates on overhead projectors. It should be noted, however, that some professionals are very skeptical about the claims made by the proponents of tinted lenses.

Your observations about your child's reading difficulties can be critically important. Does your child become frustrated whenever she reads? Is she becoming increasingly demoralized, reading phobic, and defensive about her reading errors? Is she convinced she'll never be able to read as well as her classmates? Is she failing to make reading progress in school and in the resource program? Are her teacher and resource specialist becoming exasperated by her lack of progress? If the answers to these questions are yes, you have legitimate cause for concern.

If your child is diagnosed as having a visual inefficiency problem, you must decide if you agree with the diagnosis, believe vision therapy can help your child, and are prepared to pay for the treatment. Vision therapy is costly, although some children with less severe deficits make relatively quick progress. A few sessions combined with parent instruction at home may be sufficient. It's more typical, however, for a vision therapy program to consist of twenty-four to thirty-two sessions over a three- to six-month period. Each session is generally forty to sixty minutes. The duration of the program is determined by the severity of your child's visual dysfunction, how well you are able to work with your child at home, and how well your child responds to the intervention.

The fees for vision therapy may range from $60 to $120 per hour depending on geographical area. Although some insurance companies cover vision therapy, many do not. If your child's pediatrician or ophthalmologist questions the value of vision training, the physician may not be willing to make a referral or support your claim for medical insurance reimbursement.

Some developmental optometrists do the actual vision training themselves. Others employ vision therapists who work under their supervision. Parents are usually given periodic progress updates, and, with their permission, copies of these reports may also be sent to the child's teacher and resource specialist. Most developmental optometrists request that the teacher and resource specialist complete a profile or inventory that provides specific information about the child's academic strengths and weaknesses. After several months they may be asked to complete this inventory again so that the vision therapist can gauge progress.

Recognizing that visual inefficiency problems often overlap with other learning problems, some developmental optometrists have tutors, occupational therapists, and/or educational therapists on their staff to provide supplemental remedial help. Others refer children to private providers when additional services are required. With a concurring referral from a medical doctor, some of these services, such as occupational therapy and speech and language therapy, may be covered by medical insurance, although the current trend is for medical providers to dissuade physicians from making these referrals and to decline reimbursement for any services that are not considered urgent.

The litmus test for the efficacy of vision therapy is improved visual efficiency in the classroom and when doing homework. The vision therapist may report gains, but if these gains do not translate into more accurate reading and copying skills, parents could legitimately question the practical value of the therapy.

As indicated above, educational therapy is often a critical adjunct to vision therapy. If a child has a visual efficiency deficit that is compounded by auditory memory, auditory discrimination, and visual memory deficits, it is unrealistic to expect that the reading problem can be resolved exclusively with vision therapy. The vision therapist might work on one aspect of the child's problem, while an educational therapist, speech and language pathologist, occupational therapist, or clinical psychologist focuses on other aspects. Fortunately, children rarely require all these interventions concurrently.

Some parents may be apprehensive that a vision therapist, or any type of therapist for that matter, might have a hidden agenda and may diagnose a problem simply to generate income. Certainly, there are unscrupulous professionals in every field. The best defense is to rely on recommendations from people whose judgment you trust. Ask the vision therapist to supply the names of clients whose children had problems similar to those of your child. Make a point of calling these parents and asking whether they were satisfied with the outcome and whether their child is now doing well in school. You might also request a referral from the pediatrician, teacher, resource specialist, school psychologist, parent support groups (see Appendix), or principal.

If you're considering having your child evaluated and possibly treated by a developmental optometrist, the following questions may be of value. The developmental optometrist's answers should help you understand the issues and treatment methods.

Questions for a Developmental Optometrist

Have you been specifically trained in developmental optometry?

Are you a member of the College of Optometrists in Vision Development or Optometric Extension Program?

Will you be testing my child in the following areas: near/far focusing, eye-teaming ability, visual motor integration, visual memory, vision perception, and light sensitivity syndrome?

Will we get a written report summarizing the results of your tests?

How severe is my child's visual inefficiency on a scale of one (subtle) to ten (severe)?

How long do you expect my child to remain in the vision therapy program?

Will you personally be doing the vision therapy, or will you have an assistant do the training exercises?

What are the credentials of the assistant, and how many patients has he treated?

Do you charge by the session, or is there a fee for the entire program?

What are your fees?

Are there any contracts?

If my child misses a session, can it be made up?

How much contact will we have personally with you during this training?

Will you or the assistant provide periodic updates about progress?

Will we be able to have periodic conferences with you even though your assistant is doing the vision therapy? If so, is there a charge for the conference?

Will you personally establish contact with my child's teacher and resource specialist, or will your assistant do this?

How can we gauge progress?

How much time should we spend each evening doing visual training exercises with our child?

What do we do if he is resistant to the program at your office?

What do we do if he is resistant to our efforts to work with him at home?

If our child resists working with us at home, will this defeat the program? If not, how much longer will it take to successfully complete the program?

What should we do if our child refuses to go to a session?

Can you refer us to other professionals such as educational therapists and tutors if our child requires additional assistance?

Dealing Effectively with the System

Dealing with entrenched, bureaucratic school districts can be a nightmare, especially when you want something the district is not willing to give. As previously stated, you can file a formal protest with the district and request an impartial hearing, if your child has special needs that you believe are not being addressed. A district's refusal to authorize speech and language assessment or to provide occupational therapy, adaptive P.E., or speech and language therapy services is sufficient grounds for filing a protest. (Please note that developmental optometry assessments and vision therapy are not services that schools are obligated by law to provide.)

Federal law mandates that schools provide special education services for learning disabled children. Your child's rights are specifically protected by the following: Individuals with Disabilities Act (IDEA), Section

504 of the Rehabilitation Act, Americans with Disabilities Act (ADA), and Fair and Appropriate Education Act (FAPE). Federal law also mandates procedures for registering a protest and for exercising the right of due process (see chapter 7).

Procuring special education services for your child could require skillful negotiation. For this reason you may want to have a professional advocate represent your child. If you cannot reach an agreement, your last resort is to take legal action.

Dealing with the bureaucratic rules and guidelines of insurance companies can be as infuriating as dealing with a school district's bureaucratic policies and restrictive eligibility criteria. If you can clearly demonstrate that your child requires supplemental private speech and language therapy, occupational therapy, or other types of preventative therapy, and your medical insurance provider refuses to cover the charges for private assistance, then the state (the payee of last resort) is required to pay for the intervention. Since these programs may be funded under different departments of the state government, you may need to do some detective work to identify the umbrella agency in your state. This could be the Department of Health Services, the Department of Mental Health, the Department of Developmental Services, the Department of Education, or some other agency.

Part VI
Defining Your Role in the School Success Equation

Chapter 12
Assessing the Effectiveness of the Intervention Program

You cannot assume that everything is going well because your child is enrolled in a school resource program or is receiving help from a tutor or educational therapist. You must continue to provide oversight. Even highly competent academic specialists with the best of intentions can and do make mistakes. When these professionals are less than competent, the risk of a flawed intervention strategy increases dramatically. Some of the most common blunders made by educators include:

• implementing the wrong strategy: "Trust me, a whole language approach will work with a dyslexic child."

• giving flawed advice: "Your son is not going to become responsible unless you back off and let him sink or swim on his own."

• recommending simplistic solutions: "Your child is reading below grade level and struggling because he's immature. I recommend having him repeat fourth grade."

• overlooking the obvious: "I never noticed he was squinting when he reads."

• losing objectivity: "I've used this teaching method successfully for twenty years. It will work with your child. You need to be patient."

• rationalizing: "Perhaps she's not making academic headway because of intellectual limitations."

• making cost-expedient decisions: "We have to move your daughter out of the resource program. We know she's not up to grade level yet, but we have other children with more serious problems who need help."

• lacking insight: "Your son will outgrow his reading problems. Boys often start out poorly. Be patient. He simply needs to become more motivated."

To repeat a basic postulate of this book: You must trust your intuition. When you hear advice, explanations, and proposals that do not appear logical and do not jibe with your own perceptions, you need to seek another professional opinion. You must do your research, examine your options, weigh the pros and cons, critically evaluate professional recommendations, and select an appropriate course of action.

It's also your job to oversee your child's progress. If your daughter is in a resource program or special day class, you must find out if the goals defined in the IEP are being met. You need updates about her improvement and about the problems she's facing. After allowing adequate time for your child to respond to the remedial program, be prepared to intervene if she's not advancing. This is not meddling. This is being a responsible parent.

Your goal is not to attribute blame but to find solutions. Once the obstacles are accurately defined, you and the key school personnel can work together to devise the most effective remediation strategy. If you conclude that the school cannot meet your child's needs, then you must seek solutions outside public education.

Improvement Curves

Children's learning problems are remediated at different rates, and substantive improvement can hinge on many factors, including the:

- accuracy of the diagnosis;
- efficacy of the learning assistance program;
- severity of the child's learning problems;
- child's attitude and motivation;
- teacher's attitude, skills, insight, and empathy;
- talents of the resource specialist, educational therapist, and/or tutor;
- support of parents;
- child's conviction that she can prevail.

Initially, some children do not appear to be making any headway at all, and then all of a sudden they break through and start to make significant gains. Other children make slow but steady academic progress almost immediately after beginning a resource program or private educational therapy program. And then there are children who make more erratic progress. They surge ahead, plateau, and perhaps regress slightly before they begin a new cycle and start showing progress once again. Within a four-week time frame, they may accelerate, decelerate, cruise, stop, and zoom.

These three common improvement curves can be represented graphically:

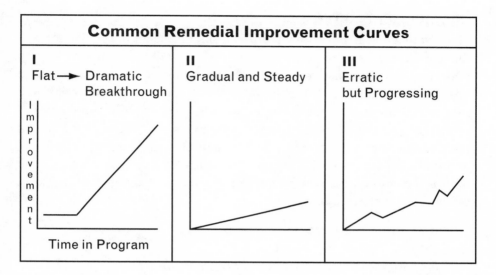

Common Remedial Improvement Curves

I	II	III
Flat → Dramatic Breakthrough	Gradual and Steady	Erratic but Progressing

Please note that two other learning curves haven't been graphically represented because they're relatively rare. A small number of children who receive resource assistance or educational therapy make dramatic gains from virtually the first day of the program. In the other learning curve, the child makes no progress whatsoever despite the best efforts of the resource specialist and/or educational therapist. A child whose learning curve remains flat for an entire year is a candidate for a comprehensive reassessment by the IEP team. Even if a reevaluation would not normally be scheduled for another year or two, parents should insist on the assessment when it's clear that their child is not progressing. Their intervention strategy may need to be modified, or it may need to be scrapped altogether and a new plan devised. A child with a protracted flat learning curve is also a candidate for an evaluation by a developmental pediatrician, pediatric neurologist, neuropsychologist, or the multi-disciplinary staff at a medical school–affiliated diagnostic center (see chapter 8). There may be neurological components to the learning problem that might explain the lack of progress. Once these components are identified and factored into a reformulated intervention strategy, the child may begin to progress.

Because it's likely that your child fits into one of the three common learning curves, your understanding the demands and implications of each category can be of critical importance. Your reactions could significantly affect the outcome of your child's remediation program.

Improvement Curve I

Since your child is not showing improvement during the initial stage of this curve, this category could be the most emotionally challenging for you. Acutely aware that your child appears to be stuck, you may begin to despair. You tell yourself that there could be a major breakthrough in a week or a month, but you wonder whether you should be patient and remain supportive of the intervention plan or sound the alarm. You can see that your child is becoming increasingly frustrated and demoralized, and you know the clock is ticking. You realize that you can't afford to sit tight if the program is clearly ineffectual. Before making any decisions, ask yourself these questions:

Have I given the remedial program a reasonable amount of time to demonstrate its effectiveness?

Is the program meeting the defined objectives?

Are there any mitigating factors or upheavals, such as a divorce, a death in the family, or a move, that could explain my child's limited academic progress?

Does my child have a good rapport with her teacher, resource specialist, tutor, educational therapist?

Could my child's limited progress be linked to concentration deficits, and should I discuss this possibility with the pediatrician?

Could there be any emotional problems such as excessive anxiety, fear, anger, or active or passive resistance that might be impeding my child's progress?

Does my child need supplemental private remedial help?

Do I have confidence in the teacher's and/or resource specialist's skills?

Is there any possibility that my child is taking drugs?

Does my intuition tell me to allow more time for my child to make improvement, or should I discuss my concerns now with the teacher and/or resource specialist?

Should I consult with a developmental pediatrician, educational therapist, educational psychologist, or clinical psychologist?

If you conclude that you need to examine the effectiveness of the remediation strategy, you might want to ask the resource specialist the following questions in a nonhostile manner. Your tone will play a major role in how they are perceived. The attitude you want to convey is one of cooperation. You are saying, "I want to work with you on the problems. To support your efforts, I need an update, and I need to know about the glitches. Then we can brainstorm solutions."

Are we still on target for achieving the IEP objectives?

Have you encountered any unexpected obstacles?

Do you have any theories about what's impeding my child's progress?

Have you observed any emotional red flags that might warrant a psychological assessment?

Do we need to adjust or fine-tune the remediation plan?

Do we need to make major modifications in the plan?

Should I consult an educational psychologist, educational therapist, developmental pediatrician, or clinical psychologist?

Is there anything additional I should be doing to help my child at home?

Are you observing excessive resistance from my child?

Is more testing appropriate?

Do you believe that my child can overcome her learning problems, or do you believe that she must learn how to compensate for them?

When would it be reasonable to expect some improvement?

Given what has happened to date, do we need to revise the goals for my child, and what revisions would you recommend?

What should we do if there is no improvement within the next three months?

If you're dissatisfied with the answers you receive from your child's teacher and/or resource specialist about the lack of progress, you are justified in requesting an IEP conference to discuss your concerns. You're entitled to request this interim meeting even though the regular meeting may not be scheduled for many months.

Let everyone at the IEP conference know that you are reasonable and realistic but that you're also very concerned about your child's lack of substantive improvement. If they agree that there hasn't been adequate progress, discuss how the program might be modified or completely reformulated. If they don't agree, request interim testing so that you can compare your child's current scores with those recorded when she began the remediation program.

In their effort to develop a more effective learning assistance plan, the school special education personnel may suggest various changes, such as:

- using a different instructional strategy or materials;
- increasing the amount of time spent with the resource specialist;
- assigning your child to a different resource specialist;
- placing your child in a different group within the resource program;
- transferring your child from a resource program to a special day class.

If you agree with their suggestions, make sure the administration understands that you expect the changes to be made as soon as possible. Inform them that you will be monitoring the program closely and that you may request another meeting in a few months to assess the effectiveness of the new strategy. Also let them know that you want to be told about any unexpected glitches.

If the school personnel argue that your child will ultimately make progress if everyone stays the course, you can either accept or reject their conclusion. If you agree to continue the current remediation strategy, establish a target date for reassessing your child's skills.

Improvement Curve II

This improvement curve is undoubtedly the most gratifying for parents. Your child's progress may be slow, but it's steady and measurable. There are tangible and visible rewards for the effort being expended by your child and the school personnel. If your child is fortunate enough to fit into this improvement curve, you should make a point of acknowledging and praising the people who are providing assistance. And, of course, you should also make a point of lavishly acknowledging and praising your child for her effort and progress. This affirmation is vital! Your child will know you are proud of her, and this will make her proud of herself and motivate her to continue working diligently.

Given your child's improvement, there aren't a great many issues that need to be raised. After expressing your appreciation to your child's teacher and resource specialist, you might ask, "Is there anything that might be done to speed up the progress even more?" When asking this question, be clear that you're not expressing dissatisfaction. Explain that your only concern is to get your child up to grade level as quickly as possible.

Improvement Curve III

This learning curve is like riding a roller coaster. For a while your child appears to be soaring, and then she either plateaus or regresses, often without any plausible explanation. The reasons for these performance, effort, and attitude swings can be elusive. The causes may involve emotional issues, fluctuations in her capacity to concentrate, chemistry between the teacher or resource specialist and your child, social factors, and/or subtle hard-to-define neurological issues. The inconsistencies, peaks, and valleys are disconcerting and do little to inspire confidence that the learning problems are being resolved. The critical issue when examining your child's performance swings is whether she has made academic gains six months after starting the resource program.

It is certainly advisable to discuss your child's erratic learning curve with her teacher, resource specialist, tutor, and/or educational therapist. They may or may not be able to explain what is happening. In addition to the previously cited explanations, mood swings, family issues, puberty, peer pressure, and many other factors can also affect a child's school performance. It could be beneficial to discuss the performance swings with your child, especially when she is in a plateau or regression phase. The explanation may be quite simple: She's having a problem with her best friend, or she likes a boy who is spurning her. Or she might tell you that she is going through a stage when it is very difficult for her to concentrate in class. Her explanations may or may not suggest solutions. To encourage her to participate actively in finding a practical solution to her erratic school performance, you might want to use the DIBS problem-solving method described in chapter 14.

Explain to your child that you would prefer to see consistent headway. You might even show her what Improvement Curve III looks like when plotted on a graph and brainstorm methods with her for evening out the peaks and valleys so that the progress is steady and more predictable.

Chapter 13
Motivating Your Child to Set Academic Goals

What you get is what you want . . .

A key trait differentiates most achieving children from their less academically successful classmates: They establish personal performance goals, and when they attain them, they quickly replace them with new ones. Good students define their short-term and long-term objectives, focus their intellectual and emotional energy on getting from point A to point B to point C, and forge ahead with a sense of direction and a clarity of purpose. They are motivated and willing to work hard because they covet the payoffs their efforts produce: pride; acknowledgment from parents, teachers, and peers; and expanded career options.

Goal-directed students strive for one hundred on the next spelling test, a math homework paper with no mistakes, and As on the next report card. This drive to excel propels them whether they're playing baseball, practicing karate, playing an instrument or doing gymnastics. They want the home run, the black belt, the highest score, or the perfect floor routine in gymnastics. They continually test themselves and push themselves to the next level of performance to find out how good they are and how much they can achieve.

Sometimes an achieving child's goal-setting process appears conscious and willful, and sometimes it seems as if the child isn't thinking about the outcome of his efforts. This appearance is deceptive. The targeting procedure can be so ingrained that the youngster may unconsciously establish goals without even being aware of it. Aiming for a perfect score on the spelling or math test just feels natural to him.

Do some children have an innate goal directedness? Certainly, inherited personality and temperament traits can affect school performance. Children who are intellectually capable, even-tempered, and meticulous are more likely to be successful in school than those who are distractible, chronically disorganized, and frenetic. The desire to achieve is a complex equation in which parents, family values, and cultural influences play important roles. Parents who encourage their children to establish personal goals, plan ahead, manage time, work diligently, suspend immediate gratification, and achieve scholastically tend to have academically successful children. Children whose parents communicate that they value and respect scholastic accomplishments will generally be motivated to learn and will covet their parents' acknowledgment of their successes. Having friends who value achievement also plays a significant role in a child's orientation.

Self-confidence is another critically important factor in the academic achievement equation. Children who learn efficiently feel confident about their ability to succeed academically. Perceiving themselves as intelligent and capable, these youngsters aim for the best grades and, ultimately, the best colleges and the most challenging careers.

Scholastic achievement is in effect a recycling loop. Good skills and goals produce success. Success produces self-confidence. Self-confidence produces more success and stimulates motivation. Stated differently, the more a child accomplishes, the more she'll believe in herself; the more she believes in herself, the more she'll want to continue achieving. Just as chocolate, pistachios, or potato chips can become "addictive" for some people, so, too, can the acknowledgment and feelings of pride and potency associated with achievement. Achieving children don't want to stop because it feels good, and they want more!

A critically important behavioral and attitude shift occurs when children get caught up in an achievement/self-confidence loop. They become convinced not only that they *can* succeed but also that they *deserve* to succeed. This same attitude is a characteristic of professional football teams that have winning seasons year after year. The players, coaches, and management become accustomed to winning and expect to make it to the Super Bowl every January. A loss is almost inconceivable.

If your child is not winning in school, she's also enmeshed in a loop, but hers is one of nonachievement. Poor skills and no goals produce little success. And little success produces little or no self-confidence, which, in turn, produces little or no success. In other words, the more she fails, the less she'll believe in herself, and the less she believes in herself, the less willing she'll be to reach for the brass ring.

Nonachievement is also a recycling loop, but the payoffs feel awful. Unfortunately, children can become resigned to the payoffs.

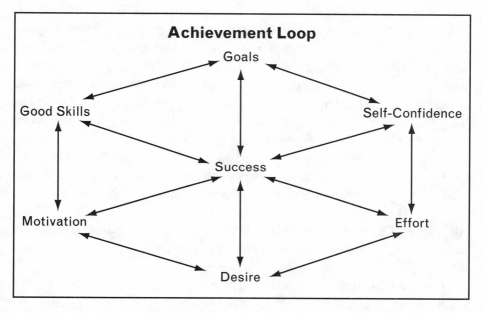

Achievement Loop

Goals

Good Skills

Self-Confidence

Success

Motivation

Effort

Desire

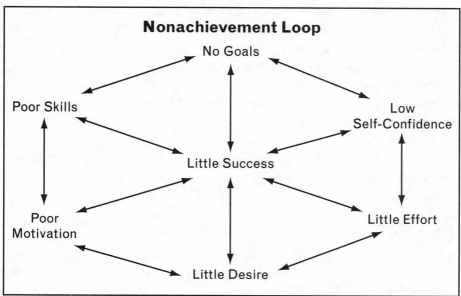

Nonachievement Loop

No Goals

Poor Skills

Low
Self-Confidence

Little Success

Poor
Motivation

Little Effort

Little Desire

Because of endless negative school experiences, many struggling children conclude that their academic situation is hopeless. They expect to lose, and this expectation becomes self-fulfilling. Negativity breeds failure, and failure breeds more negativity. In time these children often decide that they don't deserve to win. This unconscious mind-set can produce tragic consequences. Defeated learners who are convinced that they're undeserving of success are not going to establish challenging performance goals. Their defense mechanisms will not only impair their chances of overcoming their learning problems but will also spill over into other areas of their lives. A child enmeshed in an nonachievement loop may not be willing to try out for the softball team because she has concluded, "I'd never make the team anyway, and even if I did, everyone would laugh at me when I strike out or make an error."

Of course, some struggling youngsters react differently to their academic plight. These children realize that they have other areas in which they can excel. Rather than allow themselves to become demoralized, they develop their competencies and target performance goals in these skill areas. Their artistic or athletic talents can be an important psychological oasis that sustains them during the academic tribulations they experience in school.

The value of goal-setting is relevant to all aspects of a child's life. Because many academically demoralized children are not goal-directed, it's vital that parents encourage them to establish personal performance goals and strive for excellence in nonacademic areas. By orchestrating opportunities for their child to experience the thrill of achievement, they can help rebuild their child's self-confidence. Even minor victories in swimming, drama, tennis, art, or basketball can provide emotional sustenance.

The ultimate objective is for the goal-setting procedure to transfer to the academic arena. This generally happens when the struggling child realizes she's making progress in her remediation program and concludes that with sufficient effort she can succeed in school. (Specific methods for teaching children how to establish goals are explored later in this chapter.)

Learned Helplessness

The child who has poor self-confidence and no goals or aspirations is a prime candidate for shutting down academically. If she concludes that her school situation is hopeless, she may become actively resistant to learning and refuse to do her work.

A struggling child may also become passively resistant and codependent. She may become so reliant on her parents that she's unable to study or complete assignments unless one of them continually sits by her side. In an extreme case she may actually expect her parents to do her work for her. This manipulative behavior is called *learned helplessness,* and it is commonly used by children who are convinced they cannot do the work expected of them.

The parents of a helpless child are caught in a dilemma. If they refuse to provide help, their child could become increasingly frustrated, demoralized, and school phobic. If they do provide help, their child could become emotionally and academically dependent.

Figuring out how much help to offer a struggling child is tricky. To make this determination, you must have input from her teacher and resource specialist about what she can realistically be expected to do on her own. You also need clear guidelines from them about the amount and specific types of at-home assistance you should provide. Should you correct errors or simply indicate where the errors are and let your child attempt to correct them? Should you help with essays and reports, and provide feedback about grammar and spelling? Should you study with your child for tests? If your child is receiving after-school assistance, how much homework help should the tutor or educational therapist provide? Should you discuss with the teacher the advisability of modifying the difficulty level and quantity of at-home assignments so that your child can do her work more independently?

The challenge of deciding how much help to provide is compounded by the fact that the teacher and the resource specialist may not know how to handle the issue. Clearly there are psychological components to a child's learned helplessness that the school personnel may or may not fully understand. "Don't rescue her. Let her sink or swim on her own" could be good or disastrous advice. The same applies to the recommendation, "Go ahead and help her."

Yes, struggling children require protection, supervision, and assistance, but they don't benefit from being smothered with help. Excessive, unwarranted concern and parental involvement in schoolwork sends a message to children that they can count on being rescued throughout their lives.

This can cause them to become helpless. Children who learn to be helpless could remain forever reliant on their parents.

That your child may legitimately need help with her homework is not the issue. The issue is the extent of your help. You must ask yourself: Are you at school almost every day? Are you actually doing your child's homework? Are you continually making excuses for her? Do you talk in terms of doing *our* homework or having difficulty with *our* spelling test? Are you telling your child that it is her responsibility to do her work but then rush to her rescue every time she becomes slightly frustrated? These behaviors are red flags that tell you to examine your own attitudes. Whether you are driven by guilt or fear, these counterproductive feelings are clearly working at cross purposes with helping your child take responsibility for her problems.

The way in which you wean your child from codependency is critically important. Although allowing yourself to be manipulated is certainly not in your child's best interest, pulling away the safety net too quickly could be psychologically devastating for an insecure child. To extricate yourself, you must develop a plan that is implemented in increments. Totally refusing to help could traumatize your child and cause her to become emotionally or academically immobilized. You might say to your child, "I'm going to show you how to do this two-place division problem. We'll practice a few problems together. Then I'm going to let you do the rest on your own. After you finish the assignment, I'll check over one or two problems to make sure you're doing them correctly, but I will not look at all of them. It's your responsibility to check them over and find mistakes."

Struggling, insecure children often place themselves in a protective zone that reduces their risks but also restricts their development. If you have been manipulated into guarding the gates of this zone and cannot change your relationship without feeling guilty, you should consult a mental health professional who is experienced in dealing with learned helplessness and dependency issues (see chapter 9).

Assessing Your Child's Goal Orientation

If your child is not goal-oriented, it would be helpful to recognize the specific attitudes, behaviors, and deficits that are responsible. The following inventory is designed to do this. Later in this chapter your child will complete a similar inventory, and her responses will serve as a catalyst for discussion and a springboard for doing a series of goal-setting activities with her.

Goals Inventory

Code: 0 = Never; 1 = Rarely; 2 = Sometimes; 3 = Often; 4 = Always

My child defines specific short-term and long-term goals in school. ___

My child understands that carefully planned interim steps are
needed in order to attain a long-range goal. ___

My child's goals are realistic. ___

My child takes the time to plan ahead. ___

My child is able to establish priorities. ___

My child is able to budget and manage time effectively. ___

My child can develop a workable plan for attaining his/her goals. ___

My child understands the principles of cause and effect. ___

My child considers potential consequences before acting. ___

My child is willing to suspend immediate gratification to attain his/
her objectives. ___

My child bounces back from setbacks. ___

My child analyzes problems and learns from mistakes. ___

My child can handle frustration. ___

My child persists despite encountering difficulty. ___

My child likes challenges and likes to test himself/herself. ___

My child believes he/she can prevail. ___

My child is proud of his/her accomplishments. ___

My child establishes a new goal to replace an attained goal. ___

Total Score ___

If the score for your child is above 45, she is adequately goal-directed and strategic. If the score is below 45, your child would benefit from completing the inventory shown above.

Using Goals to Motivate

Because struggling students almost always have negative associations with academic achievement, it's understandable that they would resist establishing personal performance goals. For these youngsters, establishing goals in school seems pointless.

Although your child may have diminished self-confidence and painful associations with learning, it's critical that you do everything possible to encourage her to define reasonable and attainable academic goals. If she is afraid of failing to attain the objectives, limit how far you urge her to stretch initially and measure progress in small, tentative steps.

Be prepared for your child to rebuff your efforts at first, whether actively or passively. The immediate challenge is to help her overcome imprinted negative expectations and establish the habit of targeting attainable short-term objectives, such as a C+ on the next spelling test, or math homework with no more than five errors. By encouraging her active involvement in goal-setting, you're inviting her to play a participatory role in overcoming her academic deficits. This can dramatically enhance her motivation and progress.

At the same time you must beware of urging your child to set unrealistic, unattainable goals. If she cannot attain the objectives she establishes or cannot even come close, she'll become even more demoralized. You must have a realistic picture of your child's current skill levels in each academic area if you are to play an active and positive role in orienting her toward establishing goals. The information you acquire about your child's skills from the classroom teacher and standardized test scores should serve as the baseline. If the information is not current, you'll need to collect more recent data.

Let's say your child is in the third month of fifth grade (5.3), but her achievement test scores indicate she's reading at the level of third grade, ninth month (3.9). In this situation it would be unrealistic for her to target getting a B in reading on her next report card unless the teacher is willing to factor effort into grading.

It would be ideal if all teachers considered effort when grading children whose skills are significantly below grade level. Giving these students a D or an F when they're trying to catch up is unfair and insensitive. The alternative is to give them no grade or give them a special grade based on different criteria until they're able to compete with their classmates on a level playing field (see accommodations in chapter 7).

Once you have baseline information about your child's current skills, meet with her teacher and resource specialist, and get their input about realistic goals and time lines for attaining these goals. Is it reasonable for your child to target a B in math on the next report card? If she works hard, could she realistically expect a C on her next book report? If not a C, what would be reasonable, given the level of her reading and language arts skills?

It's now time to talk with your child. It would be a good idea, however, to do some planning first. Try to identify someone your daughter admires.

Is it an athlete? Her pediatrician? A famous naturalist? A singer or an actor? Her grandmother? Her gymnastics or ballet teacher? She'll probably be able to name someone. If not, suggest a person who seems to embody talents and personal qualities that you believe your child values. Once you've selected this individual, try to find an anecdote about the person or a story about someone similar who decided when she was very young to become an astronaut, a pilot, a professional skater, or a surgeon. You may need to go to the library or search the Internet for biographies of exceptional people who had firm goals and who then overcame adversity to attain these goal. Stories about well-known people such as Albert Einstein, Leonardo da Vinci, Winston Churchill, George Patton, Thomas Edison, Nelson Rockefeller, Bruce Jenner, Cher, or Tom Cruise may be especially effective because they all struggled with learning problems.

Without preaching to your child, discuss the biography of the selected person. Explore what the person's goals were and the impact these goals had on the development of that person's character. Don't do all the talking! Make every effort to get your child to talk and think and feel. You might ask, "It says here that Thomas Edison had learning problems when he was a child. Do you think kids might have made fun of him when he was in school? How do you think he felt if they teased him? Do you think he knew he was intelligent, or do you think he lost faith in himself? Do you think he had to work hard to create electricity and invent the lightbulb? Were these projects his personal goals? Did they inspire him and drive him on to overcome his learning problems?"

Listen to what your child says. If she doesn't seem enthusiastic, don't be discouraged and don't take it personally. Let the ideas percolate. She may be afraid of trying and failing again. Be sensitive to her fears and self-doubts, but also be enthusiastic and encouraging. "I bet that with some extra help and effort, you could get a B in science. Perhaps not on the next report card, but maybe on the one after that. Go ahead. Aim for it! You may not make it the first time, but many famous and successful people didn't achieve the goal the first time they tried, either. The important thing is that they kept trying and ultimately got what they wanted."

It would be a good idea to have your child complete her own goals inventory. Emphasize that you want her to give honest answers and not the ones she thinks you might want. Also make certain she understands that this is not a test. You may need to explain some of the concepts and vocabulary found in the inventory to children below fourth grade.

My Goals Inventory

I have specific goals that I want to achieve. ____

My goals are realistic. ____

I know what grade I would like in each of my classes. ____

I believe I have the ability to get what I want in school. ____

I can figure out a plan for reaching a long-term goal. ____

When I have a project or assignment, I figure out what steps to take
to reach my goal. ____

I can schedule my time so that I can get my work done. ____

I can establish priorities (do steps in order of importance). ____

I'm patient as I work toward reaching my goals. ____

I try to learn from mistakes and setbacks. ____

I enjoy learning new skills. ____

I enjoy improving my skills. ____

I'm willing to continue working hard even if I have a problem or
suffer a setback. ____

I'm willing to continue working hard even if I become frustrated
or upset. ____

I like challenges. ____

I feel good when I successfully handle a challenge or overcome a
problem. ____

I feel proud when I achieve my goal. ____

When I achieve a goal, I establish a new goal. ____

Total ____

A score below forty-five indicates your child is demonstrating attitudes and behaviors that are having a negative impact on her school performance. Her responses probably indicate specific deficits in the areas of goal-setting, prioritizing, planning, time management, and reacting to setbacks.

In discussing the inventory with your child, you could explain the results as follows: "A score below forty-five indicates that you could use some help in establishing goals and planning ahead. I'd like to work with you on an activity that can help you improve your skills in these areas."

Beware of Minefields

When working with your child on the following activity, there are comments you should avoid at all costs. The following statements may be accurate, but they are guaranteed to trigger resentment and either *passive resistance* (procrastination, irresponsibility, blaming, forgetfulness, non-cooperation) or *active resistance* (rebellion, lying, rule-breaking, cheating, delinquency, drug use).

> You need to have more self-discipline.
> You need to plan better.
> You need to be better organized.
> You need to pay more attention to details.
> You need to be more serious about what you are doing.
> You need more follow-through.
> You need to stop putting things off.
> You need to establish goals and achieve them.

Be prepared for defensiveness and resentment if you take a negative tack in discussing goal-setting with your child. A judgmental or derogatory tone will not only be ineffective but it will also be counterproductive when used with insecure, defensive children. Before your child can relate to statements about planning and establishing goals, she needs to understand the concepts. Basic cause-and-effect and time-management principles can be unimportant to a child who simply wants to get through the school day without being pummeled emotionally.

A far better alternative to delivering lectures and sermons is to make planning, organization, and time-management concepts meaningful by using concrete examples that demonstrate how to establish goals and become organized. First, you want to show your child how to use these skills, and then you want to provide opportunities for her to practice and evaluate the results of her goal-directed behavior. Your purpose is to encourage your child to experience firsthand the benefits of establishing personal performance objectives. Once she realizes that there are pleasant payoffs for the new behavior, she will be less resistant.

The experience of success can often defuse the struggling child's resistance to ideas or proposals that involve major behavioral or attitude changes. Unfortunately, attempting to orient children toward goals and orchestrate success doesn't always produce this outcome. However unhappy the defeated, insecure child may be with the status quo, she may still be unwilling to step outside of her comfort zone. The idea of becoming successful can actually be quite threatening to a child who is used to failure. To avoid having to having to deal with new and unfamiliar situations, the child may unconsciously sabotage herself and, in so doing, defeat her parents' efforts to help her become goal-directed. Establishing goals and attaining them would require a dramatic alteration in her self-perception and her modus operandi. The child who is so completely entangled in her own nonachievement web requires professional counseling.

Specific methods for teaching your child how to establish goals are found on the following pages. But first, time management must be examined because this skill is part of goal-setting.

Time Management

To get any job done, children must be able to manage the clock. If a child's short-term goal is to finish her homework before it gets dark so that she can go skating with her friends, she must be able to correlate the work that needs to be done with the time that is available. Many children with learning problems lack this planning skill. One explanation is that struggling children are so preoccupied with basic academic survival that they don't have the opportunity to focus on acquiring higher-level organizational, planning, and time-management skills.

The antidote to this deficiency is obvious: Practice some time-management activities with your child. For example, you might ask your daughter how much math homework on average she thinks she needs to do to attain her goal of a B. If her estimate seems unrealistic and she doesn't understand why, you could set up a meeting with her teacher. He could clarify how much homework and studying he expects students to do each evening. You and the teacher might also help your daughter understand that she must budget extra time until her skills improve.

Once your child understands what is expected from her in math, you can ask her to estimate how much time she needs to budget in order to complete the homework in her other subjects (a short-term goal). List the subjects on a piece of paper and write down the time estimates. After your child completes each assignment, have her note how much time the assignment actually required. With practice the discrepancies between the estimated and actual times should be reduced.

Encourage your child to add up the estimated times for all her subjects before she begins her homework each evening. This will help her think about her nightly obligations in advance and develop more precise and efficient time-management skills. She might discover that she had budgeted sixty minutes each evening for homework when she should have budgeted eighty minutes.

Combining Goal-Setting and Time Management

The way you introduce the academic goal-setting/time-management procedure can be of critical importance, especially if your child is defensive and/or resistant to change. Suggesting an experiment may reduce this resistance. You might say something like this: "Let's do an experiment. You've been getting help with your schoolwork, and it seems to be paying off. I'm very proud of your progress. I think it's time for you to begin targeting some specific goals in school. Tell me what grade you would like to aim for in each subject on your next report card. Let's make these your long-term goals. We'll write down the target grades and see how close you come to achieving them when you get your report card. Since this is only an experiment, you don't need to feel anxious. There won't be any consequences for not reaching your goal, although it certainly would be great if you did. Let's make the goals realistic so that you are not setting yourself up for disappointment. You can always raise the standard for the next grading period."

My Academic Goals

Subject	Most Recent Grades	Grades Desired on Next Report Card
Reading		
Science		
Math		
Social Studies		

"The next step in the experiment is to keep track of your grades and establish short-term goals. These goals are stepping-stones to where you want to be. It's just like using stepping-stones to cross a stream that's too wide to jump across. Your goal is to get to the other side, and the stones allow you to get there. The stepping-stones in school might be a certain grade you want on your next spelling test or math homework assignment.

Let's look at how you can keep track of your performance. The form below is simple and doesn't require much time to complete. You could tape the chart to the refrigerator door.

"During the next two weeks, choose a specific goal for each week and specific goals for each day. On Monday morning or Sunday evening, you could record your weekly goal on the form. Then each day you could record a specific goal you wish to achieve for that day. At the end of the day, check 'yes' or 'no' to indicate if you achieved your daily goal. On Friday, check 'yes' or 'no' to indicate if you've attained your weekly goal.

"To make the experiment more interesting, why don't you estimate how much time you think you'll need to achieve your short-term goal. After achieving each goal, you'll indicate how much time was actually required. In this way you will be able to see if your estimates were accurate.

"If you find this experiment helpful, you'll probably want to continue using it for the rest of the school year. We could design forms for you to use the rest of the school year. If you use them, I bet your work and grades will improve!"

Week 1

		Yes	No	Time Estimated/ Time Required
Weekly Goals				
Each Subject:	Get C or better on math quiz.	___	___	___/___
	Get a B on book report.	___	___	___/___
	_____	___	___	___/___
	_____	___	___	___/___
	_____	___	___	___/___
	_____	___	___	___/___
Daily Goals				
Monday				
Each Subject:	Get minimum of C on math hmwrk.	___	___	___/___
	_____	___	___	___/___
	_____	___	___	___/___
	_____	___	___	___/___
	_____	___	___	___/___
	_____	___	___	___/___

Tuesday
Each Subject: _____ ___ ___ _____/_____
                _____ ___ ___ _____/_____
                _____ ___ ___ _____/_____
                _____ ___ ___ _____/_____
                _____ ___ ___ _____/_____
                _____ ___ ___ _____/_____

Wednesday
Each Subject: _____ ___ ___ _____/_____
                _____ ___ ___ _____/_____
                _____ ___ ___ _____/_____
                _____ ___ ___ _____/_____
                _____ ___ ___ _____/_____
                _____ ___ ___ _____/_____

Thursday
Each Subject: _____ ___ ___ _____/_____
                _____ ___ ___ _____/_____
                _____ ___ ___ _____/_____
                _____ ___ ___ _____/_____
                _____ ___ ___ _____/_____
                _____ ___ ___ _____/_____

Friday
Each Subject: _____ ___ ___ _____/_____
                _____ ___ ___ _____/_____
                _____ ___ ___ _____/_____
                _____ ___ ___ _____/_____
                _____ ___ ___ _____/_____
                _____ ___ ___ _____/_____

Make this exercise fun! Don't be critical if your child doesn't attain her goals or misjudges the amount of time required. Suggest that she make adjustments in her goals and brainstorm a strategy for dealing with obstacles and miscalculations.

Sharing your own experiences with setbacks and frustration when you didn't attain a goal right away can have a profound impact. For example, you might say, "When I started my new job, I wanted to get a promotion within a year. It didn't happen and I was very disappointed, but I decided not to give up. I kept working hard, and I finally got the promotion a year later. I then set a new goal and began working hard to earn the next promotion. I made an important discovery: Sometimes we don't get what we want right away. We need to keep plugging. I have complete faith in you. Once you have a plan and believe in yourself, I'm certain you'll achieve your goals."

Creating an Achievement Loop

You must help your child identify:
- baseline skills;
- short-term goals;
- long-term goals;
- an acceptable fall-back position.

You must teach your child how to:
- record daily performance/accomplishments;
- plan ahead;
- set goals;
- schedule and manage time.

You must provide:
- acknowledgment/affirmation for achievements;
- appropriate assistance.

Your child must be willing to:
- work diligently;
- establish new goals.

Discussing Progress with Your Child

It's important to involve your child in the process of assessing the efficacy of her remediation program. You might want to get together ever couple of weeks and plot her progress on a graph similar to the sample improvement curves on the next page. You could use grades on tests, teacher comments, homework scores, your observations, and your child's own observations as criteria for determining how much progress was made that week. After discussing how to weigh each of these components, record progress in each academic subject on the graph. You child's personalized improvement graph might look like this:

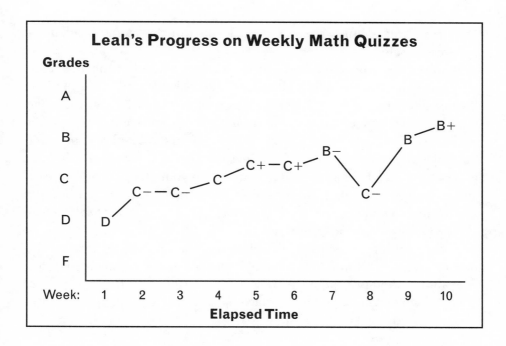

Leah's Progress on Weekly Math Quizzes

Helping your child chart her own improvement in academic skills, test scores, and classroom performance, and enthusiastically acknowledging her gains could become an enjoyable weekend family ritual. During these interactive sessions, a performance falloff should be examined nonjudgmentally. You could brainstorm ideas about how to deal with specific problems and accelerate progress. The goal is to make the graphing procedure pleasurable, informative, engaging, and motivational. The goal is *not* to find fault. Problems should be examined analytically and objectively. Your child's active participation in the remediation and charting process can play a key role in accelerating improvement and reducing performance swings. As your child sees progress and begins to prevail over her learning problems, there should be a significant boost in her self-confidence.

Show the plotted improvement graph to your child's teacher, tutor, and resource specialist. Explain that the graph has become a family project. See if they concur with your conclusions about your child's progress.

When you create an improvement graph with your child's active participation, you're clearly communicating to the school personnel that you're concerned, involved, and supportive of their efforts and your child's efforts. You're also saying that you're committed to monitoring your child's academic situation so that you can determine if adequate progress is being made.

It would certainly be beneficial to create a second graph that plots improvement in your child's attitude, effort, behavior, planning, follow-through, organization, and time management. Gains in these motivational and strategic thinking areas are as vital as improvement in specific skill areas. The "data" that you assess and plot on the graph will be based on subjective observations, but this does not negate the motivational benefits of the procedure. Your goal is to stimulate your child's desire to learn and to convince her that she is capable of learning. You can tell her that she is capable and bright until you're blue in the face. *In the final analysis, she must come to this conclusion herself.*

The overriding principle is to help everyone understand that they're part of a team. This united front—child, teacher, resource specialist, tutor, educational therapist, parents—creates a powerful force that can prevail over virtually any educational obstacle.

Chapter 14
Providing Support and Building Morale

Morale plays a pivotal role in determining whether your child ultimately overcomes his learning difficulties. That some children with learning disabilities maintain good morale is quite remarkable. Despite the academic obstacles they face, these youngsters continue to plug away resolutely and never lose their motivation to learn and achieve.

Unfortunately, most children with learning problems have poor morale. The never-ending efforts to cope with school and the daily disappointments and humiliations wear down their resolve and deplete their energy. Lacking confidence in themselves and their abilities, and unable to sustain their effort in the face of seemingly overwhelming odds, these youngsters soon accept that they are destined to either fail or perform marginally in school, and they aspire to little more than getting through each day.

The emotional fallout from learning problems assumes various forms. Some demoralized children withdraw and become shy, self-conscious, and overly sensitive. Some act out their pain and frustration through misbehavior, aggression, resistance, or rebellion. And others camouflage their upset and anger by resorting to passive aggression, such as teasing, tattling, or causing others to get into trouble, or passive resistance, such as procrastination, irresponsibility, or learned helplessness. These children often sabotage themselves and, in the process, make life miserable for everyone who cares about them.

Whether a child with learning problems exhibits his distress passively or actively, his behavior and attitudes must inevitably have an impact on the entire family. In many families the child's plight becomes the focal point of concern, and his parents find themselves increasingly occupied with helping their child solve his problems. The impact of the struggling child's school difficulties affects everyone in the family. Because the child is the focus of so much attention, his siblings may react by becoming increasingly resentful and by acting out in order to get their fair share of notice.

Although a child's learning problems and negative behavior can certainly contribute to family stress, parents must guard against attributing all family disharmony to the child and his learning difficulties. It's too easy to say, "If only Kevin would get his act together in school, we could be happy." Family discord is a complex phenomenon that is often linked to multiple causative factors. As previously stated, to blame the child exclusively for the discord is to make him, in psychological terms, the *identified patient*. This reproach can be simplistic and unfair and can hinder problem-solving.

Building Morale

Children possess good morale when they believe their efforts can produce success. Conversely, they possess poor morale when they are convinced that no matter how hard they try, they will fail.

Just as some children appear to be born more even-tempered than others, some children may possibly inherit a great capacity for emotional resilience. These youngsters are survivors; they refuse to give up when faced with great adversity. Although it is possible that genetic factors may be responsible for their willingness to keep battling despite the odds against them, it's more likely that a child's emotional resiliency is attributable to other factors. The most significant of these is supportive parenting.

The struggling child who is acting out may not consciously realize it, and certainly would not admit it openly, but he desperately wants his parents to resist his manipulations and be undeterred by his misconduct, excuses, and feigned helplessness. He wants his parents to insist that he work hard and prevail over the challenges. Their constancy provides him with strength, resolve, and security. Their unflagging faith in him encourages him to believe in himself. Their positive expectations cause him to have positive expectations. This is the essence of good morale.

The struggling child requires parents who are demanding but not unreasonable, supportive but not smothering, and involved but not interfering. Providing for these seemingly contradictory requirements is easier said than done, and many emotionally depleted parents may be tempted to throw in the towel. But they can't give up. If they are not steadfast and determined, how can they expect their child to be?

Parents need to monitor their child's behavior. They must listen carefully to his words. They may be hearing a continual litany of negative statements: *I hate my teacher! Why should I do this stupid homework? The other kids are mean and are always teasing me. Why do you always take the teacher's side? I don't need to know this dumb stuff. Everyone thinks I'm retarded. I hate school. Sometimes I just feel like killing myself.* These statements reflect pain, and they must be heeded.

Wise parents realize their limitations. When their intuition and observations tell them that their child is profoundly unhappy, excessively fearful, or extremely insecure, they seek professional help. Wise parents also realize that disregarding danger signals could have disastrous repercussions. Chronic sadness, social alienation, depression, explosive anger, continual oppositional behavior, conduct disorders, antisocial behavior, flawed judgment, excessive risk-taking, continual lying, suicidal tendencies, and self-medication with street drugs are flashing red lights that parents must notice.

The symptoms that indicate morale-depleting emotional distress range from mild to severe. Standard, run-of-the-mill emotional upsets associated with poor school performance (occasional frustration, moderate discouragement, and episodes of resistance) do not require a trip to a psychiatrist's office unless the behavior gets worse. These issues can often be handled at home by parents who are firm, supportive, insightful, empathetic, patient, and consistent.

Gathering information is the first step in addressing the issues affecting your child's behavior and attitudes, and undermining his school performance and morale. Begin by analyzing the situation objectively. Make a list of symptoms and conduct that concern you. Request input from the teacher and your child. Attempt to identify the underlying causal issues. Solicit advice from the pediatrician, the school psychologist, and any others who have expertise. Then prioritize the list of problems and start out by attempting to resolve the most critical issue. If it becomes clear after a reasonable period of time that you're not making significant inroads in redirecting the counterproductive conduct and attitudes, and in building your child's morale, acknowledge that you need help and seek the best mental health professional you can find.

Rules, Guidelines, Expectations, and Self-Concept

Children feel most secure when they know the rules of the game. Whether it's softball, cards, tennis, or checkers, they want to be certain about how the game is played and how points are scored or taken away.

Be prepared for a paradoxical reaction when you impose regulations on your child. Although he may actively or passively resist your guidelines, at an unconscious level he desperately wants you to say, "I will not accept this. I know that you can write this report legibly. I've seen the quality of your work when you make the effort and take the time. I insist that the assignment be neat and readable."

By insisting that your child conform to a reasonable standard, you're telling him that you believe in him. You're telling him that he has the ability to do what you expect. He may challenge your standards and expectations to see how you'll respond and how committed you are. Despite this periodic testing of your resolve, he wants to know what you demand in terms of behavior, effort, responsibility, and values.

The need for clearly defined rules is especially critical during the years when your child's self-concept is being formed. Without rules, your child will become confused, unsure, and willful, and he'll continue to test the limits until you finally and unequivocally define them for him.

Children with learning problems may lack academic self-confidence because of their struggle to master the content of their courses, but they can still possess healthy self-esteem. Self-esteem and self-confidence are not synonymous, and a child can have one without the other. A child's self-esteem is the composite of his feelings about himself and represent his unconscious assessment of his value as a human being. If the child likes and respects himself, he will have good self-esteem. The child's unconscious feelings can be seen in the self-image he projects. A child with a healthy self-esteem projects a positive self-image. He will figure out the math problem, climb to the top of the rope in his physical education class, master the knots he's being taught in scouting, and qualify for the junior varsity swimming team. He'll run for class president, initiate a conversation with the cute girl in his math class, and get an A on his science project. He has faith in his ability to prevail over any challenge and attain any personal performance goal that he sets.

The foundation for self-esteem is formed before birth and is comprised, on the most fundamental level, of inherited temperament, intelligence, and aptitude. During the first four years of a child's life, the superstructure is mounted on this foundation. These building blocks are composed of family values, child-rearing practices, life experiences, reasonable, clearly communicated parental expectations, fair and consistently applied rules, and social relationships. The mortar that holds the blocks together is provided by the child's parents. It's a blend of love, appreciation, encouragement, affirmation, clearly defined limits and boundaries, and a sense of security. When the foundation is solid, the building blocks well formed, and the mortar strong, a child develops self-esteem and a positive self-image, and acquires faith and pride in his own potency, connectedness, and uniqueness.

The child with poor self-esteem is at the other end of the spectrum. Because he lacks respect for himself and his abilities, he becomes convinced that others cannot possibly respect, appreciate, or love him. Feeling unworthy, he avoids establishing personal performance goals and confronting challenges. He lowers his expectations and then performs congruently with the limits he imposes on himself. To confirm his inadequacies and unworthiness to himself and others, he may unconsciously sabotage himself with poor choices, flawed judgment, and ineffectual effort.

Whereas self-esteem deals with a child's fundamental feelings about himself, self-confidence is usually linked to achievement and special talents. This is a key differentiation because it explains why some children can be self-confident but still lack self-esteem. It's possible for a youngster to be supremely self-confident in the classroom or on the playing field and yet not respect or appreciate himself. This same phenomenon can be observed when scrutinizing the personal lives of certain famous and talented movie stars and professional athletes. These luminaries appear to be the pinnacle of success, yet they often destroy themselves with drugs, seem incapable of having successful relationships, and succumb to narcissism and self-indulgence. The cause invariably involves self-esteem. Their stellar accomplishments and natural talents notwithstanding, these individuals are in conflict with themselves and are stuck emotionally at the three- or four-year-old level. Many of them are unconsciously driven to achieve as a surrogate for their lack of self-esteem.

Creating a Context for Developing Self-Esteem

If a child learns to respect himself and appreciate his abilities during the first four years of life, his self-esteem will usually remain intact despite any difficulties he may experience in school. Certainly, he may occasionally be shaken by setbacks or rejections, and his self-confidence may temporarily falter, but his positive feelings about himself will sustain him emotionally and motivate him to handle the challenge. With grit and determination he will either prevail over his learning problems or figure out how to compensate for them. He will need help and guidance, of course, but his own desire to prevail will propel him over the obstacles.

If your child has not acquired solid self-esteem during the formative years, you can help him learn to value and respect himself. The most critical component in the psychological building project is for you to provide your child with firm, reasonable constraints in the form of rules, expectations, and performance standards, and to define predictable consequences for his actions. These guidelines form the foundation on which your child can begin to establish his identity, values, and aspirations. The more solid the foundation, the more respect your child will have for himself, for you, and ultimately for society's ethics and constraints.

As an adult your child may choose to substitute rules and standards that reflect his personal needs and life experiences, but he will always carry your imprint in one form or another. Even if he ultimately rejects specific values, he may later come full circle and embrace them once again.

If your guidance is effective, consistent, and infused with your ethics, your child will learn right from wrong. He may still occasionally tell a lie, be lazy, be disrespectful, or say something hurtful. This is to be expected as children go through the process of internalizing values and learning to differentiate acceptable from unacceptable behavior.

The stability and consistency that children require might take the form of religious constants: "We say grace before our meals and go to church [or synagogue] every week." The constraints might involve chores: "You're responsible for feeding the dog and filling her water dish every morning." They might involve school obligations: "Your homework must be done before you watch TV." They might involve consequences: "If you and your sister fight and tease each other, we will not go out for pizza tonight." These positions are unequivocal and reliable. They are woven into the family cloth. The obligation to impose rules and guidelines may cause you to feel guilty. You may wonder about being too mean or too harsh. Be assured that this guilt is misplaced. Children may chafe, complain, and cry when you consistently apply the rules and impose agreed-upon consequences, but they desperately need this structure. The consistency and predictability provide security. Children want to know the rules, and they want to be clear about the consequences for breaking them.

Establishing Fair and Reasonable Standards

Defining fair standards and realistic performance guidelines for a struggling child can be a challenging and even heart-wrenching process. If your child's skills are deficient, the teacher's standards for the other children in the class may be inappropriate. Your own standards—the ones you have for your other children—may also be inappropriate or excessive.

By now, you have undoubtedly identified your child's academic strengths and deficits. Under your guidance, your child has ideally begun to establish realistic short-term and long-term goals. The challenge that you now face is to coordinate reasonable educational goals with reasonable performance standards. You want to motivate your child to stretch, but you certainly don't want to discourage or demoralize him.

Building the academic self-confidence of a struggling child requires a focused, well-conceived plan of action that must include the following components:

- carefully engineered opportunities for success
- clearly defined and realistic standards for acceptable effort and performance
- praise for accomplishments

These critical components should be applied both in the classroom and at home.

To appreciate the power of praise and success as motivational forces one need only look at the face of a two-year-old when he accomplishes a task that was previously beyond his capability. His joy and pride increase exponentially as his parents acknowledge and affirm him for his achievement. With uninhibited delight the child will clap his hands to applaud his own success.

You can play an instrumental role in helping your child acquire confidence in himself and his abilities by orchestrating successful experiences for him. For example, you might insist that he rewrite a sloppy, illegible essay or check over his math problems for careless computational errors. Although your standards for neatness and accuracy should be geared to his skill level, you want him to push himself to the limits of his current capabilities.

Your child's effort to conform to your guidelines may be quite tentative at first. Be patient. You want to nudge him from his comfort zone, but you don't want to shove him out abruptly. As he confronts challenges and obstacles, he'll need your reassurance.

Any successful strategy to help your child move from point A to point B and to point C must incorporate the fundamentals of tactical planning: setting short-term and long-term goals, establishing priorities, learning to manage time, planning ahead, and creating a schedule. Your child must acquire these skills if he is to think and act more strategically.

By communicating to your child that you expect him to work conscientiously and attain certain performance goals, you're affirming your faith in his ability. For example, you might tell your child that you consider it reasonable for a fourth grader to do an average of one hour of homework each school night. Some evenings, of course, he might not have any homework, and other evenings he may need to do ninety minutes of homework. If he contends that he never has homework or that he can get it all done in school, check with his teacher. She will tell you how much homework is assigned on average. She may also confirm that most students are able to complete the work in school. To establish a consistent standard, you might insist that even if your child completes his homework in school, you still expect him spend an hour reviewing or simply reading. You could have him review his assigned spelling words, complete a supplemental page of multiplication problems, or read a chapter in a book he has selected. You could might also request additional work from the teacher that would help your child improve his skills in his deficit areas. You could give him a timed math test for fun. If you do, make the test into a game and don't make the problems too difficult, unless, of course, he insists on being challenged. You want him to succeed, enjoy himself, and have positive associations with math and with learning. Make sure you praise him for his successes and progress. Although he may not admit it openly, he wants to please you.

The standard you establish—one hour of homework each night for a fourth grader—will become a constant, and only on rare occasions will there be a deviation. This constancy creates a sense of order and security. It also provides stability that will, in turn, produce acceptance (albeit sometimes reluctant) of society's rules. It's the equivalent of saying, "In our family, children don't tease other children. They don't ride bicycles without a helmet. They don't take drugs. They don't become involved with gangs. They study hard and work hard. They treat their parents and grandparents with respect. They finish what they start. They take responsibility for their choices and their actions. They tell the truth." These rules must be internalized if your child is going to accept society's rules.

Running into Snags

About now you may be thinking, "Okay, I understand about the value of having fair and reasonable rules, standards, and guidelines. When I establish rules about working conscientiously, my child resists them, and according to everything you've been saying, he's resistant because the work is hard and he feels inadequate. To impose additional requirements seems like an excercise in futility. It also seems like cruel and unusual punishment." If these statements express your feelings, please note the operative words "fair and reasonable." You cannot reasonably ask more than a child is capable of doing, but you can certainly insist that the child stretch for goals slightly beyond his reach. By insisting that he make a sincere effort to do a first-rate job and by setting him up to win, you're giving him a critically important vote of confidence. And when he prevails over the challenge, his self-esteem will get a needed boost. Contrast this affirming strategy with the alternative: "This problem is very hard, and I don't really expect you to be able to solve it. You don't have to do it if you don't want to." You're sending your child the message: "I don't have much faith in you or your ability to handle challenges and overcome problems."

Struggling children often hide behind a protective wall. Although this wall may provide a semblance of security, it prevents them from confronting the issues that are impeding their progress in school. Behaviors commonly associated with a fortress mentality include resisting schoolwork because it's too difficult or boring, procrastinating, and chronically avoiding responsibility. Rather than deal with the underlying issues, the child prefers to hide and pretend the problems don't exist.

Pushing a child out from behind his protective wall can be a challenging proposition. Some kids openly resist and resort to tantrums, distractions, and arguments. Others resist passively and resort to hurt feelings, excuses, and blaming. The common denominator in both reactions is that these youngsters don't want to take emotional risks and expose themselves to additional failure. They don't want to experience pain. They don't want to be forced to confront their inadequacies. This reaction is instinctive. A child battling to survive in school doesn't care about the future consequences of poor skills. The prospect of having to compete for a job ten years down the road is an abstraction. What the child cares about is getting through today.

The antidote for resistance is to provide your child with a feeling of hope. You must convince him that the problems are solvable. You must help him confront the issues, identify the factors that are causing his difficulties, and develop a plan for overcoming the problems. At the same time you must provide emotional support, affirm him for his accomplishments, and express absolute confidence in his ability to prevail over the obstacles.

Identifying Problems

Accurately defining your child's school-related problems and the underlying causative issues can be a major challenge. If you allow yourself to become entangled in the *symptoms* of the problem, you may fail to pinpoint the actual problem. For example, let's say your child is spending an excessive amount of time doing his math homework. Is the problem that he's spending too much time or that he doesn't understand the material? Well, the problem is that he's spending too much time. One of the causes of the problem may be that he doesn't understand the material.

This distinction may see contrived, but it's critical if you are to help your child learn how to resolve problems. Before you can work together effectively on finding solutions, your child must be able to define the actual problem. The next step is to identify the causal factors. Once this is accomplished, you can begin to brainstorm and experiment with solutions.

Let's look at another common problem. You observe that your child is making too many spelling mistakes, and his teacher tells you that he's having difficulty hearing accurately the sounds that different letters make, such as *o, u, i,* and *e.* Is your child's problem that he has auditory discrimination deficit or that he's making too many spelling mistakes? The problem is that he's making too many spelling mistakes. To fix this problem you need to identify the likely cause, which is apparently an auditory discrimination deficit, although there may be other causes, such as a visual memory deficit or a concentration deficit. Once the problems and causes have been accurately identified, you can brainstorm to find viable solutions. You then need to select the best of these solutions, try it out, and see if it works. This divide and conquer method will allow your child to get a handle on issues that may appear at first to be complex, overwhelming, and unsolvable.

If you're going to work successfully with your child on problem-solving, his trust in you is vital. You must convince him that you're his ally and not his enemy or his jury. Lectures, sermons, and judgments undermine trust. Once your child feels safe, he can begin to let down his defenses, and the two of you can get down to work.

The DIBS Problem-Solving Method

Let's examine a hypothetical situation. Your child's teacher reports that he seems to understand two-place multiplication but makes careless addition errors on his homework and tests. You want to help him solve the problem. At this point you can introduce a method call DIBS, which incorporates the divide and conquer principle described above.

To introduce DIBS you might say, "I have good news and bad news. The good news is that your teacher reports you understand two- and three-place multiplication. All the work you did memorizing the multiplication tables paid off. Congratulations! Now the bad news: She says you're making some silly mistakes. You may add the columns incorrectly or not align the numbers properly. This causes you to come up with the wrong answer. Let's see if we can put our heads together and brainstorm a plan for solving this problem."

Explain that you want to use a new problem-solving method called DIBS (an acronym formed from the first letter of each step in the procedure: *D*efine, *I*nvestigate, *B*rainstorm, and *S*elect). You might say, "The problem with careless errors could be solved using this method. The DIBS solution to the problem might look something like the model below. Let's examine each step and see if we agree with how the problem was solved."

<u>D</u>efine problem:	Math problems have errors
<u>I</u>nvestigate causes:	Not checking over work
	Not properly aligning numbers before adding
	Working too quickly
	Addition errors
	Not paying attention to details
<u>B</u>rainstorm solutions:	Check answers carefully before handing in
	Make sure numbers are properly aligned (in the correct column) before adding
	Take more time to do work
<u>S</u>elect idea to try:	Make sure numbers are properly aligned before adding

As you and your child examine the model, make certain that the give-and-take is enjoyable. To reinforce mastery, agree on another problem to solve. If your child is struggling to define a problem, which is quite common when children first learn the DIBS method, you might say, "Hm, 'not paying attention' sounds like it's causing your problem in reading. Let's keep working at it until we can define the problem accurately."

Once the problem is defined, the next challenge is to identify the possible causal factors. Urge your child to indicate any causes that seem plausible to him. Don't do a great deal of editing or reject an idea because it doesn't seem plausible to you.

The brainstorming phase should also be a free and open discussion. Let your child come up with any ideas that might conceivably solve the problem. You might suggest one or two, but encourage him think of as many as he can on his own. Remember, the goal is to get your child actively involved in the problem-solving process and to improve his strategic thinking skills.

Explain to your child that if the idea he selected to try out doesn't solve the problem, he can always try another until he finds one that works. He needs to learn that some problems resist easy solutions and that he has to keep plugging away until the problem is fixed or until he can figure out a way around it.

For practice, define and solve together another school-related problem or, if you prefer, a non-school-related problem. Your child will probably need your help in defining it. With practice this will get easier. If you observe that your child is becoming fatigued, schedule the practice session for another time.

Explain to your child that DIBS is a powerful tool he'll be able to use throughout his life whenever he faces a problem. When he finds himself in a bind, all he has to do is use the tool to handle the problem. After he has practiced DIBS several times, you might say, "Now you know how to use DIBS. It's pretty easy, isn't it? You figure out what's really wrong and identify the problem. Then you figure out what may be causing the problem. Next you use your head to come up with practical solutions. You select the best solution, and you apply it. If the problem is solved, you move ahead. If it isn't, you look at your list of possible solutions and select another one to try. To become really good at using DIBS, you need to practice. It's like shooting baskets or dribbling a ball. The more you practice, the better you become. One day you discover that you can sink a difficult shot without even thinking about it. One day when you're facing a tough problem, you'll automatically use DIBS to fix it. It becomes so easy that it's almost as if you're not even thinking about the DIBS steps. Your brain is thinking, of course, but the problem-solving method will be as natural for you as sinking a basketball. You could almost do it with your eyes closed!"

Teamwork

It's critically important your child understand that as a parent you have certain responsibilities in helping him solve his school-related problems. One of your jobs is to communicate with his teacher so that you can get important information that can be used to improve his learning. Another job is to make certain that he's treated fairly and receives the assistance he needs in school and after school. Your job is also to listen to what he thinks, be sensitive to what he's feeling, help him sort out problems and issues, be supportive of his efforts, and affirm his accomplishments. You may also need to provide some help when he does his homework or studies for a test.

You also want to clarify your child's job: to make his best effort, confront problems, and work conscientiously. You must communicate clearly that you have complete faith in him and in his ability to prevail over his learning difficulties. You don't require As, but you do require effort. You want him to be proud of his accomplishments, even the first small victories. You want him to realize that by working together you and he are a powerful team. With the right help and sufficient effort on his part, his team will win, and he will be the star.

Chapter 15
Supervising Homework and Studying

"Did you do your homework?"
"I did it in school."
"Are your sure?"
"Yes! You never believe me about anything!"

I f you think this dialogue occurs only in your home, you're mistaken. This conversation takes place in hundreds of thousands of homes sometime between 5:30 and 7:30 P.M. every school night.

Monitoring a child's homework can be a nightmare, especially if the child is highly resistant to studying. In most cases, resistance to studying goes with the territory when children are struggling academically.

You're probably receiving widely divergent information about the homework situation. The teacher may tell you that your daughter isn't completing her assignments and that she's unprepared for tests. Your child, on the other hand, may swear that she's doing her work. You've probably concluded that the teacher's information is correct and that your child is either deceiving herself or trying to con you. And so you find yourself interrogating her each evening like a detective, and this makes you the "heavy." Because you're continually looking over her shoulder, she has begun to resent you, and you've begun to resent her for forcing you to play this role.

Well, playing detective is part of the parental job description when your child is having difficulty in school and acting irresponsibly. You have an obligation to monitor and supervise your child if you receive reports that she is not completing or submitting her assignments. You can play this investigatory role with finesse or with clumsiness. Good "detectives" discover clever methods for eliciting information and cooperation. Less effective ones resort to heavy-handedness, threats, intimidation, and scare tactics. These are the parents who frequently end up in showdowns with their children.

No parent wants to have continual brawls with a child. In the long run, repeated confrontations can only cause hurt feelings, resentment, family disharmony, resistance, misbehavior, and alienation. Parents may be able to impose their will when their child is young, but they'll discover that they have fewer and fewer autocratic prerogatives as their child gets older. By the time children become teenagers, they can essentially tell their parents to go jump in a lake (or worse!). They may not do so openly, but they can certainly resist and rebel in countless ways. They can refuse to study or do their assignments. They can cut school, choose "losers" for friends, take drugs. The result is misery for them, although teenagers may not admit it, and for their parents.

When the parent-child relationship is based on power, the fulcrum must inevitably shift. As children mature and acquire more power, their parents have less. If, on the other hand, the relationship is based on trust, respect, and effective communication, the parent and child are far more likely to be able to work together, problem-solve, and plan for the future.

Certainly, during the formative years of a child's life, there are times when parents must put their foot down and autocratically define the rules, guidelines, and expectations. As stated in the previous chapter, this process of clearly asserting the family's work ethic provides children with an important sense of security. Youngsters may chafe under the rules and complain, but they know where their parents stand and they know what behavior and attitudes are valued in their family.

Being firm and clear with children is not the same as going to war every night. Continual skirmishes and full-blown battles about homework signal a potentially serious family problem. Wise parents realize that they must factor their child's skills, learning deficits, and emotional state into their performance expectations. Demoralized learners with abysmal skills must be treated differently from children who have simply gotten into the habit of being lazy. The former require support, encouragement, and empathy. The latter, because they have the skills to do the work, need a firmer set of rules and guidelines. They need to know that their parents expect diligence and responsible behavior from them.

Parents can be firm without being heavy-handed. They can resist manipulation without having to be intransigent and bellow and rage. Children who believe their parents are fair, reasonable, and supportive are far more likely to become teenagers who believe their parents are fair, reasonable, and supportive. Although these teenagers may also go through minor rebellious phases as they experiment with their emerging independence, they are far less likely to be out of control and beyond control.

There are alternatives to doing battle about studying with your child every night. The confrontations can be avoided if you're clever and strategically replace the "oppressed child/tough and unfair parent" scenario with a "let's work together on dealing with this issues" scenario. Depending on how you choose to play your cards, you can be perceived by your child as either an enemy or an ally.

Schedules

One of the most potent methods for avoiding confrontations about homework is to insist that your child have a study schedule. Developing a schedule for very young children who are assigned homework requires a simple and straightforward agreement. You might say, "I'd like you to have your homework done before we sit down to dinner. You can do it right after your milk and cookies when you get home from school, or you can do it right before dinner. If you want to play outside while it's still light, that's okay. But once you decide when you want to do your homework, I'll expect you to keep to your schedule every day. I don't want to have to nag you."

With children in third grade and above, the process of establishing a schedule can be more challenging. Reaching agreement early in the school year about when your child does his homework and how much time he'll spend can significantly reduce family wear and tear. Of course, you can still reach an agreement later in the school year, but your child's resistance may be more intense when you try to change the rules in midstream. Getting your child to agree to a schedule at this stage can be tricky, but it can be done. You'll need to be a bit more strategic in using the methods described below. If you conclude that you cannot work effectively and interactively with your child on scheduling activities, it might be advisable to hire a tutor to do the job. If your struggling child is ultimately to succeed in school, he must acquire effective planning and time-management skills.

Steps for Creating a Study Schedule

To avoid resistance to the idea of creating a study schedule, it makes sense to help your child understand the function of schedules. You might ask her to write down what she did the previous day. Her list might include: got up at 7:00, brushed teeth, got dressed, had breakfast, walked to bus stop, went to school, had lunch, went back to class, waited for bus, came home, had milk and cookies, played with friends, started homework, called Tamara, had dinner, finished homework, used Internet, watched TV, took a bath, brushed teeth, went to sleep.

You might say, "Pretend that you actually made up a schedule two days ago and that you planned to do the things you actually did yesterday. Let's take a look at how that schedule might look. We'll plug each activity into the following practice schedule. We'll use a different color marker to indicate each activity, and we'll show what these colors represent in the code at the bottom of the sheet. Before we start, let's look at a sample schedule that describes the study schedule of another child. As you can see, Kelly, a fifth grader, has indicated how she plans to use her time after she returns from school. The schedule shows each activity between the time she gets home on school days until she goes to bed."

Kelly's Study Schedule

TIME	MONDAY	TUESDAY	WEDNESDAY	THURSDAY	FRIDAY
8:15–3:00	########## ##########	########## ##########	########## ##########	########## ##########	########## ##########
3:00–3:30	*************** ***************	*************** ***************	*************** ***************	*************** ***************	*************** ***************
3:30–4:00	*************** ***************	*************** ***************	*************** ***************	*************** ***************	*************** ***************
4:00–4:30	*************** ***************	*************** ***************	*************** ***************	*************** ***************	*************** ***************
4:30–5:00	*************** ++++++++++	*************** ++++++++++	*************** ++++++++++	*************** ++++++++++	*************** ++++++++++
5:00–5:30	++++++++++ ++++++++++	++++++++++ ++++++++++	++++++++++ ++++++++++	++++++++++ ++++++++++	++++++++++ ++++++++++
5:30–6:00	========== ==========	========== ==========	========== ==========	========== ==========	========== ==========
6:00–6:30	""""""""""""""" """""""""""""""	""""""""""""""" """""""""""""""	""""""""""""""" """""""""""""""	""""""""""""""" """""""""""""""	""""""""""""""" """""""""""""""
6:30–7:00	""""""""""""""" ++++++++++	""""""""""""""" ++++++++++	""""""""""""""" ++++++++++	""""""""""""""" ++++++++++	""""""""""""""" ++++++++++
7:00–7:30	++++++++++ ***************	++++++++++ ***************	++++++++++ ***************	++++++++++ ***************	++++++++++ ***************
7:30–8:00	*************** ***************	*************** ***************	*************** ***************	*************** ***************	*************** ***************
8:00–8:30	*************** ***************	*************** ***************	*************** ***************	*************** ***************	*************** ***************
8:30–9:00	*************** ***************	*************** ***************	*************** ***************	*************** ***************	*************** ***************
9:00–9:30	ZZZZZZZZZZ ZZZZZZZZZZ	ZZZZZZZZZZ ZZZZZZZZZZ	ZZZZZZZZZZ ZZZZZZZZZZ	ZZZZZZZZZZ ZZZZZZZZZZ	ZZZZZZZZZZ ZZZZZZZZZZ

CODE: # School; * Free time; + Homework; " Dinner; = Piano; Z Sleep

Practice Schedule					
TIME	**MONDAY**	**TUESDAY**	**WEDNESDAY**	**THURSDAY**	**FRIDAY**
| 7:00 – 7:30					
| 7:30 – 8:00					
| 8:15 – 3:00	SCHOOL	SCHOOL	SCHOOL	SCHOOL	SCHOOL
| 3:30 – 4:00					
| 4:00 – 4:30					
| 4:30 – 5:00					
| 5:00 – 5:30					
| 5:30 – 6:00					
| 6:00 – 6:30					
| 6:30 – 7:00					
| 7:00 – 7:30					
| 7:30 – 8:00					
| 8:00 – 8:30					
| 8:30 – 9:00					

CODE: [ ]_____ [ ]_____ [ ]_____ [ ]_____ [ ]_____ [ ]_____ [ ]_____

It's now time to explain to your child the specific steps involved in creating a personal schedule.

Steps for Creating a Study Schedule

Step 1: Write down the subjects you are taking and estimate the average number of minutes you need to spend each day in each subject. This may vary from time to time when the teacher doesn't assign any homework in a particular subject or if no tests or quizzes are to be given during the week. For planning purposes, however, you want to list the average amount of homework time required each day.

Subjects	Approximate Homework Time Required Daily
Reading	_____
Math	_____
Science	_____
Social Studies	_____
_____	_____
_____	_____
Total Daily Homework Time:	_____
Total Daily Time for piano, karate, or gymnastics, etc.:	_____

Step 2: Write down the time when you get home from school, have dinner, and go to bed. (These times may vary occasionally.)

Get home from school	_____
Dinnertime	_____
Bedtime	_____

Use this information to complete your schedule, using Kelly's schedule as a sample. Let's plan how you want to use your time *before* filling in your schedule.

Step 3: On Kelly's schedule, symbols are used to indicate how she uses her time. It would be more fun to use different colored pencils or felt-tipped pens to indicate when you eat dinner and when you go to bed. If we eat dinner between 6:00 and 6:30, you would use one color to indicate that. Fill in one of the boxes with the selected color and write "Dinnertime." You would then use that color on the schedule. Fill in another box in the code with a second color and write "Bedtime."

Step 4: Use a different color to indicate when you want to study and do homework. For example, you might get home from basketball practice at 5:00, and you may want to do homework from 5:30 to 6:00. Dinner might be from 6:00 to 6:45. You may want to have some free time until 7:00 and then do your remaining homework until 7:30. The rest of the evening until bedtime is for you to use as you wish. You can watch TV, surf the Internet, or call your friends.

Step 5: Use a different color to indicate when you want to schedule free time. For example, if you get home from basketball practice at 5:00 and want to talk on the phone with your friends until 6:00, schedule this time in the color of your choice. Below the schedule, fill in the little box with the color and write "Free time."

Step 6: As an experiment, maintain your schedule for two weeks. See if your grades improve and school becomes easier.

Step 7: For two weeks record your grades on tests, quizzes, essays, and reports in every subject. This will allow you to track your performance and help you make adjustments. If, for example, your math grade doesn't improve or goes down, you'll need to schedule more time for doing math homework and studying for tests.

Step 8: Evaluate and fine-tune your schedule after the two-week trial period. If appropriate, make changes that will improve it. Remember, your schedule is your friend, not your enemy! You want it to work for you and serve you. The following form can be used to keep track of your grades. This will help you evaluate the effectiveness of your new study schedule.

Why Have a Schedule?

Help your child understand the reason for having a schedule. You don't want her to see it as another idea that's going to make her life miserable. You might say, "Once you work out the kinks in your study schedule and it begins to work, you may find that you can get your work done and that you have a lot more free time. The key is to keep to the schedule even if

My Study Schedule

TIME	MONDAY	TUESDAY	WEDNESDAY	THURSDAY	FRIDAY
| 3:30 – 4:00					
| 4:00 – 4:30					
| 4:30 – 5:00					
| 5:00 – 5:30					
| 5:30 – 6:00					
| 6:00 – 6:30					
| 6:30 – 7:00					
| 7:00 – 7:30					
| 7:30 – 8:00					
| 8:00 – 8:30					
| 8:30 – 9:00					
| 9:00 – 9:30					
| 9:30 – 10:00					

CODE: [ ]_____ [ ]_____ [ ]_____ [ ]_____ [ ]_____ [ ]_____ [ ]_____

it is occasionally inconvenient or requires sacrifices. Make changes only when absolutely necessary. For example, if we want to go out for dinner with you on a particular evening, you'll obviously have to make changes in your schedule that night. This situation would be the exception, not the rule. Keeping to a schedule can sometimes be a challenge. You might be playing with friends when you realize it is 4:30, the time *you* decided to begin studying. Telling your friends 'I gotta go home and do my homework' isn't easy. You have to remind yourself that you made a commitment because it was the smart thing to do."

Daily Grade Record

Subjects	Tests/ Quizzes	Reports	Homework	In-class Work
_____	_____	_____	_____	_____
_____	_____	_____	_____	_____
_____	_____	_____	_____	_____
_____	_____	_____	_____	_____
_____	_____	_____	_____	_____
_____	_____	_____	_____	_____

An Experimental Study Schedule Contract

You might want to propose that your child sign a contract that commits her to keeping her schedule for an agreed-upon period of time. You could explain why it is a good idea to have a contract in this way: "A training schedule for an athlete, such as running three miles every day and doing seventy-five sit-ups and one hundred push-ups can be hard to keep. It's very tempting to let things slide when it's raining or you have a slight sore throat or headache. Then you discover that you're tempted to let things slide the following day. It becomes easier and easier not to follow the schedule. Before long you abandon the schedule altogether.

"As an experiment, use the contract that follows to help you keep your schedule. This contract is an agreement between you and yourself. Remember, keeping your commitments, especially those you make to yourself, is an important part of getting the job done!"

Assignment Sheets

Another practical solution to homework resistance is to have your child use an assignment sheet on which she carefully records all her assign-

> ## Contract Between Me and Myself
>
> Date: _____
> Dear Me:
>
> I, _____, being of sound mind (not crazy!),
> agree to use the study schedule I created for a two-week trial period.
> If after using the schedule for two weeks I decide that my schedule
> should be changed or fine-tuned, I will do so. Once I make these
> changes, I agree to use the revised schedule for a minimum of four
> weeks. If I'm pleased with the results and my grades improve, I'll
> continue to use the schedule for the rest of the school year, making
> changes and adjustments every four weeks. Finally, I agree to keep
> to my schedule without having to be prodded or reminded by my
> parents.
>
> _____
> Your Name
> Witnesses (for fun):
>
> _____   _____

ments, notes the due dates of reports, indicates the dates of quizzes and
tests, and checks off that she has completed each assignment.

Your child may already have an effective assignment recording system.
It's also possible that his teacher wants all students to use the same system.
Some teachers eliminate the homework recording problem by providing
a sheet that lists the weekly assignments at the beginning of each week.
Students put the weekly assignments in their binders for reference. Your
child should use the recording method preferred by the teacher, of
course, but if the teacher hasn't provided one, have your child use the
system described above.

Teach your child some easy to remember abbreviations, such as *rpt.,
p., Sci., ans., cmplt., etc.* These will reduce the amount of time required to
write down assignments and allow her to fit all the important information
and instructions on the recording sheet.

Sample Assignment Sheet

WEEK OF: _2/3/97_____

SUBJECTS	MONDAY	TUESDAY	WEDNESDAY	THURSDAY	FRIDAY
MATH	P. 93 PROBLEMS 1–10 P. 96				
SPELLING	WORDS P. 26 QUIZ WED. 2/5				
HISTORY	READ P. 156–161 ANSWER QUES. 1–5 COMPLETE SENT.				
SCIENCE	READ P. 87–90 KNOW DEF. 10 WORDS P. 91 REPORT 2/10				
READING	READ P. 67–70 ANSWER QUES. 1–6 P. 71				
TESTS AND REPORTS	SCI. RPT 2/10 SPELLING QUIZ 2/4				

My Assignment Sheet

WEEK OF: _____

SUBJECTS	MONDAY	TUESDAY	WEDNESDAY	THURSDAY	FRIDAY
MATH					
READING					
SPELLING					
SCIENCE					
SOCIAL STUDIES					
TESTS AND REPORTS					

Afterword

F inding assistance for your child and helping her get on track in school is not a one-time event that you handle and then forget about. Identifying, assessing, and resolving your child's learning difficulties is an ongoing process with many overlapping, interrelated components.

Unfortunately, the progression from academic difficulty to academic competence is not always smooth and straight. Whereas certain remediation methods work miraculously with some children, they may not work at all with others.

The wise parents of a struggling child carefully monitor what is happening in school and regularly request updates about problems and progress. When appropriate, they solicit advice from specialists in the public sector, such as teachers, resource specialists, and school psychologists, and, when expedient, from specialists in the private sector, such as educational therapists, pediatricians, and psychologists. The parents analyze why their child is having difficulty and why a particular remediation strategy may or may not be working. After assessing the situation and attempting to identify the underlying causal factors, the parents brainstorm alternative solutions and select the most promising options available.

Seeking help for a child is not like throwing a dart at a board and seeing where it hits. Rather, it is a calculated, strategic procedure in which you must play a key role. Your evaluation of the situation and the decisions you make about the support services your child requires can have a profound effect on the outcome. For example, if your child is receiving counseling to deal with recurring behavioral or attitude issues and you begin, after six or seven sessions, to question the efficacy of the counseling, you and your child are at a major crossroads. How do you handle your concerns about whether your child has rapport with the therapist? How do you resolve your doubts about the therapist's skills? You may decide to wait a while to see if the situation improves, or you may make an intuitive judgment call and decide that it is time to seek another therapist. Your third option is, of course, to discontinue all therapy.

Unfortunately, there is no question-and-answer template that will help you make these decisions. You may decide to discuss your concerns with the therapist, or you may consult other professionals to help you resolve your dilemma. As you wrestle with your choices, all you can do is carefully weigh as best you can the pros and cons of each course of action. In the final analysis, you must ultimately trust the voice within you.

The same analytical process also applies to decisions about educational therapy, tutoring, and participation in a school resource program. If you have doubts and concerns, you may decide to discuss these issues with the resource specialist or the school administration. You may request changes and additional in-class accommodations. If you're profoundly dissatisfied with your child's progress, you may want to discuss during an IEP conference the advisability of having your child transfer to another resource class, another school, or perhaps even another district. If this request is denied, you would then have to decide if you want to dispute the decision, accept it, or consider enrolling your child in a specialized private school that offers educational therapy and tutoring resources.

Deciding what to do in this situation requires another difficult judgment call. You realize that your child will have to interact with many people in her life with whom she may not have rapport. Learning to handle these less-than-perfect situations can be an important learning experience, and rescuing her could be a disservice. On the other hand, to insist that she stay in a situation that is clearly not meeting her needs could also be a disservice. You must evaluate each situation, carefully weigh the pros and cons, and then trust your intuition.

In chapter 1, a basic flowchart of services and intervention options was represented. You are now aware of the many alternatives available to you as you seek help for your child. Below you will find a more complete listing. Take a moment to study it. You may not need or want to avail yourself of all the listed services and alternatives, but you will at least know how the many pieces fit together.

To fully appreciate what you now know about finding help for your child, take an inventory. You have the information you need to understand your child's learning problems and the emotional fallout that is commonly associated with academic deficiencies. You understand the different educational remediation options that might be used. You are aware of medical options and psychological services. You are familiar with the educational jargon that describes learning problems. You know what your child's federally mandated rights are, and you know the specific laws (and pesky acronyms!) that protect these rights. You know the strengths and weaknesses of the public school system. You know how to find additional resources that exist in your community. You know what questions to ask the professionals who provide services for struggling children, and you have criteria for evaluating the efficacy of these services and any recommendations that are made to you. You also realize that you may need to go beyond your local community in your search for assistance, especially if you live in a rural area that has more limited educational and therapeutic resources.

Finding Help: The Process
1. Recognition of the learning problem
2. Parent-teacher discussion
3. Possible in-school help:
   - child study team
   - school psychologist
   - resource specialist
   - occupational therapist
   - speech and language pathologist
   - school counselor
   - social worker
4. Possible outside help:
   - educational psychologist
   - clinical psychologist
   - child psychologist
   - neuropsychologist
   - pediatrician
   - developmental pediatrician
   - pediatric neurologist
   - child psychiatrist
   - social worker
   - marriage and family therapist
   - occupational therapist
   - speech and language therapist
   - developmental optometrist
   - educational therapist

- tutor
- corporate-owned or franchised learning and reading center
- locally owned learning center
- publicly funded specialized private school
- privately funded specialized private school

Whether your child needs a diagnostic assessment, learning assistance, language therapy, or counseling, you can find it if you follow the blueprint outlined in this book. If your child requires help, don't hesitate. Pull out all the stops. Do it now. Make it happen.

Appendix

The following agencies and parent support groups may be able to provide you with information and guidelines for finding help for your child.

American Occupational Therapy Association, Inc. (AOTA)
4720 Montgomery Lane
P.O. Box 31220
Bethesda, MD 20824-1220
(301) 652-2682
(800) 668-8253
Website: www.aota.org

American Speech-Language-Hearing Association (ASHSA)
10801 Rockville Pike
Rockville, MD 20852
(301) 897-5700
(800) 638-TALK
Website: www.asha.org\ASHA\
E-mail: irc@ahsa.org

Association of Educational Therapists (AET)
1804 West Burbank Boulevard
Burbank, CA 91506
(818) 843-1183
E-mail: aetla@aol.com

CHADD (Children and Adults with Attention Deficit Disorder)
499 N.W. 70th Avenue, Suite 101
Plantation, FL 33317

(954) 587-3700
(800) 233-4050
Website: www.chadd.org

Council for Exceptional Children (CEC)
1920 Association Drive
Reston, VA 20191
(703) 620-3660
(888) 232-7733
Website: www.cec.sped.org

Independent Educational Consultants Association
4085 Chain Bridge Road, Suite 401
Fairfax, VA 22030
(800) 808-IECA
(703) 591-4850
Website: www.educationalconsulting.org
E-mail: IECAassoc@aol.com

International Dyslexia Association (formerly Orton Dyslexia Society)
8600 LaSalle Road
Baltimore, MD 21204-6020
(410) 296-0232
(800) 222-3123
Website: www.ldonline.org/index.html

Learning Disabilities Association of America
4156 Library Road
Pittsburgh, PA 15234
(412) 341-1515
(888) 300-6710
Website: www.ldanatl.org
E-mail: ldanat@usaor.net

National Association of Private Schools for Exceptional Children
(NAPSEC)
1522 K Street, N.W., Suite 1032
Washington, D.C. 20005
(202) 408-3338

Website: www.napsec.com
E-mail: napsec@aol.com

National Attention Deficit Disorder Association
P.O. Box 972
Mentor, OH 44066
(800) 487-2282
(440) 350-9595
Website: www.add.org
E-mail: NatlADD@aol.com

National Center for Learning Disabilities
381 Park Avenue South, Suite 1420
New York, NY 10016
(212) 545-7510
Website: www.ncld.org

National Information Center for Children and Youth with Disabilities
(NICHY)
P.O. Box 1492
Washington, D.C. 20013-1492
Website: www.nichy.org
E-mail: nichy@ade.org

Office of Civil Rights
U.S. Department of Education
400 Maryland Avenue, S.W.
Washington, D.C. 20202-4135
(202) 401-3020
Useful information about Section 504 of the Rehabilitation Act and
parents' rights under the Individuals with Disabilities Act [IDEA]

Parent Educational Advocacy Training Center (PEATC)
10340 Democracy Lane, Suite 206
Fairfax, VA 22030
(703) 691-7826
Website: http//members.aol.com/peatcinc/index.html
E-mail: peatcinc@aol.com

Parents' Educational Resource Center (PERC)
1660 South Amphlett Boulevard, Suite 200
San Mateo, CA 94402
(650) 655-2410
Website: www.perc-schwabfdn.org
E-mail: perc@perc-schwabfdn.org

Index

Achenbach, Thomas, 74
achievement loop, 230–232, 244
acting out, 138, 139, 143, 157, 197, 247
adaptive physical education specialist, 180
adolescents, 262, 263
advocates, 90–92, 106, 126, 173, 218
after-school programs, 23, 139, 193
agencies, government, 218, 279–282
American Board of Professional
    Psychology, 127
American Speech and Hearing Association
    Hotline, 201
Americans with Disabilities Act (ADA), 98,
    108, 218
anger, 38–39, 141, 142–143, 154, 156
Anser System (Aggregate Neurobehavioral
    Student Health and Educational
    Review), 75, 122
aphasia, 202
apraxia, 206
articulation, 198–201
assignment sheets, 270–273
Association of Educational Therapists
    (AET), 170, 171, 174, 175, 182, 185,
    279
ataxia, 206
attention deficit disorder (ADD), 25, 28, 29,
    62, 74, 75, 98, 113, 116, 117, 118, 119,
    120, 122, 127, 129, 130–132, 148, 149,
    155, 157, 181, 186
attention deficit hyperactivity disorder
    (ADHD), 25, 74, 75, 98, 116, 117, 118,
    120, 122, 129, 130–132, 148, 186
attitude, 19–20, 32, 44, 159, 231–232, 236
auditory discrimination defects, 53, 62, 63,
    76, 83, 184, 200, 201, 256
Auditory Discrimination in Depth (ADD),
    62, 84–85
auditory sequencing defects, 76
Ayres, A. Jean, 207

balance problems, 204
Beery-Butenika Developmental Test of
    Visual Motor Integration, 72–73, 208
behavior:
    checklists for, 18–19, 74
    confrontational, 262–263
    coping, 38–40, 86, 138–139, 141, 174
    disruptive, 10, 140, 141, 142, 144, 149,
        154, 158, 192
    pattern of, 31, 44
    self-defeating, 138, 174, 247
    standards for, 249–256, 262
behavioral therapy, 150–151
Bender Gestalt Test for Young Children,
    72, 84
Better Business Bureau, 164
bilateral crawling, 204
biofeedback, 129
blame, 38, 46
brain function, 114, 121, 127, 128–129,
    198, 204–205, 211–212
Brigance Diagnostic Inventory of Basic
    Skills, 69
Broad Knowledge, 65, 66
Broad Math, 65, 66
Broad Reading, 64–65, 66
Broad Written Language, 65, 66, 83

California Achievement Test (CAT), 23,
    67–68
California Tests of Basic Skills (CTBS), 23,
    180
central nervous system, 130, 205
cerebral hemispheres, 128–129, 204–205
certificate of clinical competence (CCC),
    202
certification, 124, 127, 130, 168, 169,
    170–171, 175, 179, 182, 183, 184, 185,
    189, 193, 198, 202–203, 209, 216

Certified Educational Therapist (ET), 170–171
Child Behavior Checklist (CBCL), 74
child psychiatrists, 130, 146–150
child psychologists, 116, 150–155, 172
children, learning disabled:
  abuse of, 148, 158
  boys vs. girls as, 3
  communication with, 37–47, 261–263
  developmental stages of, 141–143
  emotions of, 30, 38–40, 44, 45, 141, 147, 173, 192, 227, 248–249
  expectations of, 249–251
  frustration of, 20–21, 95, 137–138, 139, 174, 247
  humiliation of, 92–93, 196–197
  independence of, 86
  rights of, 95–110
  role of, 156, 157, 248
  self-confidence of, 230–234, 235, 250, 251, 253
  self-esteem of, 1, 2, 19, 30, 32, 38, 45, 85, 92–94, 110, 142, 152–153, 169, 173–174, 250–252
  self-evaluation by, 41–44
Children and Adults with Attention Deficit Disorder (CHADD), 110, 279–280
Child Study Team, 21, 24, 51, 52, 59, 196
class size, 9–10, 13, 188, 193
clinical psychologists, 116, 150–155, 172
College of Optometrists in Vision Development, 216
comfort zone, 166, 174, 239–240
concentration difficulties, 25, 31, 101–102, 113, 117, 119, 186, 212
conferences, parent-teacher, 24
confidentiality, 153–154
Conner's Rating Scale, 74, 75, 118, 132
consultants, educational, 188
content area specialists, 166, 168
context-appropriate educational counseling, 173
contracts, 183, 184, 270, 271
coordination, 18, 84, 195, 196, 198, 204–207
corpus callosum, 204
counseling, 25, 29, 122, 123, 132, 145, 146, 155–159, 173, 179, 180, 275
cranial nerve exam, 131
crawling, 204
crisis intervention, 146, 152
criteria-referenced instruments, 180
curriculum, modification of, 53, 86, 91, 93–94, 95, 100–105, 169, 176, 276

Cylert, 132, 149

day classes, 59, 139
decoding, 196, 198
defense mechanisms, 37–38, 39, 43, 46, 138–139, 147, 151–152, 158, 232
deflection, 38
denial, 38, 46
depression, 132, 141, 142, 143, 149
despair, 38, 141, 142, 174
Detroit Test of Learning Aptitude (DTLA-3), 68
developmental optometrists, 198, 210–217
developmental pediatricians, 116, 120–123, 130
Dexedrine, 132, 149
diagnosticians, 113–133
Diagnostic Statistical Manual (DSM IV), 132
DIBS method, 227, 257–259
diet, 123
differential diagnosis, 32–33
directionality, 212
Disopramine, 132
disorganized thinking, 144
divorce, 141
drug abuse, 119, 150, 194
dysarthria, 199
dysfunctions, 197–198
dyslexia, 28, 31, 45, 53, 83, 84, 114, 117, 168, 184, 185, 211–212, 221
dysphasia, 202
dyspraxia, 205
dystaxia, 206

ear infections, 200
educational support services, 176n–177n
educational therapists, 22, 23, 25, 28, 33, 47, 59, 84, 88, 116, 168, 170–176, 179, 180, 181, 184
Education for All Handicapped Children Act, 97
Educator's Checklist of Observable Clues to Classroom Vision Problems, 212–214
electroencephalogram (EEG), 114, 133, 199
employment, 97, 109, 139–140
encoding, 196
Equal Employment Opportunity Commission, 108
evasion, 38
expressive language, 195, 198, 201, 202
eye–hand coordination, 204, 213

Eye Movement Desensitization and Reprocessing (EMDR), 151
eye-teaming, 210, 213

Fair and Appropriate Education Act (FAPE), 99, 190, 192, 218
families:
  child's role in, 156, 157, 248
  counseling for, 155–159
  problems in, 13, 32–33, 45, 132, 141, 155–159
  in rural vs. urban areas, 165
  values of, 250–251, 252, 262
  see also children, learning disabled; parents
family counselors, 155–159
fatigue, 142
feedback, 1, 2, 14–15, 31, 33, 37, 47, 198–199
finances, 99–100, 110, 131, 151, 152, 158, 164, 165, 172, 173, 177–178, 180, 181, 187, 188, 190, 203, 208–209, 215
finger tracking method, 166
504 SED (Severely Emotionally Disturbed) Schools, 192
flash cards, 166, 167
focusing deficits, 117, 210
fortress mentality, 255
free time, 268
functional magnetic resonance imaging (fMRI), 114, 133, 211–212

generalists, 166
goals:
  academic, 236, 241–246
  inventory of, 235, 238
  setting of, 229–246, 251, 253
Goodenough-Harris Drawing Test, 73
grades, 19, 102, 159, 236, 241–246
Gray Oral Reading Test (GORT-3), 70–71
grievance procedures, 99, 104–106, 218
group counseling, 180

handwriting, 20, 31
health maintenance organizations (HMOs), 147, 151, 209
homework, 3, 22, 89, 95, 102, 129, 140, 168, 169, 171, 175, 233, 234, 240–241, 252, 254, 261–273
homolateral crawling, 204
hyperactivity, 25, 74, 75, 98, 116, 117, 118, 120, 122, 129, 130–132, 148, 186

identified patient (IP), 156, 157, 248

Illinois Test of Psycholinguistic Abilities (ITPA), 69–70, 83
"I'm Dumb!" Syndrome, 137–140
Imipramine, 132
impairments, 197–198
Independent Educational Consultants Association, 188
Individual Educational Plan (IEP), 33, 52, 79–94
  advocates in, 90–92, 106, 126, 173, 218
  conferences for, 79–85, 87–89, 120, 122, 127, 133, 155, 170, 173, 175, 178, 196, 203, 276
  document for, 80–81, 85
  jargon in, 80, 87
  legal aspect of, 79, 90–91, 94, 99, 105
  objectives of, 85–87, 222, 223, 225
  procedural checklist for, 82–83
  questions about, 81, 83–84, 88–90, 189
  recommendations of, 80–81, 95
  remediation plan and, 85–90, 113, 145, 224, 225, 226
  reviews of, 89–90
  school psychologists and, 79, 80, 81, 89
  tests and, 81, 83–85, 87, 90, 92
Individuals with Disabilities Education Act (IDEA), 97–99, 108, 187, 189, 191, 217
insurance, medical, 120, 121, 123, 125, 147, 148, 151, 152, 155, 158, 203, 208–209, 215, 218
International Dyslexia Association, 110, 280
IQ, 57n, 64, 68, 72, 84, 108–109, 124, 128, 133
Irlin Test, 214

jargon, 62–63, 80, 87

kinetic tracking deficit, 211

laboratory tests, 114–115
language problems, 157, 195, 198–204
laterality, 212
laws, 95–110
  accommodations mandated by, 100–105
  grievance procedure for, 99, 104–106
  Individual Educational Plan (IEP) and, 79, 90–91, 94, 99, 105
  plan of action based on, 105–107
  specific examples of, 97–100
  testing and, 63, 106
lawyers, 107–108, 110, 187
learned helplessness, 232–234, 248

learning, auditory vs. visual, 167
learning assistance providers, 163–164
learning centers, 25, 28, 59, 164, 165,
    176–186
  franchised, 176, 183–186
  independent, 176, 179–183
  university-affiliated, 176–179
learning curves, 86, 222–227
learning disabilities:
  assessment of, 41–44, 51–60, 63–64, 82
  causes of, 3–4, 31–33, 44–47
  compensation for, 139–40, 152–153
  deficits in, 20–25, 31, 53, 56–57, 76
  diagnosis of, 32–33, 113–116, 132,
    197–198
  dysfunctions vs. impairments in,
    197–198
  identification of, 2, 4, 9–25, 28, 32–33,
    53, 113–116, 275–278
  macro vs. micro perspective on, 11
  nonorganic basis of, 198, 199
  nonspecific, 109
  organic basis of, 74, 114, 116, 121, 198
  prognosis for, 113, 133, 139
  psychological basis of, 137–145, 155, 165
  questions on, 2–4, 28–29
  remediation plan for, 85–90, 113, 115,
    125–126, 139, 145, 165, 174, 224, 225,
    226
  symptoms of, 29–30, 32, 44–47,
    114–115, 142–145
  see also special education
Learning Disabilities Association Newsbrief,
    100n
learning disabilities lab, 178
learning strategies, 102
Levine, Melvin, 75
licensed clinical social workers (LCSWs),
    159–160
licensed marriage, family, and child
    counselors (LMFCCs), 155–159
Lindamood Auditory Conceptualization
    Test (LAC), 62, 68, 74
Lindamood Auditory Discrimination in
    Depth Program, 84–85, 165, 170, 201,
    211
litigation, 106–108, 218
Local Education Agency (LEA), 191
lying, 38

magnetic resonance imaging (MRI), 114,
    131, 133, 211–212
management, classroom, 101
marriage counselors, 155–159

math skills, 76–77, 166–167
medical history, 116, 117, 119, 146
medications, 29, 113, 114, 117–118, 119,
    120, 127, 132, 133, 148, 149–150, 151,
    152, 155
mental health professionals, 137–160
methylphenidate, 118, 119, 132, 149, 150
Mr. Holland's Opus, 13
morale, 38, 141, 142, 174, 247–259
mothers, 157
motivation, 12, 102, 164–165, 169, 173,
    175, 229–246
Motor-Free Visual Perception Test, 73
motor skills, 18, 84, 195, 196, 198, 204–207
multiple births, 199
muscle tone, 205

National Association of Private Schools for
    Exceptional Children (NAPSEC),
    188–189, 280–281
National Board Certification of
    Occupational Therapists (NBCOT),
    208
National Educational Association, 13n
Neurolinguistic Programming (NLP), 151
neurologists, 116, 130–133
neurology, 114, 130, 131, 132–133, 199,
    204–205, 223, 227
neuropsychologists, 116, 127–130
neurotransmitters, 114
Norpramine, 132

occupational therapists, 58, 82, 87, 180,
    199, 204–210, 215
ocular motility, 213
ocular-motor pursuit, 63
Office of Civil Rights, 99, 281
"open enrollment," 177
ophthalmologists, 198
Optometric Extension Program, 216
optometrists, 198, 210–217
oral apraxia, 199
organizations, 110, 174–175, 279–282
Orton-Gillingham method, 62, 165, 211

Parent Perceptions Inventory, 33–35
parents:
  anecdotal information from, 73–74
  concerns of, 1–5
  counseling for, 156–157
  decision-making by, 29, 275–278
  expectations of, 17, 46, 86–87
  intuition of, 1, 30–31, 59–60, 88, 143,
    222, 249

perceptions of, 27–35
rights of, 21, 24, 95–100, 105, 188–189, 217–218, 277
role of, 13, 103, 230, 233–234, 248–249, 261–263
Parents' Educational Resource Center (PERC), 110, 174–175
Parents' Rights Manual, 21, 105
Peabody Individual Achievement Test–Revised (PIAT-R), 66–67, 83–84
Peabody Picture Vocabulary Test (PPVT-R), 68
pediatricians, 116–123, 130, 200, 201
pediatric neurologists, 116, 130–133
peer assistance, 103
perceptual processing deficits, 63, 109, 115, 184
peripheral nervous system, 130
preferred provider organizations (PPOs), 147, 151, 209
premature births, 199
President's Commission on the Employment of Persons with Disabilities, 108
problem-solving strategies, 27–28, 40–41, 43–44, 227, 248, 256–259
procrastination, 141
proprioception, 206
psychiatrists, child, 130, 146–150
psychological overlay, 44–47, 132, 141, 155, 157, 159
psychological support, 103
psychologists, clinical, 116, 150–155, 172
psychologists, school, 150–155
  evaluation by, 3, 21, 58, 113, 116, 124, 145, 150–155, 172
  Individual Educational Plan (IEP) and, 79, 80, 81, 89
  information from, 9
  referrals and, 25, 106–107
  tests administered by, 61, 64, 71–74, 106
psychosocial factors, 125

quantitative electroencephalograph (QEEG), 129–130
questions:
  for diagnosticians, 119–120, 122–123, 126–127, 130, 133
  about Individual Educational Plan (IEP), 81, 83–84, 88–89, 189
  for learning assistance providers, 169–170, 175–176, 178–179, 181–183, 185–186, 189–190, 193–194
  on learning curves, 224–225

on learning disabilities, 2–4, 28–29
for mental health professionals, 148–150, 153, 154–155, 158–159, 160
for specialized clinicians, 203–204, 209–210, 216–217

rationalizations, 38, 221
reading, 13, 22, 31, 39, 43–44, 63, 84, 95, 108–109, 126, 166, 168, 210–216
receptive language, 195, 198, 201, 202
referrals, 23, 25, 106–108, 118, 122, 125, 129, 130, 132, 145, 146, 155, 158, 164, 168, 170, 172–176, 215
refractive status, 213–214
Rehabilitation Act, 98–110, 119, 192, 218
release forms, 20
report cards, 236, 241
resistance, active vs. passive, 239–240, 247, 250, 255
resource specialists, 3–4, 21, 23, 25, 39, 46, 47, 58, 62, 64, 79, 80, 81, 89, 94, 171, 174, 177, 186
retardation, mental, 92
Ritalin, 118, 119, 132, 149, 150
role models, 236–237
rules, 249–256, 262

schedules, 263–273
school boards, 59, 106, 110
school districts, 91, 105–106, 107, 109, 110, 145, 187, 191, 192, 201, 202, 217, 218
schools:
  bureaucracy of, 16, 21–22, 54–56, 58, 96, 217–218
  disadvantaged, 23
  magnet, 145, 191n
  nonpublic (NPS), 145, 190–194
  obligations of, 96–97
  parochial, 186–187
  private, 28, 59, 165, 186–190, 276
  residential, 187
scotopic sensitivity syndrome, 214
Section 504, 98–110, 119, 192, 218
Sensory Integration and Praxis Test (SIPT), 207–208, 209
Sensory Integration International, 207
sensory integrative dysfunction, 205–208, 209
sensory modalities, 125
severely emotionally disturbed (SED) programs, 145, 192
shame, 39
skills, mental, 19, 89–90, 159, 166–167, 170, 173, 175, 180, 183, 232, 262

Slingerland method, 85, 165, 170, 211
Slingerland Test for Identifying Specific
    Language Disabilities, 62, 70, 83, 84
Slosson Oral Reading Test (SORT-R), 70
small-group instruction, 172–173, 175–176,
    179
social problems, 13, 32–33, 137–145, 155,
    165
social workers, 58, 83, 95, 132, 159–160
sound blending, 83
spatial organization, 212
special education:
    adequacy of, 54, 95–96, 97, 221–227
    assistance process in, 28, 30, 52–54, 59,
        277–278
    eligibility for, 51–60, 75–77, 79, 91,
        108–110, 113, 118–119, 163, 218
    funding for, 1–2, 54
    guidelines for, 55, 56–57, 96, 275–278
    information on, 16–24
    legal aspect of, 53, 54, 58, 63, 95–110
    private, 88, 163–194
    progress in, 91, 163, 169, 173, 181,
        222–227, 236, 241, 244–246, 276
    staffing of, 54, 63
    see also learning disabilities
specialized clinicians, 195–218
speech pathologists, 58, 82, 198–204
speech problems, 195, 198–204
spelling mistakes, 256
standardized diagnosis, 132
Stanford Achievement Test, 23
static tracking deficit, 211
stress, 4, 39, 248
studying, 19, 261–273
stuttering, 199
suicide, 143
symbolic language, 157
symptoms, presenting, 32

tactile/kinesthetic manipulatives, 129
tactilely defensive, 205
Tactual Performance Test, 128
"talk therapy," 147
Teacher Checklist, 17–23, 29, 33
teachers:
    accommodations made by, 53, 86, 91,
        93–94, 95, 100–105, 169, 176, 276
    class size and, 9–10, 13, 188, 193
    communication with, 15–16, 23–24
    competency of, 10–12, 15, 16
    exceptional, 12–14
    feedback from, 14–15, 31, 33
    information from, 9–25, 73–74

referrals by, 23, 25
respect for, 13, 15
training of, 104
updates from, 17, 23
teamwork, 259
temper tantrums, 144
"testing package," 58
Test of Auditory Perceptual Skills (TAPS),
    73, 84
Test of Variables of Attention (TOVA), 118
tests, standardized, 61–77
    administration of, 61, 63–64, 71–74, 106,
        124–125, 172, 180, 183, 184
    cost of, 172
    eligibility for, 24–25
    evaluation of, 23, 61–77, 118, 121–122,
        126, 127–128
    Individual Educational Plan and, 81,
        83–85, 87, 90, 92
    interim, 225
    jargon and, 62–63
    legal requirements and, 63, 106
    procedure for, 51, 52, 53, 58, 59
    readministration of, 126–127, 172, 180
    types of, 64–73
    see also individual tests
thought field therapy, 129n
time management, 103, 239, 240–241, 246,
    254, 263
Title 1 program, 23, 99–100
Tourette's syndrome, 130
trauma, 45
triangulation, 157
tricyclic drugs, 132
trust, 44
tutors, 23, 25, 33, 44, 47, 59, 87, 88, 123,
    163–164, 166–170, 171, 179, 180–181,
    184, 185, 187

underachievers, 53
university-affiliated programs, 115, 116,
    176–179

values, family, 250–251, 252, 262
vision therapy, 198, 210, 212, 214–216, 217
visits, in-class, 24
visual discrimination defects, 63
visual efficiency, 196, 198, 204
visual memory defects, 53, 76, 129
visual–motor integration defects, 84
visual perception, 213
visual problems, 210–216
visual sequential memory, 83, 184
visual tracking problems, 53, 210–211

Visualizing Verbalizing Program, 85, 165

Wechsler Intelligence Score for Children (WISC-R), 128n
Wechsler Intelligence Score for Children III (WISC-III), 64, 71–72, 84, 128, 172
Wepman Auditory Discrimination Test, 69, 74, 83

Wide-Range Achievement Test (WRAT-3), 68
Woodcock Johnson Psycho-Educational Battery (Revised) of Academic Achievement, 64–66, 67, 83, 172, 180
work ethic, 262

X rays, 131